Role-Sharing Marriage

ROLE-SHARING MARRIAGE

AUDREY D. SMITH
and
WILLIAM J. REID

New York
Columbia University Press
1986

Library of Congress Cataloging in Publication Data

Smith, Audrey D.
Role-sharing marriage.

Bibliography: p.
Includes index.
1. Marriage—United States.   2. Division of labor.
3. Communication in marriage.   I. Reid, William James,
1928–   .   II. Title.
HQ536.S65 1985   646.7'8   85-9650
ISBN 0-231-06110-2 (alk. paper)

Columbia University Press
New York   Guildford, Surrey
Copyright © 1986 Columbia University Press
All rights reserved

Printed in the United States of America

To our sons,
Stephen and Steven

CONTENTS

ACKNOWLEDGMENTS

We were fortunate to have the encouragement and cooperation of a large number of people throughout this study, which could not have been done without them. We are deeply appreciative of their help.

First, our gratitude to the couples who agreed to participate in the project and so graciously made time in their already overloaded schedules for hours of interviewing. Their thoughtful responses, insightful comments, and voluntary additions made them collaborators rather than merely respondents.

While the senior author was on the faculty at the School of Social Welfare, University of Wisconsin-Milwaukee (UWM), she enlisted the aid of graduate students who were interested in obtaining research experience in the instrument development and data collection phases of the study. We are particularly grateful to these students for the many hours they spent interviewing couples, possibly learning more about role sharing than they ever wanted to know. Graduate student assistants at the School of Social Welfare, State University of New York at Albany (SUNYA), conducted the interviewing in New York and helped to process the data. Our sincere thanks to all of these able, dedicated students, who so willingly and enthusiastically participated in the study. Kathy Dahlk, then a graduate student at UWM, was especailly helpful since she was involved in the conceptualization of the study, helping to identify issues to be pursued.

Many colleagues of the senior author at UWM and later of both authors at SUNYA provided encouragement and support through the interest they showed in the research, the discussion of ideas, and the review of drafts of part of the book. Special thanks to Catherine Chilman, UWM, and to Bonnie Carlson and Liane Davis, SUNYA. We would also like to thank Linda Haas, Sociology Department, University of Indiana at Indianapolis, for her thoughtful review of the manuscript and helpful suggestions. Our dean, Stuart A. Kirk, provided tangible and intangible support both at SUNYA and at UWM, where he was formerly acting dean.

We are grateful for a grant from the Research Foundation of the State University of New York and to the Rockefeller Foundation, which through its Scholar-in-Residence Program at Bellagio Study and Conference Center, provided an idyllic retreat on Lake Como, Italy for us to begin writing the book. John D. Moore, Director of Columbia University Press, and Maureen MacGrogan, assistant executive editor at the Press, were most supportive throughout. Their sense of humor and good natured teasing of us when we argued over points and despaired of ever completing the book may be partly responsible for the survival of our own role-sharing marriage during the writing.

And finally, thanks to Gail Texter for typing numerous drafts of the manuscript.

Audrey D. Smith
William J. Reid

Role-Sharing Marriage

1

A Perspective on Role Sharing

Consider these vignettes:

- The Harris family faces a crisis. Joan, the wife and mother, and a teacher, has been offered an important administrative position in another city, a good distance away. She wants to take the job, but Phil, her husband and an accountant, is reluctant to leave his position in a firm where his chances for a partnership look good. Ann, their eight year old, doesn't want to move either. After considerable agonizing, Phil decides to look for another job in the city where Joan's job would be and finds one that is adequate but less promising. They both accept the new positions and move.
- In the Allen household, Joe does the cooking and cleaning while Beth does the laundry and takes care of minor car repairs.
- Two weeks after her baby was born, Jeri went back to work. Hal took off the next two weeks from his job to stay at home with the infant.
- Doris and Bob Hill each contribute equally to common household expenses but keep the rest of their earnings for themselves. Neither knows how much the other has in savings.

A generation or two ago these examples might have been uniformly interpreted, by expert and laypersons alike, as signifying that something was wrong with the marital relationship or with one or both partners. Joan Harris might have been seen as an overly ambitious wife ready to sacrifice her family's interests for the sake of her own career. The Allens might have been seen as a case of role reversal. Questions would have been raised about Jeri's attitudes toward motherhood and

Hal's possible identity problems. The Hills would have been seen as two self-centered people linked together in a marriage of convenience.

Although these examples would often be interpreted the same way today, a new perspective has emerged. According to this view, these couples are participating in a different kind of marital relationship—equal partner, egalitarian, role-sharing, modern, and progressive are among the terms used to describe it. One way of defining this marriage is that both partners have equal claims to the breadwinning role and equal responsibilities for the care of home and children, including the obligation to contribute equally or equitably to family expenses. Activities of partners as spouses or parents are no longer tied to gender or tradition but become interchangeable (Scanzoni and Fox 1980). Within the framework of this kind of marriage, the actions of our illustrative couples become understandable and legitimate.

Although this kind of marriage is very much in the minority and probably still a rarity for families with young children, it is becoming the ideal for many couples who subscribe to new values of equality between the sexes at work and at home. For that reason alone, it is of interest, albeit other reasons may be found in its likely growth as a style of marriage and its possible implications for children, work, and society.

Any important development in the family soon finds itself the subject of study. The role-sharing marriage made one of its first appearances in the Rapoports' (1969, 1971, 1976) studies of couples in which both partners had careers. During the last fifteen years, many other studies of dual-career or dual-worker couples have followed. In this research, role sharing has been dealt with as one aspect of marriages in which both partners are employed. Although role sharing as we define it cannot occur unless husband and wife are both working, most working couples do not share roles fully, since not many husbands participate to any great extent in their wives' traditional domestic and child care roles. There have been relatively few studies explicitly addressed to the subgroup of "two paycheck" couples who define themselves as egalitarian or role sharing (Haas 1980b, 1982; Smith 1980; Kimball 1983). Of these only Haas and Smith have obtained detailed data from in-depth, in-person interviews from both partners on behavior and attitudes concerning role sharing. Thus, not a great deal of knowledge has been accumulated about how role-sharing couples actually manage their relationships, what problems they face, and how they handle them.

In this book we hope to extend this knowledge base. The contribution of the volume, we hope, will be of interest to three types of readers: researchers and scholars of family life, individuals who are or may be involved in role-sharing marriages, and professionals who provide educational and counseling services to married couples and to persons considering marriage.

Our general thesis is that couples who are attempting to achieve a role-sharing marriage are struggling to define and implement emerging values about marital relationships, values that include equality of opportunity for career development and fairness in division of domestic and parental responsibilities. These egalitarian values often run counter to long-held traditions concerning the institution of marriage. Because of these traditions, a man and woman are not entirely free to form a relationship based on egalitarian values. They enter it with abilities, expectations, and attitudes shaped by their earlier socialization, find their choices constrained by market-place realities, and face continuing pressures from society at large to maintain conventional conceptions of marital and parental roles. The result is usually a set of compromises between the modern and old-fashioned marriage. Although role-sharing couples may view their fresh half-loaves as much better than the old standard fare, the compromises create a unique set of issues. These issues will grow in importance as role-sharing marriages increase.

Our examination of the role-sharing marriage focuses on these issues. Our work is based largely on a study of sixty-four couples who identified themselves as having such a marriage. Through joint and individual in-depth interviews—approximately 190 in total—we obtained a considerable amount of detailed data on role-sharing phenomena. In addition to these data, our analysis draws upon results of other research and upon the theoretical literature concerning dual-earner and role-sharing marriages.

To begin the development of our thesis we shall first consider the kind of role-sharing marriage that might be projected from the newer egalitarian values and how this marriage differs in conception from traditional forms. This exposition will, we hope, clarify the issues that arise when role-sharing marriages are attempted.

New Relationship Values

The role-sharing marriage of interest in this book is one in which partners subscribe to newer values about the relationship between men and women. These values, which have emerged from contemporary feminism, espouse an essential equality of worth and opportunity between the sexes. In practical terms this equality means that women should have the same options as men in developing their lives; in the pursuit of these options they should not be discriminated against because of their sex. For example, a woman should be as free as a man to embark upon a career and to develop it without being handicapped by traditional values that make being a wife and mother any more demanding or restricting than being a husband and father. By the same token, a father should be as free as his wife to be a nurturing parent and caregiver to his children. Aspects of functioning that are inextricably linked to biological differences, such as childbearing, need to be recognized but also viewed as minor qualifications of the equality principle.

Partners in traditional marriages may certainly view one or another as being of "equal worth" and may object, with some justification, to calling role-sharing marriages "egalitarian." The issue is not so much one of value as human beings (although the feminist literature presents a convincing case that women and "women's work" are not valued as highly in our society as men and their work) but of the extent to which partners claim equality in respect to entitlements, obligations, and rewards in their family roles. A role-sharing wife who becomes a mother may regard herself as equally entitled to pursue her career as her husband, who in turn is obligated to help her do this. A traditional wife who becomes a mother may view her husband and herself as having a quite different, that is, unequal, set of obligations, entitlements, and rewards. For example, she may feel obligated to subordinate her career to her role as mother but would regard her husband as obligated to provide her with financial support.

Claims to equality of entitlements, obligations, and rewards are being made by increasing numbers of women. These claims run counter not only to traditional values but also to traditional sociological and psychological theory consonant with these values. One example is the structural-functional conception of the family as a role-differentiated unit in which the wife and mother is responsible for "expressive" and the husband for "instrumental" functions (Parsons and Bales 1955). Another is the view that mothering provides inherent qualities conducive to child development that cannot be provided by other caretakers, including the father (Bowlby 1951, 1958, 1969).

A corollary of this new notion of sex equality is increased autonomy for both sexes, especially women. As equals, men and women should be free to form interdependent relationships in matters of love, sex, marriage, parenting, and so on to achieve "maximum joint profit" (Scanzoni 1979: 440). Dependency on the opposite sex should not be a requirement to achieve important life goals. Thus, a woman should not *have* to depend on a man for economic support because she is a woman. Nor is a man obligated to depend on a woman to provide necessary care for his children. Neither is required to engage in sex unless he or she wants to. Rather than be programmed by the social order, interdependencies are to be entered into by choices between equals. Moreover, equal partners are not constrained to follow any particular course but are free to determine the shape and conditions of these interdependencies. Gender-linked custom becomes replaced by the negotiated contract.

The value placed on autonomy does not mean that role-sharing partners operate with an unusual degree of independence in their daily lives. In fact, in respect to such tasks as child care, food preparation, and housework, their interactions may be more interdependent than one finds in traditional marriages in which these tasks may be largely the wife's responsibility. Interdependence in respect to companionship, emotional support, and other more purely relationship aspects of the marriage may be no less, possibly even greater, in the role-sharing than in the traditional marriage. Autonomy refers rather to freedom to control one's interdependencies. Autonomy becomes a higher order principle, a metarule (Haley 1963, Wertheim 1975, Reid 1978) used to generate more specific rules having to do with the specifics of marital interaction.

Increased autonomy also has implications for relationships outside the marriage. Role-sharing partners may not consider themselves as "one" in respect to social or familial contacts. Each partner may feel free to maintain the kind of relationship with her or his own family of origin that he or she wants, without any expectation that one's spouse will be involved unless the spouse wants to be. Activities with friends who are not also one's spouse's friends are permissible. When opposite sex friends are involved, tension may arise and couples may find that they need to define the limits of autonomy for themselves in order to have a mutually satisfactory marital relationship. Whether or not sexual relationships outside the marriage are to be considered acceptable may be an issue to be dealt with by egalitarian couples.

Relationship in the Role-Sharing Marriage

When values of sex equality and autonomy are strongly held by the partners, the result may be not only a symmetrical division of labor but also a distinctive kind of marital relationship. The characteristics may, in fact, underlie and shape the resulting division of labor. Sharing of marriage roles may be accompanied by attitudes and behavior that protect the partners' equality and autonomy. Thus, a couple may decide that the wife should move to another city, forcing an indefinite long-distance commute in order to advance her career. The move may complicate their division of labor and may actually result in less net income after costs of commuting and maintaining two dwelling units are taken into account. The move, however, preserves the wife's parity and freedom of action. To have refused the position might have been viewed as subordinating her career to her husband's, an option they would reject as violating the value premises of their relationship. Another example may be found in partners who regard the earnings of each as "individual" rather than "family" income. Each may contribute to carefully defined joint expenses but retains the right to use the remainder as he or she sees fit. Each thereby preserves independence through actions that go beyond division of labor.

Moreover, the relationship formed by role-sharing couples may have implications for various aspects of interaction between the partners and the family as a whole—that is, for family structure (Minuchin 1974, Aponte and Van Deusen 1981). Traditional distributions of power in the family may be altered. Husband and wife should be equal in power, and that power should be shared over important domains of family life—unlike a common pattern in the traditional marriage in which the husband may control decisions about major expenditures and geographic mobility, and the wife, matters concerning the household and children. Greater involvement of parents with children may make less likely coalitions often found in traditional marriage such as the isolated, detached father, on the one hand, and the mother aligned with the children, on the other. Because of less specialization, there may be greater need for communication between the parents, and there is some evidence (Kimball 1983) that this may occur.

Not all implications may be positive, however. Issues concerning who is in charge may be heightened and spread across a broader front; parents may become competitive with one another in forming alliances with their children. Greater need and opportunities for communication may simply add up to more quarreling. Increased emphasis on autonomy may threaten the intimacy that most couples regard as the essence of marriage.

Role sharing then does not necessarily mean a marriage that is inherently more or less fulfilling than traditional arrangements. It simply means a marriage that differs in some respects from the conventional. These differences are of interest in their own right and may have consequences of great significance for the roles of men and women in our society, for conceptions of work and family life, and for the rearing of children. But the differences and consequences can be best explored if the role-sharing marriage is seen as differing from other forms of marriage rather than as superior or inferior to them.

Division of Labor

Although general characteristics of the relationship in role-sharing marriages may be distinctive and fundamental, specific attributes of the marriage can best be approached by considering how labor is divided. Again, our interest is in a projection of how the role sharing might look if its organizing values were implemented.

In most societies, and certainly in ours, adult family members are expected to contribute a certain amount of work for the family's benefit. Income must be obtained, children provided for, the dwelling unit cleaned, food prepared, household finances managed, cars kept in working order, and so on. Although some of the tasks done at home are difficult to separate clearly from the nonwork aspects of family life, they involve the sort of expectations and efforts that are associated with work, and some families, in fact, hire people to do them.

Although the range of such activities is diverse, three principal groupings emerge: *earning income, domestic chores,* and *child care.* Earning income through work outside the home is the usual way families support themselves, although, of course, income can be secured by other means such as public assistance, retirement benefits, inheritances, and investment income. Domestic chores are made up principally of food preparation and clean-up, housecleaning, and laundry. We use this category broadly to include, in addition, a range of usually minor tasks that are done in and around the home, such as bill paying, serving as social secretary, yard work, house repairs and projects, and car maintenance. The presence of children requires a special class of effort for which the terms child care and child socialization (Nye and Gecas 1976, Gecas 1976) seem the best descriptors. Most of the tasks in the domestic and child care groupings consist of what has traditionally been regarded as "women's work," although some, such as house repairs and car maintenance, have traditionally been within the man's domain, and child socialization, in both parents' role.

PATTERNS OF ALLOCATION

In most American families these three work-family roles, as Pleck (1977) has called them, are assumed largely by the husband and wife. Many patterns of allocation occur. The *traditional* division, to put it most simply, has been for the husband to earn the income and for the wife to take care of the children and the home. To put it less simply this theme has occurred with infinite variations. The husband may take varying amounts of responsibility for childrearing and domestic chores. The wife may supplement the family income with part-time, episodic, or less remunerative employment. Even with both partners working full time the wife may still retain a disproportionate share of child-care and domestic responsibilities. This latter variation, which we term *"quasi-traditional,"* is increasing in frequency as wives in growing numbers become full-time employees. The inequities inherent in this arrangement have been a major impetus, as we shall see, for the development of the newer *role-sharing* pattern, in which husbands and wives are coparticipants in the work-family roles. But the line between this newer form of division and older ones, such as the quasi-traditional, are by no means clear cut. Even if a marriage can be said to be clearly role sharing, many variations can still occur—in respect to who takes responsibility for what tasks. Another pattern of allocation, less common than those mentioned above, but a pattern that may also be increasing in frequency is the *reversed traditional* pattern: the wife is the primary breadwinner and her "househusband" is responsible for child care and domestic tasks.

Another source of variation arises from the family's circumstances or stages in its development. The arrival and departure of children have the greatest impact. This dynamic produces the familiar shifts between traditional and quasi-traditional styles. A couple may begin marriage in a quasi-traditional mode. Both partners work but the wife assumes major responsibility for domestic chores. With her first pregnancy the wife leaves paid employment and becomes a full-time homemaker (traditional). After the last child enters school (or earlier or later depending on circumstances) the wife reenters the labor force but still carries a disproportionate share of domestic tasks and, in addition, the lion's share of work in caring for the children (quasi-traditional).

With couples who maintain a full and consistent role-sharing relationship, children provide another responsibility to be shared. When children are young, child care arrangements may be used or both parents may take time from work. However, for many couples who consider themselves to be basically committed to egalitarian values and practices, the appearance of children may cause a disruption in role sharing. The wife may leave paid employment or work part time to become the principal child caregiver while the husband continues his employment full time. While these arrangements may resemble traditional or quasi-traditional divisions of labor, certain differences are apparent. Role-sharing couples are likely to view their situation as temporary and atypical. The husband may take on a greater share of domestic and child care responsibility than a husband would in a traditional marriage. The wife's staying home is seen, not as fulfilling her womanly obligations, but rather as a career sacrifice for which her husband should be indebted. Thus, it might be agreed that the next such sacrifice would be the husband's.

Couples currently in this phase of development are neither easily identified nor classified. They are role sharing in values and orientation but only partially so in behavior. In some cases, in fact, the egalitarian goals may never become fully realized as the wife's attachment to her career may attentuate with the passage of time, the arrival of additional children, or the advancement in her husband's career. We assume that most such couples will in fact return to role sharing but because role sharing is a new phenomenon, there is lack of knowledge about longitudinal patterns. Linda Hass and Teresa Jump have suggested to us in personal communication that these couples who are not now role sharing but have been and seem inclined to in the future be referred to as *transitional*. Their suggestion seems apropos, especially to a sizable portion of the couples in our study.

The notion of a transitional couple in a role-sharing context can also apply to other kinds of disruption: one spouse may become temporarily unemployed for reasons other than child care, may become ill or disabled for a period, and so on. In general, to be considered transitional there would need to be evidence of a preexisting role-sharing pattern, the occurrence of an event viewed by the partners as causing a temporary departure from their regular pattern, the continuation of role sharing at some level during the period of disruption and continued adherence to a role-sharing orientation, and finally indications of a plan to return to full role sharing once the temporary event has passed.

BEHAVIORAL DESCRIPTION

Like any complex aspect of family life, division of labor has a number of aspects that need to be sorted out. Basic to all other considerations is the behavioral dimension—who actually does what.

At the behavioral level, the key distinction between traditional and role-sharing marriages lies in how the partners spend their time doing work for the family's benefit. Which of these forms a marriage takes can be determined for the most part from accurate reports of time spent on different tasks. In the pure traditional marriage the husband and wife spend the bulk of their work time in different task domains. Who is the wife and who is the husband can be readily identified from the content of the work performed. The bulk of the husband's work time would be spent in earning money, most of the wife's, in domestic and child care tasks. In the pure role-sharing marriage it is not possible to make this distinction. The husband's and wife's "time sheets" for different types of tasks would look much alike. Each would report similar amounts of time spent in money-making, child care, and domestic chores. In theory, there would be no reliable way to tell them apart no matter how the tasks were categorized or how fine the categories. They would show similar amounts of time on tasks classified as enjoyable, interesting, disagreeable, menial, and so forth. Perhaps the only clues would be provided by tasks involved in earning income, which are somewhat beyond the control of the partners and would reflect sex-role differentiation in the world of work. Here types of task (not total time) might show some differences.

It is this quality of interchangeability that defines the role-sharing marriage in operational terms. The quasi-traditional marriage shows up as an imbalance: the husband and wife showing similar amounts of time earning income and the wife showing greater amounts of time in domestic and child care roles. This maldistribution is frequently referred to as the "wife's two jobs"—one in the home and one outside the home (Myrdal and Klein 1956).

RESPONSIBILITY AND CONTROL

Behavioral descriptions do not paint a complete picture, however. Questions of task responsibility and control must also be considered. A husband and wife can be observed to be sharing meal preparation in a more or less equal way but when the task is completed the wife thanks the husband. The "thank you" is a tip-off to what might be learned through an interview with the partners. Meal preparation is the wife's responsibility—her job. The husband in this instance, and perhaps in others, "helps out." Having responsibility for a task adds to the burden because it involves planning, decision making, picking up loose ends, worry, and taking blame if the outcome is less than desirable. Moreover, the partner helping out may accrue credit on the implicit ledger of debts and obligations that families keep (Boszormenyi-Nagy and Ulrich 1981). The husband in this instance has been assisting the wife in her job. A favor given deserves one in return.

Taking responsibility for a task does not necessarily mean having to do all the work, as the example suggests. In fact, responsibility may not entail any implementing effort if domestic help is used. Still the person responsible has to cope with the administrative headaches just described—which involve labor of a different sort. Because most American households do not enjoy the luxury of servants, we shall assume that taking responsibility for a family work role means doing it oneself or with the help of other family members.

Being responsible for a task inevitably results in having a certain amount of control over how it is done, at least control over particulars. The person immediately responsible may still be taking orders from another and hence may have only a limited amount of discretion. Thus, when children are involved in division of labor, responsibility for a task may be given to the child while a parent assumes control. At the adult level, the spouse responsible for a task generally has the most to say about how it is done, but the other spouse may share control or in some cases try to assume it. A good deal of marital discord is, in fact, sparked by such issues. For example, a wife may "veto" a decision that her husband has made regarding repair of the family car—an area he takes responsibility for. She may do this on grounds that they cannot afford to get the vehicle fixed—perhaps justifying her attempt to exercise control on grounds that her responsibility is to keep the family budget in balance.

In regard to most family tasks, marital partners assume the right to evaluate the other's efforts and, if need be, to take corrective action. A partner is likely to exercise this right if the effort of the other does not come up to his or her standards. When partners have joint responsibility and control, as is characteristic of role-sharing marriages, conflict over standards assumes particular importance.

BASIS FOR ALLOCATION

Perhaps the most intriguing aspect of division of labor between spouses has to do with the basis of task allocation. How is the work divided up and what determines the resulting division? Our interest is in the principles or rules used for deciding who does what. These range from beliefs about what is proper to such mundane considerations as possession of skills. We shall develop our major ideas within the context of the traditional and quasi-traditional marriages, which will provide needed background for understanding the allocative rules used by role-sharing couples.

In the traditional arrangement, the gender of the spouse provides the principal rationale for division of labor: the man is the breadwinner and the woman's place is in the home—to use the familiar clichés. In quasi-traditional arrangements, this rationale may be modified in different ways. A typical formulation is that a woman has responsibility for care of children and the home but in order to improve the economic well-being of the family, elects to obtain paid work in addition, with the understanding that she can rely on her partner to help her with the home and child care responsibilities. Allocative principles in these marriages are based on more than custom, however. Socialization, skill development, societal attitudes, and economic realities have prepared husband and wife to move into traditional roles and continue to keep them there. A young working couple decides to have a baby. The wife is more likely than her husband to see the care of an infant as an agreeable task, to be better at it and more interested in improving her knowledge and skill in this area. Her husband is more likely to have the higher paying job, to see receiving a paycheck as an indication of personal worth, and to have the stronger investment in career advancement. People expect the wife but not the husband to stop working when the child arrives.

Given this set of forces, it is not surprising that the usual shift in division of labor when the baby arrives is for the wife to trade time at work for time with the infant. The same pressures operate, although perhaps less obviously, to keep the wife in the kitchen and the husband in the garage. Nor must the pressures be strong to have an effect. When it is a question of who shall do what task, minor considerations (competitive edges) can be decisive.

This gender-linked division can also be viewed within a conception of a fair exchange or equity (Rapoport and Rapoport 1975). It is usually assumed that the husband's efforts as breadwinner and the wife's responsibilities for home and children constitute the basis of a fair exchange. Various exceptions can be accommodated by this balance and in fact may help to preserve the fairness of the exchange; for example, the husband may be expected to do certain domestic chores and, as father, assume certain child care responsibilities; the wife may be expected to take responsibility for work-related entertainment. Partners may feel obligated (or be expected) to carry out traditional responsibilities even though they may be assuming a disproportionate share of the effort. A husband may work two jobs so that his wife can remain at home, although with only one older child and a small apartment she may have time on her hands. The division of labor may be unbalanced in an objective sense but still perceived as equitable because both partners are fulfilling their obligations. The wife may be seen as simply more fortunate than her husband in this instance.

Traditional expectations and obligations attached to the more generic roles of spouse may override considerations of gender and put ideas of equity in still another light. Spouses have customarily felt obliged to take over responsibilities the other cannot perform because of illness, disability, or other circumstances beyond the person's control. A husband may do the housework if his wife is sick or a wife may work full time plus do the greater share of domestic and child care tasks if her husband loses his job. The overworked spouses may not see their positions as inequitable if their partners are "doing what they can."

Wives who work full time outside the home while carrying the larger share of domestic and child care tasks may well complain about having to assume an unfair burden. The husband may argue from a traditional perspective that as a wife her obligation is to care for the home and children and not to work outside. Hence, her employment is a burden she chooses to assume; if she feels this is unfair she can simply stop working. The wife may reply that for her to do so would be unrealistic considering their need for income or that she has as much right to work as her husband, who should feel obliged to share the load at home. In stable quasi-traditional arrangements a wife may accept the inequity as a part of a woman's lot while attempting to extract as much "help" as she can from her husband. In addition, or instead, she may stress the gratifications from her sense of competence at carrying so many roles—the well-known "superwoman syndrome." Or she may hold on to her domestic and child care roles because of the sense of power, control, or satisfaction she gets from them, particularly if her outside work role gives her little satisfaction or autonomy.

Feelings of altruism and devotion—or at least the expectation that spouses should act as if these feelings existed—modify other aspects. A spouse may do "more than is fair" or expect his or her mate to do likewise "out of love." To be sure genuine caring can override the equity principle in the short run and in the longer term can serve to blur its edges. However, the very existence of mutual affection between spouses is dependent to a large extent upon their beliefs that they are being treated in an equitable manner by one another. Love is blind, but not for long.

In role-sharing marriages, the rationale for division of labor usually offered is based on the notion that partners have equal capacity and responsibility for performing work-family roles. Assumptions linking roles to gender are rejected. Women have as much right to pursue occupational and career interests as their husbands, who in turn are as obligated to care for home and children as their spouses. Guided by this value orientation, the partners may allocate tasks on the basis of special interests and aptitudes, as well as considerations of the moment. A different rationale may be offered by couples who share roles out of what they consider to be a necessity. The couple may share wage-earning and domestic roles down the middle, with the husband a full participant in the latter. However, neither see themselves as embracing a noble principle. In fact, both may prefer a more traditional arrangement and may be striving to attain one. Role sharing is seen as a fair way to divide the work under the circumstances. In addition, it may be the most practical: because of work schedules and side jobs only one spouse may be at home in the evening.

As might be expected, the first rationale is more likely to be found in middle-class couples in which the wife is well educated and career oriented (ideological role sharing). The second rationale is more likely to be seen in working-class marriages in which the wife works simply to augment family income (pragmatic role sharing). The first rationale provides legitimacy to the division of labor; it is the way things should be, an ideal to be attained. The second rationale explains why things have to be the way they are.

Our interest in this book is in the role-sharing marriage based on notions of equal capacity and responsibility—the more revolutionary of the two forms. It may appear on the surface that the rationale for division of labor in these marriages is straightforward: equal work for equal partners. In theory this may be so but reality usually complicates matters considerably. Role-sharing couples have not escaped the processes of socialization and skill development that lead to traditional arrangements. Moreover, they face the same social and economic pressures and constraints as more traditional couples. Even if role-sharing partners succeed in equalizing roles of husband and wife, they still find themselves part of the configuration of obligations, expectations, attachments, and feelings that make up married life and that can influence division of labor.

The role-sharing couple has eschewed a gender-linked basis for division of labor in favor of a principle based on equality. But beyond the notion that both should participate in work-family roles, matters are left open. In other words the gender-linked principle has not been replaced by anything nearly as well programmed. Concepts of equal responsibility and capacity provide no specific directives on the order of "this is man's work and that is woman's work." The very vagueness of the notions permits other, generally more traditional, bases for allocating tasks to enter the picture, particularly when practical decisions must be made. A wife brought up to believe in the immaculate kitchen and with skills as a cook may find herself somehow spending more time in meal preparation and clean-up than her husband, even though they are to participate in these tasks equally. Ideals of altruism and devotion may preclude a couple from rationalizing an equal division through "mechanical" devices such as keeping track of time spent on different tasks. Abstract principles that one is loath to spell out in specific terms are easily corrupted.

Conceptions of Role Sharing

We have projected an image of what the role-sharing marriage might look like if its egalitarian ideals were fully implemented. The resulting picture is by no means unclouded. It is, perhaps, clearest in respect to the unlinking of family roles and gender. It is least clear in respect to autonomy, especially the extent to which egalitarian values lead to change in traditional norms concerning mutual responsibility and subordination of individual interests to the benefit of the family unit. In any case egalitarian principles are open to many interpretations and to transformations as they are applied. As the play-out of different possibilities is considered, it is apparent that different varieties of the ideological role-sharing marriage can emerge. These can be ordered roughly in terms of the degree to which they break with tradition. At the more conservative end would be marriages one step from the quasi-traditional. There would be significant sharing of the work-family roles but traditional values and division of labor would be in evidence. For example, the husband might have the higher paying and more demanding job and the wife would do more of the traditional female domestic tasks, the husband more of those traditionally male. The wife would have the edge in child care. They would accept conventional norms about financial and other forms of interdependency. The husband's career interests would take precedence in the case of a relocation decision.

A less conventional variation would approach a complete stripping of gender from work-family roles. In this kind of marriage husband and wife would be on parity in respect to careers and share domestic and child care roles equally. Their norms concerning interdependency would still be fairly traditional, however. A more radical form of role sharing would likewise show little connection between gender and work-family roles but in addition would have a different conception of autonomy. Partners would see themselves, not as having a single income, but as being independent wage earners with control over their own money. They might work out contractual agreements about responsibility for one another in case of disability. Sexual fidelity might also be open to negotiation as in the "open marriage" (O'Neill and O'Neill 1972). As these possibilities are carried to extremes the marriage begins to resemble a cohabiting pair who find living together to be mutually convenient for the present.

One can easily imagine many other possibilities falling in between these examples or at angles to them, such as the transitional situations noted earlier. Which of these variants one wishes to call "real" role sharing is a question we shall leave open for now. By considering these different strands as a part of the role-sharing phenomenon we can better examine the full range of issues that arise as couples move away from conventional forms of marriage.

2

Tradition and Change

To comprehend the revolutionary aspects of the role-sharing marriage and the variety of issues and compromises characterizing its development, we need to understand what it departs from. To this end we consider the origins and nature of the traditions that have defined husband-wife relations and division of labor. In the latter part of the chapter we consider to what extent and how these traditions may be changing. Our own investigation, to be presented in subsequent chapters, examines these changes in depth as they have occurred in one group of role-sharing couples.

Traditional Roles in Marriage

Role sharing among husbands and wives is not normative behavior today and was even less so in the past. As far as we know there has always been some division of labor between women and men in family groups, although the work has not always been divided in the same way in all cultures and at all times. However, some principles, apparently based on biological differences—most notably that women bear the children and men are usually stronger—seem to apply rather generally. Women have tended to be more homebound in order to care for infants and young children while men have not been so restricted. For example, in prehistoric times men were the hunters of wild animals, often venturing far from home and staying away for days at a time, while women were the gatherers of wild plants and the preparers of food—tasks that could be done in and near the home while they cared for children. Such specialization may well have been the most efficient and rational way of organizing the work to be done.

Today, with the advancements in contraceptive technology and in knowledge from research indicating that fathers can be as competent as mothers as nurturers and caretakers of infants and with so little work inside or outside the home requiring a great deal of physical strength, there seems to be little if any biological reason for maintaining a division of family roles based on sex. Yet, the ideal of a sexual division of labor in families is still held by most people and only recently has come under question. The explanation seems to be that gradually the social basis for specialization of labor according to sex became more important than its biological origins. Whether this sexual division of roles was viewed as "natural" or "God-ordained," it was seen as necessary to maintain the social order. Inherent in the social order was the concept of status differential, men having higher status than women; consequently, men were the dominant sex while women were the submissive, subservient one.

The separation and specialization of sex roles within families reached its most exaggerated form in the United States after the Industrial Revolution. We are still greatly influenced by the notions and attitudes held during that period. Indeed it is the family life of the late nineteenth and early twentieth centuries that is nostalgically viewed as the ideal by many people today concerned about the changes occurring in families. To understand how this ideal evolved we need to take a step further back in history—to the settlement of this country by the first wave of European immigrants in the early 1600s.

Colonial Times

The historian William Chafe (1977:15) points out that "one of the remarkable themes of women's history has been the constancy of prescriptive attitudes toward woman's 'place' over three and a half centuries" in spite of great changes in the social and economic circumstances during this time and in the behavior of women, which was responsive to these changes. In colonial America, when this country was largely agrarian and the household the center of production, women were an indispensable part of the family's economic activities.

The division of family labor was complicated but was characterized essentially by men engaging in production for the market, that is, in the fields, and women engaging in production for the family, that is, in the home (Smuts 1971; Matthaei 1982). According to Matthaei (p. 32) the husband "worked as a property owner and family head, to establish his identity as a man" while his wife "worked as a homemaker, in order to aid her family." Although such a division was perceived as "natural," that is, in keeping with the social order, it was not and could not be always adhered to. Women engaged in men's work when it was necessary to do so. This included wives whose husbands could not or would not provide for their families, white women without husbands, and black slave women who were made to work in the fields alongside slave men (Matthaei 1982).

It is clear that during this period both men and women were expected to work for the family, though their tasks differed (Kessler-Harris 1982). The domestic work that fell primarily to the wife was considered as essential to the household as the husband's work, though hers had less status and her role was secondary to her husband's. Yet there is evidence that people were more relaxed about sex roles than they were later to become; the social and economic conditions did not yet afford the luxury of a rigid sexual division of labor. For example, wives and female servants helped in the fields at times, wives engaged in "putting-out" work (work done at home for pay or barter) when necessary to supplement the family's income, husbands sometimes helped with the spinning and weaving when their farm work was done, male apprentices often did household chores, and mothers taught young children while fathers tended to take over the educational responsibility as the children got older (Kessler-Harris 1982).

SEPARATION OF WORK AND FAMILY

Prescriptive attitudes about what constituted women's work and what was men's work became more pronounced during the Industrial Revolution, when the workplace became separated from the home-place. The family-centered economy of farming and household production gradually became replaced by the wage economy operating largely through the factory system. As work, that is, paid employment, moved out of the home, so did men. In other words, men worked outside the home in industry while women stayed at home to take care of the children and the home. At least that was the way family responsibilities were divided in middle- and upper-middle-class families.

According to Chafe (1977), it was at this time that the activities of women divided sharply along class and ethnic lines. While white middle-class wives became full-time homemakers and mothers in small nuclear families, black and immigrant women—wives, as well as women without husbands—became a source of cheap, marginal labor. In poor white families in which the husband could not earn enough to support the family, wives continued to help out as they had under the family economy system. Sometimes poor wives could stretch their husbands' wages through shrewd management and bargaining enough to make ends meet. Generally it was necessary for poor wives to continue producing at home for the family and often for the market, for example, "putting out." As soon as children were old enough, they might be sent into the labor market. As a last resort, a small number of wives in poor white families joined black and immigrant wives in the cheap, marginal labor force. Although sex inequality was a salient characteristic of the marketplace for women without families, work conditions were even worse and more exploitative for wives, who were seen as temporary workers and who took jobs that would permit them to continue fulfilling their primary roles as mothers and homemakers (Tentler 1979).

Normative behavior—that is, prescriptive attitudes about what was women's work and what was men's—was determined by the middle class. Husbands were to be the breadwinners, and wives, full-time mothers and homemakers. Clearly women's place was in the home, women being financially supported by their fathers before marriage and by their husbands afterward. This situation was to change somewhat for single women later, after women gained the right to obtain higher education.

The behavior described here could be engaged in largely by white middle- and upper-middle-class families, but this did not affect the norm, nor did the fact that it was only in the latter part of the nineteenth century that even these women were able to devote much of their lives exclusively to mothering and homemaking. For the first time social and economic conditions allowed some women to fulfill the norm.

Thus, the norm was firmly entrenched regardless of behavior. Chafe (1977) argues, however, that in fact two standards arose: black and immigrant women were expected to toil in fields and factories. This did not prevent the widespread notion that those who could not live up to the prescriptive norm were failures. One reason for this was the moral overtones to the prescribed behavior, together with changed circumstances, which opened up economic opportunities for men. In colonial times land ownership was a prerequisite to wealth, but the Industrial Revolution changed that. With the advent of the wage economy, the opportunity arose for men to improve their economic position through hard work and shrewd dealing. It was believed that every man had the chance to rise to the top of the economic ladder. In spite of the inequalities in conditions and opportunities that still existed (to take an extreme example, recently freed slaves were at a competitive disadvantage vis-à-vis white men from wealthy families), a man's economic position came to be seen as a result of his hard work—or lack of it—and therefore a measure of him as a man. One indicator of a man's success, proof that he was a good breadwinner, was a homemaker wife who devoted herself full time to her family (Matthaei 1982). For middle-class women this resulted in what some have called the "cult of domesticity" and the "cult of motherhood," terms used to depict the glorification of these roles and the exaggeration of the responsibilities attached to them.

The Industrial Revolution resulted in a sharp division between occupation and family roles, not only in terms of where they were to be performed and who would perform them, but also in terms of the requirements for each role (Dizard 1972). Where cooperation and mutuality had been stressed in both of these roles earlier, now competition, aggressiveness, and individualism were necessary for the successful performance of occupational roles. Since men's time and energies were depleted in the competitive occupational struggle, women were responsible for the family roles, which included almost total responsibility for parenting children and providing love and comfort to the husband. Since increased affluence permitted families homes of their own, nuclear families proliferated. This, in addition to the increased mobility that occurred, made families less connected to kin and long-term friendships. Within this context, wives became more and more preoccupied with their children and homes. Increasing technological advances that made domestic chores easier tended to raise their homemaking standards and added consumerism to their domestic role. The decreasing family size from having fewer children enabled mothers to concentrate more attention on the children they did have. The increased importance of the mothering role was encouraged by child care experts and by society generally.

Wives Move into the Labor Force

The ideal of sexual specialization of family roles continued to be unchallenged until the 1960s, when the most recent feminist movement began. Women's behavior had already changed, however. Black, immigrant, and poor white wives had always had great difficulty behaving, or were completely unable to behave, in the prescribed sex-role stereotyped manner. Many of these wives were already in the labor force, along with women without husbands, and they were to be joined later by white middle-class women—educated single women first, then gradually educated married women as well. The rate of women's participation in the labor force has been steadily increasing throughout this century, with only one period of decline. This exception was immediately after World War II, when some middle-class wives returned to their homes after contributing to the war effort; this resulted in the "baby boom" and a renewed emphasis on domesticity and motherhood with societal sanctions.

It is clear that wives are in the labor force to stay. Although less than 6 percent of wives were gainfully employed at the turn of the century (Hayghe 1982), currently more than half of the wives living with husbands in this country are in the labor force, about half of whom work full time (Masnick and Bane 1980). The sharpest increase in labor market trends in recent years has been among mothers of preschool age children; in 1981, 45 percent of children under six years had mothers in the labor force (Grossman 1982). Currently most mothers of preschool age children who are employed outside the home work part time or part year. As Masnick and Bane (1980:71) conclude, "though fewer mothers are dropping out of the labor force, they continue to adjust their work lives to the demands of home and children."

Another way of viewing wives' employment outside the home is to ascertain the proportion of the family breadwinner role they may be assuming. On the average, working wives brought in about a quarter of the family income in 1977 (Masnick and Bane 1980). Younger wives have slightly higher labor force participation and attachment (working full time more continuously) rates and contribute a slightly higher percentage of the family income. Masnick and Bane conclude that wives' contributions to family income may increase as their labor force attachment increases.

The labor market behavior on the part of wives has done little to change the societal norm of sexual differentiation of family roles or the attitudes of most families. Husbands are still seen as the breadwinners, or at least the primary breadwinners, while wives are still responsible for the home and children even if their role set has expanded. Because of the sex inequality that still exists in the job market (although progress is being made), men generally have better job opportunities and can earn more than women. Husbands and wives, in addition to employers and society in general, often rationalize and play down the importance of the wife's employment and financial contribution to the family. Although wives are generally no longer considered to be working only for "pin money," they are usually perceived as working for self-actualization, only temporarily to achieve a family goal such as a down payment on a house, to raise the family's standard of living because the wife is not content with what her husband can provide, or for some similar reason. Since most wives still see their primary roles as home-maker and child rearer, when they do participate in the labor market they generally do so in such a way as to put their families first, and this practice often limits the type of jobs they can get (Masnick and Bane 1980). The type of behavior referred to includes not preparing for a career, because they expect to get married; choosing careers that will permit them to combine work with their family roles, careers that usually require less commitment and are of lower status with lower pay; working only part time or part year; taking jobs at lower skill levels than they possess for reasons such as proximity to home, or liberal policies about taking time off to handle family responsibility, or its being the best job she can get in the area to which they have moved because of the husband's job.

There is some evidence, however, that this behavior is beginning to change. According to Masnick and Bane (1980) the revolution yet to come—one that may be an even more far-reaching change that is just beginning within families—is in women's *attachment* (full-time, year-round work on a more permanent basis) to the labor force. Greater attachment will increase women's contributions to family income. Recent trends, especially among younger women, seem to point to the likelihood of such a revolution.

Changes in Family Roles

HUSBANDS' BEHAVIOR

The changes in women's roles—particularly their employment outside the home—have not been matched by changes in men's roles. Since cultural norms about sex roles and socialization practices to ensure these expectations have not prevented women from expanding their role set, one might wonder why men have not expanded theirs. Specifically, why have wives been able to share the financial provider role with their husbands, in addition to fulfilling their roles as homemaker and child rearer, while husbands have been restricted largely to the breadwinner role?

We think there are a number of political, economic, social, and psychological factors that have contributed to this difference; only a few are mentioned here. One is the status differential between men and women and accordingly the different values placed on the roles assigned to the sexes. Since, by all obvious indicators, paid employment is valued more highly in our society than domestic work or child care, it is not surprising that persons of higher status do not choose to participate in less esteemed roles. The fact that both the homemaker and parenting (in reality, mothering) roles have expanded, changed in content, and become more specialized over the last two centuries may have acted as a deterrent to men. As these changes occurred, women became increasingly invested in these roles; even now many women resent sharing these roles and the power and satisfaction that come with them. Unlike women who have historically played a role in production for the family—in fact, as Breckinridge (1928) points out, women have always worked although not always for wages—men have had no comparable experience with women's family roles. Historically, unmarried, divorced, and widowed men have had the domestic and child care roles performed by women, usually their mothers, other relatives, or hired help. In addition, while some women, especially unmarried women, have been employed outside the home since the Industrial Revolution, no such parallel development has been in evidence for unmarried men. Until very recently, men continued living with their families until they were married (their mothers and sisters performing the domestic role). Even the few who remained unmarried seldom established their own households but often continued living with relatives or with other families as boarders.

Study after study on time use and time allocation within households show little change in the husband's behavior when wives participate in the labor force (e.g., Walker and Woods 1976; Robinson 1977; Vanek 1974; Berk and Berk 1979; Nickols and Metzen 1982; Geerken and Gove 1983). Wives continue to do most of the cooking, housework, and child care for their families (Masnick and Bane 1980). The change this research does show is in the wife's behavior: employed wives spend less time on housework and leisure activities than nonemployed wives do. Consequently, even though husbands do not increase the number of hours (absolute time) they spend on family work when their wives are employed, the *proportion* of time they spend on family work relative to wives' time increases simply because employed wives cut back on the family work they do (Pleck 1979). Pleck illustrates with the Walker and Woods (1976) data, which show that husbands of nonemployed wives spend an average of 1.6 hours per day in family work to their wives 8.1 hours or 16 percent (1.6 divided by 9.7). When the wife was employed, the husbands spent the same number of hours in family work—1.6. Since the employed wife reduced her hours of family work to 4.8 hours, the husband's proportion increased to 25 percent (1.6 divided by 6.4). The Walker and Woods study further showed that employed wives average only one hour less per day than husbands in paid work. Consequently, the average work day of employed wives (family work and paid work) is more than two hours longer than husbands'. This is in contrast to studies that show that full-time homemaker wives and husbands spend approximately the same amount of time in total work hours (Pleck 1979). There is indication, however, that husbands of employed wives may finally be increasing the amount of time they spend in child care and housework. So far, the increase is small, and without question women still have primary responsibility for family work (Pleck 1979).

This last point is underscored and illustrated by Vanek (1980:277), who states that an examination of work done reveals a sharp division of household tasks by sex. "Men's work clusters in only a few activities:

yard work, home repairs, shopping, travel on household errands, and to a limited degree, child care. The wife is still responsible for routine home and family care, which includes such tasks as meal preparation and clean-up, home care, laundry, mending, and care of children." The only tasks divided roughly equally are shopping and travel on household errands. Even child care tasks are sex typed since wives perform almost all the physical care activities such as feeding, bathing, and diapering (Vanek 1980).

Numerous studies have come to the same conclusions—that employed wives still do by far the largest share of the housework and child care and that the activities involved in performing these roles are sex-segregated (Blood and Wolfe 1960; Lopata 1971; Poloma and Garland 1971; Rapoport and Rapoport 1971, 1976; Holmstrom 1972; Oakley 1974; Curtis 1976; Walker and Woods 1976; Weingarten 1978; Robinson 1977; Lein et al. 1974; Berk and Berk 1979; Ericksen et al. 1979; Pleck 1979; Kamerman 1980; Vanek 1980; Bryson and Bryson 1980; Geerken and Gove 1983). Further, one study, which examined the household activities of husbands and wives in minute detail, concluded that generally when husbands spent time doing routine household tasks it was because practical circumstances (e.g., wives at paid employment or busy with other household duties) prevented the wives from doing them (Berk and Berk 1979).

Although studies designed to ascertain the division of domestic and child care tasks among husbands and wives reach similar conclusions, there is some variation in the findings of different studies, depending upon the chores included. Some studies limit themselves to the domestic responsibilities traditionally considered "women's work" while others also include the family work that men traditionally do (for example, heavy yard work, house repairs, and car maintenance). The extent to which husbands participate in the domestic role could be expected to differ according to which operational definition of the role is used. This would affect only comparisons between studies, however, and not those made within studies.

DUAL-CAREER COUPLES

One might reason that more change in the division of household work would be evident among dual-career and professional couples, since wives in these families may view their wage employment as something more than a job. The Rapoports (1976:9) define a career as "those types of job sequences that require a high degree of commitment and that have a developmental character." Careers include professions that generally require years of training to prepare for. Thus, since career and professional women have a higher investment in their outside work (and generally earn more than women with jobs), one might expect their husbands to participate more in the household and child care tasks.

Indeed a number of writers who have studied dual-career marriages (e.g., Rapoport and Rapoport 1969, 1971, 1976; Holmstrom 1972; Bird 1979; Pepitone-Rockwell 1980; Smith 1980) by and large see dual-careerists, to quote Hunt and Hunt (1982:41), as "in the vanguard of societal movement toward fuller employment of women, greater sex equality, and more 'symmetrical' (Young and Willmott 1973) families." (See Hunt and Hunt 1982 and Bohen 1984 for dissenting views.) Some researchers (Dizard 1968; Bailyn 1970; Holmstrom 1972; Bahr 1974; Rapoport and Rapoport 1969, 1971, 1976) have indeed found evidence of movement toward a more egalitarian pattern among dual-career couples in which husbands assumed some of the domestic and child care responsibilities that traditionally fell to wives. Some evidence was found in these studies of interchangeability of tasks and of division of household labor according to availability, skill, interest, and enjoyment rather than exclusively according to sex (Yogev 1981).

However, one must conclude that this movement seems to be coming about very slowly, for the egalitarian behavior described here seems characteristic of only a minority of dual-career couples. Research on dual-career couples suggests that wives still have most of the responsibility for the domestic and child care roles. Role sharing is not often found among dual-career and professional couples (Epstein 1971; Poloma and Garland 1971; Weingarten 1978; St. John-Parsons 1978; Bryson and Bryson 1980; Yogev 1981). Professional couples, like other dual-career couples, tend to divide household responsibilities in the traditional manner and to place differential values on their careers (Bryson and Bryson 1980). The Brysons, in a study of couples in which both were psychologists, found not only that both husbands and wives consider the wife's employment as secondary and tend to subordinate her career to the husband's but also that wives were more likely to hold attitudes supportive of this behavior than husbands were. They concluded, as had the Rapoports (1971) earlier, that "most of the wives in these couples accepted as inevitable that they would have to bear the major burden of responsibility for child care and domestic organization, resulting in more strain on their careers than on their husbands" (Bryson and Bryson 1980:250). In a study of women lawyers in partnership with their husbands, Epstein (1971) found the traditional division of labor in the law partnership, as well as in the home. Haas (1980b:289) sums up the research on allocation of family roles among dual-career couples thus: "While the wife is committed to a career, her basic family responsibilities typically remain intact and her husband's career has precedence over hers."

In spite of the overload, stress, and conflict resulting from the two roles (career and family) that researchers have identified (Rapoport and Rapoport 1976; Johnson and Johnson 1976; Bryson et al. 1978; Holahan and Gilbert 1979), it is not clear that women want a more nearly equal division of family roles. Poloma (1972) discovered some techniques professional women in her study used to manage role conflict, but expecting or asking her family to help her to adjust to the demands of her two roles was not one of them. Some researchers (Rapoport and Rapoport 1971; St. John-Parsons 1978; Bryson and Bryson 1980; Kamerman 1980) have found that outside help, especially with the housecleaning, may be employed, but this does not alter the traditional division of household and child care responsibilities. St. John-Parsons (1978) reports that in his case study of ten dual-career families, not one wife expressed resentment of the sex-stereotyped division of household work they followed. From her study of married university faculty women, Yogev (1981:868) discovered that the traditional pattern in the home existed "not only because the husbands might be resistant and reluctant to increase their participation in housework and child care, but also because the women do not want or expect their husbands to share these responsibilities equally. It is important for them to have this unfair division so it will enable a wife to feel that she is 'the mother' in the family." Yet these women perceived themselves as essentially equal to their husbands. Yogev explains this apparent contradiction on the wives' part as due to what the Rapoports (1971) coined "identity tension line," which describes "how far individuals are able to go toward establishing their ideal new definitions of sex roles before reaching the point of discomfort, when these new behaviors threaten individual notions of self-esteem" (Yogev 1981:869). The author suggests that an egalitarian sharing of the domestic and child care roles may be beyond the identity tension lines for both men and women today.

Yogev's findings are consistent with those of other researchers who find that the maternal role is the Achilles' heel of dual-career wives. Role conflict among professional women is due primarily to guilt from perceived neglect of the maternal role (Johnson and Johnson 1977; Gilbert et al. 1981). Women in dual-career couples find their role as mother more limiting than their role as spouse (Heckman et al. 1977). Heckman and the Brysons (1977:328) conclude that the traditional norm about "woman's place" is still in place and that "women often fit their careers around children and husbands" because they believe "the children will suffer if they do not have their mother's care."

The "responsibility of motherhood" implicit in such statements is a reflection of the way society, including child care experts, have equated parenthood with motherhood, particularly since the middle of the nineteenth century. The importance of the father in the child's development has only recently been recognized. Because of the salience traditionally given to motherhood, for many women this role is still an important part of their sense of self and is a tremendous source of gratification (Hoffman 1983). Consequently, sharing the parenting role with their husbands may be threatening to the mothers; it may mean a loss of autonomy and control in a valued role, loss of a sense of unique competence in the family—and diminution of an intense mother-child relationship (Hoffman 1983).

Be that as it may, there is no solid evidence that the effects on children are deleterious when mothers work outside the home or when fathers share the child care role. Reviews of research on the effects of maternal employment on children have concluded that the mother's employment status per se seems to have limited influence on children's development and adjustment but have suggested that other variables (e.g., age and sex of children, family circumstances, parents' attitudes about the mother's working, child care arrangements) may mediate the effects (Etaugh 1974; Hoffman 1974). A recent longitudinal study, examining the effects of maternal employment on children at one, three, and six years of age, again found no negative effects on the children's social, emotional, and cognitive development attributable to the mothers' absence due to their employment (Zimmerman and Bernstein 1983). Similarly, research on the effects on children with high paternal involvement in child rearing indicate no cause for concern over shared parenting. Specifically, sex-role development, cognitive development, and the development of social competence have been found not to be affected adversely by high father involvement (Radin 1981, 1982; Radin and Russell 1983; Sagi 1982; Carlson 1981). Even with newborn infants, fathers have been found to be as competent as mothers in providing affection, stimulation, and the necessary care (Sawin and Parke 1979).

Regardless of their behavior women are more egalitarian in their attitudes about family roles than men are (Rapoport and Rapoport 1976; Araji 1977; Sexton 1979). Less educated husbands hold even more traditional attitudes than more educated husbands do (Lopata et al. 1980). However, these highly educated husbands do not necessarily translate their egalitarian attitudes into practice (Lopata et al. 1980).

In addition to noting the discrepancy often found between attitudes and behavior, researchers have tried to identify the characteristics of husbands and the situations in which husbands are more likely to help with the domestic work and child care. So far little is conclusive. The evidence is conflicting regarding social class; some studies indicate that working class or lower income husbands do less housework than middle-class husbands (Schneider and Smith 1973; Oakley 1974), but other studies seem to contradict this (Blood and Wolfe 1960; Ericksen et al. 1979). One problem is that researchers have tended to study one class or the other and thus have made direct comparisons difficult. Several studies have found that black husbands participate more in housework than white husbands do (Farkas 1976; Ericksen et al. 1979; Model 1981; Beckett and Smith 1981; Maret and Finlay 1984), but at least two studies have found the opposite (Blood and Wolfe 1960 and Pleck 1983). Generally education of both husbands and wives is positively related to role sharing, but this association may be tempered by the husband's income. The higher the wife's education, the more likely housework and child care are to be shared (Ericksen et al. 1979; Haas 1982). Not surprisingly, the same association holds for husbands; that is, compared to husbands with lower education, higher educated husbands are more involved in housework (Farkas 1976; Hesselbart 1976;

Mortimer et al. 1978; Aldous et al. 1979; Model 1981; Geerken and Gove 1983) because highly educated women tend to marry highly educated men. However, studies have also found that as the husband's income goes up, he is less likely to participate in domestic work (Ericksen et al. 1979; Model 1981). The wife's status and income relative to her husband's seems to be a key factor in these contradictory trends. Model (1981) found that the higher the wife's status relative to her husband's, the more likely she is to work and he to perform tasks at home. High education and relatively equal incomes of husbands and wives are associated with greater sharing of family roles (Mortimer et al. 1978; Aldous et al. 1979; Model 1981). Domestic role sharing also seems more likely when the higher education of the husband is combined with an egalitarian ideology on his part (Hesselbart 1976; Perrucci et al. 1976; Bird et al. 1984).

ROLE-SHARING COUPLES

A few other researchers have done as we have—identified couples who purport to share one or more family roles in order to examine the role-sharing behavior. Several of these researchers (DeFrain 1979; Radin 1981, 1982; Russell 1982; Sagi 1982; Carlson 1981, 1984) have concentrated on the child care role.

The extent to which fathers who share the child care role also share the domestic role is not clear. For example, DeFrain (1979) studied 100 androgynous parents, defined as those who shared child care and job or career responsibilities relatively equally. As measured by contact hours, mothers in his sample had 54 percent (and fathers 46 percent) of the child care duties, while fathers did 54 percent (and mothers 46 percent) of the labor involved in jobs and careers. In spite of relatively equal divisions in these two spheres, the couples divided housework in a more traditional manner. "The mothers did 77% of the cooking, 68% of the dishwashing, 73% of the cleaning, 68% of the grocery shopping, 74% of the laundry, and 87% of the ironing. Fathers did 79% of the servicing of the car, 77% of the lawn work, 85% of the household repairs, and took out the garbage 71% of the time" (DeFrain 1979:238).

However, Carlson (1984) found that fathers who shared child care, as contrasted with fathers who did not, did more housework. In this study Carlson interviewed a self-selected sample of 60 parents of preschool age children. The sample was divided into three groups according to the mother's employment status and the level of paternal responsibility for child care: (1) mother primary caregiver; (2) dual-career, mother primary caregiver; and (3) dual-career, shared caregiving. Not only did Carlson find that fathers in the third group (n = 20) performed significantly more housework than fathers in the other two groups, she also discovered that the fathers in the third group performed significantly more housework than their wives!

After careful screening, Haas (1982) was able to locate 31 couples (primarily young professionals) who shared family decision making and all of the family roles more or less equally. At least three-fourths of these couples were sharing the breadwinner role equally, but some were having difficulty with the idea that wives should have the same obligation to work as husbands. Overall, husbands and wives had relatively equal decision-making influence, spent approximately the same amounts of time on, and assumed the responsibility for, domestic, kinship, and child care tasks, but husbands did most of the handyman chores. Haas (1980a, 1981) also studied domestic and child care role sharing in Sweden. These findings are particularly interesting since Sweden is unique in its support (attitudinal and structural) of equality between the sexes in the home, as well as in the labor market (Haas 1981). The findings from Haas's mail survey indicated that although Swedish couples "share household chores more evenly than do American couples, . . . practice lags considerably behind ideology" (p. 957). There was also hesitancy on the couples' part to make the wife equally obligated to provide economic support and for men to share child care equally (Haas 1980a, 1981).

Kimball (1983) interviewed by phone 150 reportedly egalitarian couples, that is, couples who shared "money-making, housework, child care, and decision-making" (p. ix). The findings led the author to conclude that less than half (71 couples) were egalitarian in attitude and behavior. On the basis of her study, Kimball (p. xii) reported that "egalitarian marriages tend to fall into the three categories: (1) those that began traditionally and changed to role-sharing after the woman returned to paid work (these were the most troubled relationships), (2) second marriages that successfully react against a traditional first marriage, and (3) intact marriages that began equally (usually younger couples influenced by feminism)."

The Future

This brief historical overview and review of some recent research and thought on the division of family roles, while far from exhaustive, will provide, we hope, a background for considering the findings of our study and the issues we discuss in the subsequent chapters. The studies cited in this chapter are meant to be illustrative only; during the last decade or so, research on changing sex roles, women's labor force participation, family allocation of roles and responsibilities, and related topics has been burgeoning. We believe, however, that the research reviewed presents a fairly accurate picture of the state of our knowledge at this point about how couples currently handle family roles. (Readers interested in additional recent reviews may want to see Moen [1982], Miller and Garrison [1982], and Pleck [1983].)

One must conclude that the norm concerning the sexual division of labor is still alive and well. There are indications, however, that it may be beginning to weaken a little. Predictions about how much it might decline or to what extent it might be replaced by an egalitarian norm vary according to who is making them. Although our own opinion is that such predictions are risky, there is some evidence to suggest the possibility of a change. For example, Masnick and Bane's (1980) data suggest the likelihood of women's becoming increasingly attached to the labor force, which has different implications from merely participating in the work force. Nickols and Metzen (1982) found in a longitudinal study that while traditional role patterns still predominated, a few more husbands reported doing housework each year over the six-year period. Farkas (1976) found that *young* highly educated husbands shared housework more than older less educated husbands. Pleck (1979) reports that data from a 1977 representative national sample show a small increase in the amount of time husbands spent on housework when their wives are employed. Scanzoni and Fox (1980) conclude that while behavior seems to be slow to change, there is evidence of a gradual shift in preferences or attitudes away from the traditional. They also conclude that children with better educated parents are "less exposed to traditional preferences and stereotypes than children from less-advantaged homes" (p. 752).

A *New York Times* poll conducted in November 1983 (*New York Times* 12/4/83) found that women and men are growing much closer in their attitudes about work outside the home. Compared with a Virginia Slims poll in 1970, women seem to be moving toward viewing their place as on the job. Whereas only 9 percent of the women listed paid work as an enjoyable part of their lives in 1970, thirteen years later 26 percent did. Similarly 14 percent had mentioned general rights and freedom (independence) earlier, but this had increased to 32 percent by 1983. On the other hand, a dramatic difference was found in their reported enjoyment of their traditional family roles. In 1970, 53 percent of the women listed being a mother and raising a family as an enjoyable part of their lives; in 1983, only 26 percent did. Being a homemaker was mentioned by 43 percent in the earlier poll but by only 8 percent in the later one. Similarly, being a wife had fallen from 22 percent to 6 percent over the thirteen years. In the recent poll when women were asked whether they would prefer to have a job outside the home or to stay home to take care of their houses and family if they were free to do either, the women were divided almost equally between the two choices. However, the younger the woman, the more likely she was to choose the job over staying home.

If we are moving—albeit slowly—toward more egalitarian or symmetrical family patterns as these data and the writings of other experts on the family suggest (Bernard 1971; Young and Willmott 1973; Matthaei 1982; Scanzoni 1983) we can expect role-sharing behavior to become more common. Although such behavior may be rational or functional for many families, we do not see it as a panacea. Like any other lifestyle, it has its rewards and problems. Our major concern in this book is to identify and examine some of the problems and issues involved when couples attempt the sharing of work-family roles at this point in time.

3

Extent of Role Sharing

Between 1978 and 1982 we interviewed 64 couples with a role-sharing lifestyle. These couples had been referred to our study because they seemed to meet our criteria, the most important of which was sharing the major work-family roles—an assessment with which the couples agreed was generally true although a minority were in a transitional stage at the time of our data collection. During the interviews, we obtained rather detailed information about how they handled these roles and about issues that arose in sharing the responsibilities involved.

This chapter describes the couples and the amount of role sharing we found. It concludes with a discussion of some of the problems involved in trying to measure role sharing. (See appendix A for a description of the study design and methods.)

Characteristics of the Couples

The couples we interviewed were middle class, white, and urban, living in or near Milwaukee, Wisconsin, or Albany, New York. The large majority were dual-career, as opposed to dual-worker, couples. A wide variety of professions was represented. Because most of the couples had been recruited through faculty and students in schools of social welfare, it is not surprising that many of our respondents were social workers, psychologists, psychiatrists, other mental health workers, and university professors. In addition, there were teachers, nurses, physicians, lawyers, businessmen and women, artists, law enforcement officials, clerical workers, salesmen, and so on. Almost all were college educated, more than half of the husbands and almost half of the wives having an advanced degree, that is, a masters, doctoral, medical, or law degree.

The median age of both wives and husbands was 32 years. However, there was a great spread in ages, for they ranged from 22 to 55 years. Most of the couples had been married for a number of years, with the range from 1 to 29 years. Two-thirds had been married for six years or longer. It was the first marriage for all but eight husbands and eight wives, not always in the same couple.

Of the 64 couples, 37 had children. Almost half of the couples with children had only one, and most of the rest, only two. The ages of the children living at home ranged from a few weeks to 22 years, but the large majority were ten years of age or younger.

Role Sharing

Although the sharing of each of the three major work-family roles are considered separately in chapters to follow, the roles are looked at together here to obtain a composite picture of role sharing on a more or less equal basis. The indicators of role sharing used here have been simplified considerably and do not deal with many of the complexities of the data that the later chapters do. Only the couples' behavior at the time of our interviews is considered in this section; no attempt is made to take into account temporary imbalance or a view of the relationship over time. Consequently, the "transitional" couples (defined in chapter 1) who basically share the role-sharing lifestyle show up in this description of current behavior as not sharing one or more work-family roles. This transitional group consists of 21 couples in which one spouse, usually the wife, was temporarily not employed full time. The majority of these spouses were employed part time; most of the rest were either on leave or attending school.

Across Roles

The breadwinner role was considered to be shared if both spouses had full-time paid employment or if both engaged in paid employment part time. There were 41 couples in the former category and two in the latter.

Following Haas (1980b) we used the 40- to 60-percent range to define shared domestic and child care tasks. The domestic role was considered shared if neither spouse performed less than 40 percent or more than 60 percent of the following tasks: cooking, after-meal cleanup, planning meals, grocery shopping, vacuuming, scrubbing floors, and laundry. (See appendix B for descriptions of scales used in this section.) These tasks were selected from a longer list of domestic chores we inquired about because they, unlike the others, are usually done on a regular basis. They also represent tasks traditionally considered "women's work." According to our criterion, 51 couples shared the domestic role. Husbands in two of these couples were rated as doing slightly more than 60 percent but were included here because the tasks were those traditionally performed by women.

Child care was considered shared if neither spouse did less than 40 percent or more than 60 percent of the child care and socialization tasks in the following areas: routine care, child's development, emotional support, and child's entertainment. Of the 37 couples who had children, 31 met this criterion.

When one looks at the sharing across roles in the families, it is clear that children make the role-sharing pattern harder to attain. Of the 27 couples without children in the home, 21 (78 percent) shared both the breadwinner and domestic roles. Only 13 of the 37 parents (35 percent) shared the breadwinner, domestic, and child care roles. Thus, at the time of our interviews 34 (53 percent) of the 64 couples were sharing all applicable work-family roles on a fairly equal basis.

The majority of our sample could be defined then as "clearly role sharing" according to our criteria. The remainder fell along a continuum of role sharing ranging from amounts close to what was found in the majority to amounts perhaps only one step removed from traditional or quasi-traditional styles. We shall examine the extent of sharing in different subgroups.

Although by definition the 21 transitional couples did not fully share the breadwinner role, a good deal of sharing took place in remaining roles. Ten of these couples shared both the domestic and child care roles according to our 40- to 60-percent criterion. An additional eight shared either the domestic or child care role. This amount of sharing of domestic and child care roles suggests that the couples as a whole were truly transitional; that is, one could expect sharing of these roles to continue or be augmented when the nonemployed spouse returned to work outside the home.

The remaining nine couples (of the 64 interviewed) shared the bread-winner role and seven of these the child care role as well. There was no case of a couple with children who shared the domestic tasks but not child care responsibilities. The other two couples, both childless, shared just the breadwinner role; that is, they fell outside the 40- to 60-percent range on domestic tasks. Of all the couples we interviewed, these two came closest to the quasi-traditional style: a working wife carrying a disproportionate share of domestic and child care chores. A closer look at their division of labor, however, revealed noteworthy sharing of the domestic role with a similar pattern in each: the majority of domestic tasks were shared, the remaining tasks falling to the wife.

To summarize, the majority (53 percent) of the couples studied shared all available roles; an additional 39 percent shared either the domestic or child care role—often both. Thus, in the great prepon-derance of cases—92 percent—men and women shared at least one role traditionally assumed by women.

COUPLES WITH YOUNG CHILDREN

There is, of course, a good rationale for focusing on couples with young children to ascertain the extent of sharing what has been tradi-tionally considered "women's work." When there are children, the tasks and responsibilities of the family role are greatly increased over those of couples who do not have children. We are referring not only to the addition of a major set of responsibilities described variously as child care, child rearing, socialization, or parenting but also to the greatly expanded domestic role that comes with having children. There are more of all the domestic tasks—cooking, laundry, cleaning, and so on—to do and also more urgency about doing them. For example, if a couple without children do not feel like cooking dinner, they have several options such as going out to dinner, ordering a pizza, heating up a can of soup to go with the leftover pie, or leaving it to each person to fend for herself or himself. The options are much narrower, and cannot be resorted to as often, in families with young children.

To look at this expanded role set more closely, we selected the 33 couples with children under 12 years of age and divided them into three groups according to the amount of time the mother was engaged in paid work: full time, part time, or temporarily not employed. As one might expect, nonworking mothers were the most likely to have very young children (age three or under), and mothers working full time, the least likely. Fathers were more likely to share in child care tasks when mothers worked full time outside the home and less likely when mothers were employed only part time or not at all. These findings are consistent with those reported by Hoffman (1977) and Pleck (1977).

When we examined domestic tasks among these three groups, again we found fathers more likely to share when the mother has full-time paid work than if she is not employed or works only part time. When individual couples are looked at across the domestic and child care roles, there is a high correspondence between the husband's sharing both sets of tasks. In other words, fathers who share child care tend to share in housework also. Fathers who share one of these roles but not the other are more likely to have wives employed part time.

One other comparison may be of interest. One might wonder if husbands are more likely to share housework when there are children in the family than when there are not. To answer this question, we looked only at couples in which the wives were in full-time paid work. We divided these couples into two groups: childless couples (n = 23) and families with children under 12 years of age (n = 13). We found that fathers were less likely to share housework than men without children were. This finding is consistent with some other studies (Blood and Wolfe 1960; Silverman and Hill 1967; Model 1981). However, Pleck (1983) reports finding just the opposite. Model (1981) suggested that husbands participate less in housework when children are available as substitutes. Although couples in our study indicated that older children helped with the domestic work, they seldom mentioned participation by children under 12. In our reporting of data, tasks performed by children or paid help are not credited to either the wife or husband.

As we have indicated, the couples we studied were not a sample of marital pairs who shared all of the work and family roles equally. To our knowledge, no such pristine sample has been studied. The closest to this ideal among American couples is Haas's (1980b; 1982) sample of 31 couples. Our sample is more varied but not dissimilar to hers in respect to numbers of role-sharing couples studied. The present sample certainly differs sharply in proportion of role-sharing marriages from usual samples of dual-career or dual-worker couples.

The couples in our study are not intended to represent a cross section of role-sharing couples. In addition to its bias toward mental health professionals, it doubtless contains more "happy marriages" and partners with positive attitudes toward role sharing than one might expect to find in some hypothetical cross section of such couples. People with troubled marriages or in conflict about role sharing are likely to steer clear of studies such as ours. Nevertheless, as we shall see, our couples are sufficiently diverse to reveal a wide range of practices, attitudes, and issues relating to role sharing, a range that we assume is reasonably comprehensive.

Measurement of Role Sharing

Role sharing, like many other useful and interesting concepts, is difficult to pin down. Implicit in our discussion so far is the imprecision of the term. In the first chapter we tried to convey what we mean by role sharing on an abstract level and in this chapter we defined it operationally. It is clear from the latter, however, that a number of problems are inherent in any attempt to measure role sharing. In this section, we briefly discuss some of these difficulties. Because they involve the essential meaning of role sharing, the difficulties are of more than technical interest.

Researchers have employed one of two major methods for obtaining data used to ascertain whether or not, and to what extent, role sharing occurs. One is referred to as time use, time budget, or time allocation.

Here the actual amount of time husbands and wives spend on various activities is obtained by techniques such as having respondents keep a record of the time they spend on certain designated activities or keep a time diary of all their activities for a specified period. An alternate and less precise technique is to have respondents estimate the amount of time they spend on specific activities. The second major method—the one we used—is a proportional measure: husbands' and wives' performance of activities is obtained relative to their spouses. For example, couples may be asked to estimate what percentage of each of a number of designated tasks each spouse does. Or, as in our study, the couple may be asked to rate a list of tasks on a scale indicating who performs or takes responsibility for each task. Scale values may be: husband, husband mostly, both, wife mostly, wife, or something similar. Data obtained with this second method are relative; that is, they answer the question of what proportion of a particular role or task is performed by each spouse. This method does not provide the additional information that time-use studies do, that is, how much absolute time each devotes to a task or group of activities. For example, we cannot ascertain from our data how much more time one spouse may spend on a given task or set of tasks than her or his mate. Nor can we tell if Mr. A, who does all of the cooking in his family, spends more or less time on this task than Mrs. B, who also does all of the cooking for her family. Although these are limitations, information about absolute time is not crucial to measuring role sharing, which by definition is relative.

Whether or not absolute or relative data are used, a decision must be made about when a task or role is to be considered shared. For example, how much time must a husband, compared with his wife, spend doing laundry before he is considered to be sharing the task? Is the response "husband mostly" to yardwork to be counted as shared? What proportion of domestic tasks must a husband perform or share to be considered sharing the domestic role? Such questions are not easily answered, and any cutoff point must necessarily be arbitrary. To insist on exactly 50–50 sharing of the domestic and child care roles is to limit drastically the number of role-sharing couples. On the other hand, occasional help from a spouse with a task in one's role set is not what we mean by role sharing. Our compromise of a 40-60 performance ratio may not be considered acceptable by everyone.

Some tasks are more important than others. For example, cooking is usually considered more important than dusting according to any number of criteria; it is essential to the welfare of the family, is necessary rather than optional, requires regular as opposed to occasional performance, requires a great deal of time and effort, and so forth. In view of the differences in importance, regularity of performance, time and effort involved, and so on, should all tasks in a role set be counted equally? If not, how does one weight them?

Implicit in this discussion are specific measures of performance. But what should these measures be—time, effort, results, or what? Should we be concerned about who performs a task or who has responsibility for it if these are not the same person? To illustrate, is the breadwinner role shared if the husband is employed full time and the wife works outside the home three days a week? One day a week? Fills in occasionally during regular employees' vacations? If she earns money occasionally typing manuscripts at home? In all these examples, it is clear that the husband would be considered the primary breadwinner, but would he also be considered the sole breadwinner for all intents and purposes in some of these cases? Also, does it matter how much the wife earns, compared with her husband, in considering whether the financial provider role is shared? Even harder to determine is a 40-60 ratio in the performance of the breadwinner role. Our solution was to use roughly equal amounts of work effort (husband and wife both full time or both part time). This differs from most studies that consider the role shared if the wife has any paid employment, although the analyses may consider whether the wife is in full-time or part-time employment. Since few wives earn as much as their husbands, neither actual salaries nor the proportion of the family income each spouse provides is generally considered a fair indicator of the extent to which the breadwinner role is shared.

Much variation exists in studies of the performance of family roles in terms of which roles, tasks, and activities are included. Probably the most striking difference is between the studies that define the domestic role as including household tasks traditionally performed by men, as well as those usually performed by women, and the studies that limit themselves to the traditional female domestic role set. The latter studies are usually interested in ascertaining the extent to which husbands are sharing in "women's work" in view of wives' increasing involvement in "men's work" (earning money for the family). In our effort to determine role sharing across the three major work-family roles, we limited our indicators to those domestic tasks usually performed on a regular basis. These tasks are also the ones traditionally performed by women. However, we obtained data on the domestic role more broadly defined; these data are presented in chapter 5.

In addition to the variation mentioned above, researchers do not always use the same set of tasks to designate the domestic or the child care role. Some tasks may be included in one study but not in another, and this variation makes comparisons difficult. The tasks used as indicators of a role may vary in inclusiveness and specificity. For example, one researcher might inquire about housecleaning but another might ask about vacuuming, dusting, picking up, scrubbing floors, cleaning bathrooms, etc. Even the work-family roles included in the study may vary. The roles most often studied are the three with which we are concerned. Haas (1980b) suggests the following typology of traditionally sex-segregated family roles: the breadwinner role, the domestic role, the handyman role, the kinship role, the childcare role, and the major/minor decision-maker roles.

Earlier we mentioned the difficulty in deciding when a role is shared. Trying to decide if a task is shared presents additional complications. Luckily, the latter may be considered different ways of sharing, and this stratagem avoids our basic dilemma. A consideration of these variations may help in understanding our findings. Here we are referring to the varied behaviors of couples when they told us a task was shared or that they both performed a task. Sometimes this meant that both participated in the task at the same time (e.g., in washing dishes, one spouse might rinse the dishes and the other stack them in the dishwasher); at other times, sharing meant that each performed the task alone at different times (e.g., taking turns); at still other times, it meant that each spouse did the task for herself or himself (e.g., doing their own ironing or taking care of their own cars).

Regardless of how one decides to measure role-sharing behavior, cross-sectional data or data obtained at one point in time generally will be limited to that point in time. (One can ask about past behavior, usual behavior over a long time span, or even anticipated or planned behavior, but often such data are fraught with difficulties such as incomplete or inaccurate recall, global and impressionistic generalizations, and guess-work.) Since one of the hallmarks of successful role sharing is flexibility or adaptability (a point developed in later chapters), some of the couples who usually share work-family roles may be in a transitional status—for example, the wife staying home temporarily to care for an infant—at the time of data collection. Although one may obtain a picture of the usual pattern of handling family roles, which behavior "counts"—what they are doing now, what they did at an earlier time, what they plan to do, or does one try to make a global assessment of the marital relationship? How one resolves this dilemma may depend on what question one is trying to answer.

Biases in self-report data in studies of this kind are particularly problematic. When respondents know what a researcher is looking for, they often "help out," consciously or unconsciously, by giving it to him or her, particularly if the behavior or attitudes being studied are socially acceptable. At this point in time, it might be easier to find the proverbial needle than the dual-career couple who has any doubts about how anyone studying role-sharing or egalitarian marriages evaluates such relationships. This is not to imply that respondents try to deceive the researcher or deliberately distort information; they generally do not. It simply means that ambivalent attitudes or perceptions of ambiguous behavior may temporarily shift in the direction of "social desirability" when couples are queried about them. For example, a husband's occasionally helping to fold clothes taken from the dryer may be elevated to sharing in "doing the laundry" when the couple is asked who does this task. As the example suggests, the social desirability bias probably operates in the direction of inflating the husband's participation in traditionally female tasks.

Another bias somewhat related is what we refer to as the "talking dog syndrome"—the exaggeration that occurs when one spouse does anything that his or her sex does not ordinarily do or that is not expected of that sex. In our study it is more likely to involve things the husband does since most of the domestic and child care tasks we asked about are generally assumed to be "women's work." For example, a husband with modest culinary skills may be elevated to the status of gourmet cook. Or a husband who does a considerable amount of housework may be described as a househusband, though he may have full-time paid employment and a wife who does as much (or more) housework as he.

Although these biases may have distorted somewhat our picture of the husband's role sharing, they were kept in check, we assume, by use of in-depth joint interviews with both husbands and wives who could, and often did, correct one another's reports. Moreover, as noted, evidence of husband's participation in domestic and child care tasks was interpreted conservatively.

4

Earning and Spending Money

The breadwinner role is the pivotal role in a role-sharing relationship. It is only when the wife shares this role that any serious consideration is given to sharing the family roles. But as the research reviewed in chapter 2 amply demonstrates, the sharing of the breadwinner role has triggered little general role-sharing behavior in families so far.

Whether or not and to what extent wives participate in the breadwinner role traditionally assigned to husbands is usually ascertained in a straightforward, objective manner. One can simply look at whether or not the wife has a paid job, the number of hours she works outside the home (generally broken down into full time or part time), and the percentage of the family income she earns. Family income is generally assumed to be equal to the sum total of the husband's and wife's earnings; income from other sources may or may not be considered.

Far more complex and interesting, we think, is how who earns the money in families affects other aspects of the marital relationship and how the money is managed in families. These two phenomena may vary in different types of marriage, and consequently different problems and issues may arise. A great deal of research has been done on the first of these two topics. For example, chapter 2 reviewed a number of studies that looked at the extent of the husband's participation in housework and child care when wives are employed. Power or decision making in families has also been studied, with the general conclusion that as wives' earnings increase relative to their husbands', their family power increases (Blumstein and Schwartz 1983). When money management in dual-earner couples is studied, it is generally assumed that there is one combined pot to be managed. An exception is Bird (1979), who described four types of couples, depending on how they viewed the wife's earnings: pin money couples (hers to spend as she pleases); earmarker couples (wife "helps" by working for specific items or goals); pooler couples (combining income into a family pot); and bargainer couples (each spouse controlling own paycheck).

Thus, although this chapter presents data on the earning of money, most of the chapter is devoted to the less clear-cut matter of money management—the other side of the coin, so to speak. Issues related to the two approaches to money—family ("poolers") or individual ("bargainers")—that couples in our study used are discussed at some length.

Responsibility for the Breadwinner Role

All 64 of the couples in our sample saw themselves as sharing the breadwinner role, though not necessarily continuously or equally. In fact, at the time of the interviews, some of the spouses were temporarily working outside the home only part time, and others, not at all. As expected, spouses not employed full time were far more likely to be wives. Of the seven wives temporarily not working outside the home, three were full-time students, one had just completed a professional degree and was looking for a job, and the others were staying home to care for infants or preschool age children. An additional fourteen wives—a student, three mothers of infants, eight mothers of preschool-age children, and two mothers of school-age children—were employed part time. Almost all the wives had full-time employment before having children or returning to school. All planned to return to full-time work outside the home at some future time.

Only four husbands were not employed full time. Two husbands in couples without children were temporarily unemployed: one was a full-time student and the other was doing work he enjoyed without pay while taking his turn at being supported by his wife. The latter couple had agreed before marriage to take turns supporting each other to give the other spouse the opportunity to obtain further education or to explore career options. The wife had already taken three years to obtain a professional degree. Two husbands were working part time: one temporarily to take turns with his wife, who also worked part time, in taking care of their preschool-age child; and the other because he and his wife had agreed that each would work only part time to have more time to enjoy each other and other things in life. The latter husband had recently increased his work hours and his wife had decreased hers owing to the birth of their son.

RELATIVE INCOMES

We asked each spouse about his or her annual gross salary using income brackets of $5,000. Not surprisingly, husbands generally earned more both because they were more likely to work full time and because their salaries were often higher than their wives even when both worked full time. Of the 57 couples in which both spouses indicated an annual salary, 18 consisted of spouses in the same income bracket. Nine of the husbands had incomes one bracket higher than their wives, and 24 husbands' salaries were two to seven brackets higher than their wives. Only six wives' salaries were in a higher income bracket than their husbands. When we looked at only the 41 couples in which both spouses were employed full time, we found the following changes: 15 couples with spouses' salaries in the same salary range, eight with husband's salaries one bracket above their wives, and 12 husbands with salaries two to seven brackets above their wives. (The other six couples were those in which the wife earned more than the husband.)

PERCEPTION OF BREADWINNER ROLE

More important for our study than actual salaries, however, was how the couples felt about responsibility for the breadwinner role. Taking into their calculation unemployment, part-time work, and sometimes salary differentials, 35 of the couples saw the provider role for the unit as being shared and 19 couples perceived the husband as the major breadwinner, at least temporarily. In addition, the husband was the sole breadwinner in eight couples and the wife in two. This is a snapshot picture of the way the breadwinner role was viewed at the time of our interviews. Many couples indicated the fluidity of their financial arrangements, sometimes with one spouse supporting the unit at one time and the other spouse at another time. Almost all seemed to feel that viewed over a long time perspective, the provider role was shared.

When each spouse was asked specifically if he or she felt financially responsible for the other spouse, the larger number of husbands and wives said no. They explained this by saying that there was no need to since the other spouse could take care of herself or himself financially. However, most spontaneously indicated that if the other spouse could not work, then of course they would provide financial support for the other. A few spouses even said that if the other did not work, they would be financially responsible for him or her. Most of our couples made a clear distinction between not being able to work and choosing not to work, indicating that they expected the other spouse to work if he or she could, barring a mutual decision for that spouse to return to school, stay home with children, or something similar. While they did not go so far as to say they would not provide for the other if he or she simply chose not to work, they did indicate that such a situation would be problematic, as well as unexpected. This seems consistent with the notion of a shared breadwinner role.

Views and Management of Money

We were interested in learning if values relating to spouse autonomy were reflected in how these couples handled family expenses and finances. Specifically, we wondered to what extent there might be a shift from regarding money earned by each spouse as "family money" to viewing it as "individual money." By "family money" we mean that the spouses put their money in a common pot without regard to who earned it or the type of expenditure (i.e., family or individual) for which it is used. "Individual money" would be the converse; that is, the contribution of each spouse is taken into account, as well as the type of expenditure, with a distinction made between whether the expenditure is for the couple or family as a unit or for one of the spouses individually. Generally, partners who view their money as individual money do not pool their incomes except perhaps enough to cover certain agreed upon common expenses. Although we were aware that spouses who might see their incomes as their personal money would still need to make some arrangement for handling "common" or family expenses, we wondered if couples who viewed both incomes as family money also have a need for personal money in addition. Obviously, the more radical of the two orientations is the individual money perception on the part of both partners, made possible for most couples only by the wife's obtaining paid employment.

We emphasize "on the part of both partners" since we are aware that historically some husbands and wives (rarely in the same families) have viewed all or part of their incomes as their individual money. For example, some husbands, as sole family breadwinners, have felt the money they earned was theirs, though they contributed part of their incomes to the family unit. The salaries that some women earn are regarded by both the wife and the husband as her money; in such cases the wives do not contribute financially to the support of the family, though on occasion they may voluntarily spend money on other members of the family or on the household. Other employed women who view their salaries as personal money may use it, not for themselves, but for obligations they do not share with their husbands such as paying a parent's medical bills, contributing to the support of an elderly parent, or paying off a college loan. In none of these examples is the breadwinner role shared by husband and wife.

A related but slightly different pattern that was probably more common in the past than now is for the wife's income to be used for the family but only for extras or one-time expenses, such as vacations, private schools for the children, a down payment on a house, a child's orthodontia, or a boat. In such families, the husband is generally perceived as the breadwinner since he provides for the family's basic necessities, though the wife may be viewed as "helping out." In such cases, the wife's income may be viewed by one or both spouses as her individual money or as family money. If viewed as her money while the husband's income is family money, this pattern has the same asymmetry as in the previous examples, and it is questionable whether the breadwinner role should be viewed as shared. If the wife's income, like her husband's, is viewed as family money, this financial arrangement may be considered one of the patterns used by couples sharing the breadwinner role.

FAMILY PERSPECTIVE

Regardless of who earned the money, how the breadwinner role was viewed, or how family expenses were handled, the large majority of these couples (all but 11 couples) viewed their incomes as family money at the time of our interviews. Most of the partners in these couples had worked before marriage, and of course, each had managed his or her own money. Even the few couples who had lived together before getting married had continued their individual orientations to money while cohabitating, though they had worked out arrangements for sharing common expenses. Yet most of the people in our sample who had been financially independent before marriage began, upon getting married, to pool their incomes as family money. However, there were some couples in this group who had continued in their individual orientation for a while after marriage but had later changed to combining their incomes as family money. In some cases the change occurred when one spouse's paid work effort was reduced, for example, when having a child, but in other cases the couple simply decided pooling was less complicated.

Although these couples pooled all or most of their incomes, almost all of the partners considered it necessary to have some money to spend as they pleased. In fact, one or both partners in 60 percent of these couples had individual savings or checking accounts. Both spouses were generally involved in the management of family money, decisions for major purchases being made together and those for small purchases often being made independently by either spouse. In no case was the wife reported to have the edge in decision making regarding the commitment of money for a major purchase, but the husband was in several couples. Almost invariably in these instances the husband had the higher salary and managed the family money.

It is possible that the control of the family's financial resources is more tilted toward the husband than these findings indicate. Some wives who earned less than their husbands stated that they did not feel they had as much right as their husbands to commit the family money; some even saw family power as being related to one's financial contribution. A few wives expressed displeasure with their husbands' withholding money from the family pot to spend or save as they pleased when the wives pooled all of their incomes. Consequently, some wives felt a larger proportion of their salaries than of their husbands' went for family expenses. Some wives seemed concerned that their husbands spent family money more freely and in larger amounts than they themselves did. A few wives indicated that they wanted more control over the family's financial resources. None of these feelings or complaints were expressed by husbands in our sample. It is also important to remember that only a minority of wives expressed any feelings of dissatisfaction or inequality regarding the management of money. The large majority of spouses were very pleased with their financial arrangements and emphasized the agreement, mutual trust, and shared values concerning money existing between husband and wife.

INDIVIDUAL PERSPECTIVE

At the time of our interviews, only 11 of the 64 couples seemed to have an individual, rather than a family, orientation to their incomes. Six additional couples had viewed their incomes as individual money when both spouses were employed full time but shifted to the family money perspective when one partner became the sole or major breadwinner. Each spouse in these 11 couples managed his or her money independently, and only three of these couples had joint checking or savings accounts in addition to the separate ones.

Although an individual orientation to money is easier to maintain if there are two incomes, preferably equal ones, the individual perspective is possible even when this is not the case. Spouses in only two of the 11 couples with an individual money perspective had approximately equal incomes. In fact, the husband was viewed as the primary breadwinner in two cases and the wife was temporarily the sole provider in another.

The wife who was the sole breadwinner simply deposited part of her salary into her husband's checking account and the rest into hers as her husband had done earlier when he was the sole wage earner. Joint expenses were paid from either account. This couple discuss and decide together about major expenditures but reluctantly admit that the one bringing in the money does have more say in these financial decisions even though they do not believe it should be this way.

In the two couples who viewed incomes as individual money but in which the husband was the major provider, the wives were employed full time but earned much less than their husbands. These two couples handled their incomes in very different ways. In one—a family with two school-age children—the husband gave his wife a check each month for groceries and the children's clothing. In addition, he paid most of the large family bills, while his wife paid the rest out of her income. Both have money left over for personal expenses.

The other couple, who have no children, tried various ways of splitting common expenses before finding a method satisfactory to both of them. At first, they tried dividing their joint expenses so that each paid half, but the wife was broke all the time because of her low salary while her husband was building up his savings account. Even when they agreed to lower the percentage of the joint expenses she was to pay, they found that she still had far less left over than her husband did. Although this situation was quite satisfactory to the husband, it was perceived differently by the wife. After several days of her complaining, his resisting, their arguing, a stalemate of silence and sulking ensued. Soon they were ready to discuss the situation rationally in order to find a solution satisfactory to both. The plan they arrived at consisted essentially of the husband's subsidizing the wife: both salaries are pooled, all joint expenses are paid out of this pool, and the money left over is divided so that each spouse gets half. She reported feeling happy about the arrangement and still financially independent, while her husband believes the new system is fairer and better since, in his words "half the fun of making money is sharing it with my wife."

The other eight couples with an individual-money perspective considered the breadwinner role fully shared. This group, which consisted of spouses all employed full time, handled common expenses in a variety of ways. In all but one case, the common expenses were handled so that the partner earning more—usually the husband—paid more of the family expenses. In two families, the husband moved in with the wife and her children by a previous marriage. In both of these cases, the husband gave his wife a check each month, in an amount agreed upon by the couple, for household expenses. Four couples split the common expenses by having each spouse pay certain agreed upon bills out of his or her account. The person earning more pays the larger bills. The other two couples split the household expenses by having either spouse pay the bills and keep track of what he or she has spent, the couple settling accounts on a regular basis. Both couples split the bills on a fifty-fifty basis, with the exception that the husband in one couple (the Ys, discussed later) also pays for all of the couples' food and entertainment. Because the husband earns more than his wife, the couple sees this as a way to have each contribute to the family unit proportionately to his or her income. Although the husband in the other couple (the Zs, discussed later) also earns more, both spouses are committed to equal contributions to joint expenses. This arrangement has resulted in the wife's being in debt to her husband since she had difficulty managing her half, while the husband is accumulating money in an individual savings account.

PROS AND CONS OF THE TWO
APPROACHES TO MONEY MANAGEMENT

Family Orientation. Couples who regarded their income as family money cited many advantages and both real and potential disadvantages. Prominent among the former was their belief that it was simply more efficient to handle money in this manner. For them it took less time, thought, and energy to pool their money than to figure out who should pay for what and to devise a system for handling common expenses from separate accounts. Yet, some of the poolers saw this method as being inefficient, particularly when both partners were writing checks on the joint account. Good record keeping and both spouses' constantly being aware of the financial picture were cited as requirements when the money was managed jointly. Overdrawn accounts occurred from time to time. Some of these couples thought that not only was it harder to know where they stood financially, it was also harder to plan, since control of the money was shared. Apparently this was not a disadvantage to all poolers, since some cited as an advantage their ability to save more money and to pursue joint goals better by putting their money together.

Some of the poolers also liked the fact that the spouse who was the better financial manager could handle the family finances. Thus, the less capable partner in this area or the one who simply did not want to be bothered did not have to. Indeed, several of these spouses did turn over all or most of their paychecks to the other to manage. Most of the individuals in the sample, however, found it necessary to have some money—no matter how little—to spend as they chose.

Shared decision making was seen positively by many of these couples but negatively by others. Whereas some couples valued the necessity of joint decisions about family money, believing that better and less impulsive decisions were made that way, others complained that the necessary joint decision making was slow and found it sad that impulse spending was virtually eliminated. Some regretted lack of freedom in spending and sometimes found it a burden to always have to consider the other spouse before spending. The result, according to some poolers, was to spend less money on themselves than they thought they would otherwise. One wife went so far as to mention self-sacrificing as a disadvantage of this method.

Some couples stated that pooling made them feel closer to each other, more like a family unit. They thought it prevented feelings of competition that might otherwise arise if one partner earned more or had more money at her or his disposal. With some couples, however, the control issue was not settled by pooling. It was not uncommon for the lower wage earner, usually the wife, to feel that she or he had less right to participate fully in the family's financial decisions. Generally the higher earning spouse did not feel he or she should have more power in the relationship, but some admitted they did, especially in disputes over spending. The closeness in the marital relationship that some couples achieved by pooling all their financial resources had the drawback of preventing these spouses from feeling that they could ever give the other a gift. They explained this feeling by asking, "How can you really give another person a gift if he or she is paying for part of it?" and "How would you like to receive a gift from your spouse and have to write out a check for it when the bill came due?" In other words, they saw it as tantamount to the spouse's buying his or her own gift.

A number of the couples pointed out that pooling worked well for them because they had similar values regarding money and trusted each other. They thought this method would cause problems if there was a lack of mutual trust, or if one spouse spent more than the other, spent money for things the other did not approve of, felt too constrained in spending, and so on. Some couples who were quite satisfied with pooling mentioned another potential disadvantage of the method that would occur in the event of divorce or death of one of the spouses. They thought pooling would make financial disentanglements more complicated and problematic. Couples in which one partner managed the family money also saw a potential disadvantage in the other partner's not knowing how to manage money.

A large group of poolers, particularly those in which each spouse also had some money to manage independently, saw no disadvantages to their method of handling money. Regardless of advantages or disadvantages they cited when asked, some couples admitted they had never considered any other way of handling money.

Some pooling couples who were aware of the option of each spouse managing her or his own money volunteered that they thought the latter method too complicated, likely to cause hassles and problems, and "a pain" having to keep track of who spent what. They did not like what they described as a "this is mine, that is yours" attitude that they saw as petty. Some also described the method as inefficient, for it prevented family budgeting and planning, which they seemed to see as preferable to budgeting and planning on an individual basis.

Individual Orientation. Needless to say, couples in which each spouse did manage his or her own money saw things differently. They believed their method, compared with joint management of pooled money, was more efficient and involved fewer conflicts. They liked the fact that financial dependence between the spouses was reduced and that each had the freedom to spend her or his money as he or she chose. For example, one partner would not have to be involved or affected by the other's financial investments; support of or gifts to children by a previous marriage; expenses of property purchased before marriage or individually after marriage; costs of separate trips to visit, or vacation with, one spouse's family or friends; or purchase of expensive clothing or equipment that only one partner wanted. Although these couples often chose to discuss individual financial plans with each other, this seemed to be primarily for informational purposes and perhaps feedback to be taken into account in one's individual decisions.

The only disadvantage of this method mentioned by a few couples who used it was their not saving as much as they thought they should. These spouses believed they spent more than they would have under the constraints of joint finances and management.

Case Examples

The financial arrangements of two of the 11 couples with an individual money orientation will be elaborated further to illustrate two different effects of this approach. Both arrangements for handling joint expenses are precise and businesslike, but one raises many issues that the other does not.

The Ys. This is a professional couple—he, a self-employed architect and she, a psychologist—in their late thirties who have decided not to have children. Both were married previously and Mr. Y has a son by his first marriage whom he supports. Although her income is rather high, his is higher still even after child support payments. The Ys enjoy a very comfortable standard of living. In addition to owning a well-appointed home in the city, they have a summer home on a lake. They own a boat, each has a small luxury-class car, a cleaning service comes in twice a week, and the Ys entertain rather lavishly and often eat out.

By the time the Ys married eight years ago, both were well on their way to becoming established in their careers and were used to living independently. Each has continued to maintain her or his financial independence since marriage. Their system of handling common expenses, worked out in principle before their marriage, has worked well for them, they say. Each contributes half to things they purchase jointly—the houses, furnishings, boat, etc. Each pays for and maintains his or her own car. All household expenses, except for groceries, are shared equally. Under their management system, either one pays bills or makes joint purchases. Each keeps a running record of money expended for the common good, and these accounts are settled at the end of the month. Since Mr. Y's salary is higher than his wife's, he buys the groceries and pays for the couple's dining out and entertainment outside the home. Each pays her or his own expenses for vacations and other trips away from home, whether taken together or separately.

Although the rules concerning who pays for what are clear, the Ys are flexible enough to vary this at times in order to let one spouse treat the other if she or he wants to. For example, Mrs. Y may treat her husband to dinner out, Mr. Y may treat his wife to an unexpected trip, or either may purchase something for the home without charging the other for half. The Ys seem to enjoy treating each other at times, just as they enjoy buying each other gifts. Of course, it is easier for the Ys to be generous in this manner than it would be for a less affluent couple, but altruism and affluence are not always directly related.

The Zs. Mrs. Z, a secretary, is in her mid-twenties, and her husband, a criminal lawyer, is ten years older. They have been married for two years and have no children. This is the second marriage for both, their first marriages having ended in divorce. Mr. Z pays alimony to his ex-wife and child support for his two daughters. Even after these expenses, however, Mr. Z has far more money at his disposal than his wife earns. In fact, since his income is rapidly rising, the gap in Mr. and Mrs. Z's incomes will soon widen even further.

In spite of the disparity in disposable incomes, both spouses are committed to maintaining their financial independence and to the equal sharing of common expenses. The latter has resulted in problems that they have not yet been able to resolve. Their financial arrangement was agreed upon before the marriage. A few months before their marriage, Mrs. Z had moved in with Mr. Z in the large cooperative apartment he had recently started buying. Then, as now, Mr. Z pays the mortgage and all of the regular household expenses (except food), keeps a record of these expenses, and each month gives his wife an itemized bill for her half. Either one can buy groceries or items f .· the house, with the understanding that the other will pay half. Although Mr. Z has greatly enlarged his savings account and investments during the time they have been living together and sharing expenses, Mrs. Z has gotten further and further in debt, especially to her husband, since she has not been able to keep up her share. She does not know how she will ever catch up, for she cannot anticipate much increase in salary. In addition, she owes on some outside debts and badly needs a new car. She does what she can to try to hold down expenses, such as trying to do the grocery shopping before her husband gets to it since he is a more extravagant shopper or trying to talk him out of vacation trips that she cannot afford. At the same time that she feels she is going under financially, she feels responsible for holding her husband's standard of living down. He would now like to purchase a home in the suburbs, travel abroad, and generally live in a style more commensurate with his income. But she cannot afford her half!

Yet neither seems willing to break the verbal contract made before their marriage. At that time—as now—neither wanted to feel that Mr. Z was supporting Mrs. Z. She believes it is very important to the maintenance of the relationship and to her own self-image for her to remain independent. Although the cooperative apartment is still in Mr. Z's name alone, Mrs. Z feels that by splitting the mortgage payments and the upkeep, the home is "theirs" and that she is paying her way. Mr. Z admits that he likes this financial arrangement and wants his wife to continue paying half, though he could well afford to renegotiate their contract and pay a larger share of the expenses. At this time, he seems willing to put up with the inconvenience the arrangement is causing both of them. A recent example of sacrifice on both of their parts for the principle of financial equality (but not equity) was a European trip he wanted to take. Since his wife could not afford it, he offered to lend her the money, but she refused to go further in debt. He then offered to treat her to the trip. She refused, believing that if she accepted he would feel resentful about having to pay her way. He admitted that this was so and plans for the trip were dropped.

Issues

As these findings indicate, some of the issues concerning money raised in families with two earners are new, but some are similar to issues that may be present in more traditional families with the husband as sole breadwinner. However, even when the issues are the same, couples sharing the financial provider role may perceive these issues differently, and perhaps more importantly, they may have a wider range of options for resolving the issues because each has her or his own income. Of course, the range of options is also greatly influenced by the amount of discretionary income the family has. If the family barely has enough money to pay bills, it may not matter how many breadwinners the family has or which options it decides to use.

AUTONOMY

One rather complicated issue concerns autonomy. In conventional marriages, wives are dependent on husbands to provide financially for the family while husbands are dependent on wives to take care of the home and children. Role-sharing couples are not dependent on each other in these ways, for each partner is capable of performing and does perform, at least in theory, each of these roles. Thus, each partner can function autonomously or independently by supporting himself or herself financially. As we have seen, several couples in our study do exactly that with no pretense that their money is family money; each contributes to joint expenses more or less as roommates might. At the other extreme, a number of the role-sharing couples consider that type of financial arrangement petty, cold, uncaring, and more competitive than cooperative. They see it as more appropriate to business arrangements between friends or strangers, not family members. In fact, they view treating their incomes as individual money as antithetical to marriage, which to them means traditional sharing of almost all assets and liabilities.

As we have seen, most of the couples in which each partner managed his or her own money and couples who had done so when both had incomes valued the financial independence and freedom they were able to maintain after marriage—occasionally at great inconvenience to one or both. Although practically speaking, this freedom applied only to what was left after joint or family expenses were paid, psychologically it applied to their entire take-home pay. It may be that one's orientation to money is symbolic of how one views oneself in a marital relationship more generally: as one-half of a married couple or as an individual who happens to be married. If so, one might expect couples who divide work-family roles in the traditional manner to perceive themselves more in terms of the marital or family unit, and role-sharing couples to be more likely to have an individual orientation as their primary one. Although most of our role-sharing couples did not approach financial management in an individual manner, almost all of the individuals in our study needed some money—if only an allowance—to spend as they pleased. Perhaps the need for financial independence (as an individual, not as a couple) among role-sharing couples is only a matter of degree—or in this case, of how much.

The potential for financial autonomy is present for any couple in which each spouse can support himself or herself, but this potential is not realized unless the spouses also perceive themselves as financially independent and manage their money independently. Having children may complicate the financial arrangement (each partner would contribute to their support) but does not have to affect each spouse's financial independence. Yet, most of the individuals in our role-sharing couples preferred to think of themselves solely as part of a financial unit rather than as financially independent. At the same time, they recognized that they and their spouses were capable of being self-sufficient if they chose to be or needed to be, for example, in the event of divorce or death of a spouse. Furthermore, there was some evidence that some of the couples in our study did change from a family orientation to money to an individual orientation and vice versa (more often, vice versa), depending primarily on their stage of family development or the circumstances in which they found themselves. Perhaps, for some husbands and wives, the knowledge that they could be financially autonomous was the crucial factor.

CONTROL

Closely related to the issue of autonomy is the issue of control. Couples who viewed and managed their incomes as individual money maintained complete control over their discretionary money but may have been faced with the control issue over joint expenses. To the extent that there is room for decision making concerning joint expenses (when or whether to purchase an item, which of several models to buy, or even if an item should be a joint or individual expense), who has the final say may be important if the two spouses do not agree. However, none of the couples with an individual money orientation in our sample indicated any problem with control, possibly because they did not make joint expenditures unless both agreed to it—that is, each person had veto power. Apparently, control was not an issue with these couples, since each person felt he or she maintained sole control over her or his own money.

Control of money is more likely to be an issue when all or most of the money is in a family pot. As we proceed with this discussion, we should take care not to confuse bookkeeping or accounting functions in handling money (the writing of checks, balancing accounts, etc.) or the implementation of previously made decisions (e.g., the selecting and purchasing of items) with the decision-making function, that is, the power to commit money. Traditionally, men as the wage earners have had the major say in the larger decision-making arena. It is not uncommon, however, in male breadwinner families for the husband to give his wife a certain amount of money to run the household, with the wife's having discretionary power to allocate the money to cover these expenses. In the event of a disagreement over what is a household expense and what is not, it would not be unusual for the husband to have the final say. Thus, wives have traditionally made decisions about money at one level because husbands have delegated this function to them. In other words, the wife's making the smaller financial decisions may be viewed as part of her domestic role or as the husband's delegating this portion of the financial management to her, or as both, since the two notions are not incompatible.

For the most part, our role-sharing couples resolved this power issue in the same way traditional couples do—the one who earns the money has the greater control over it. The issue becomes more complicated for role-sharing couples, however, since both are wage earners. Some of our couples struggled with whether they should have equal control over combined money when one (usually the husband) earned more and had contributed more. Sometimes the issue was resolved one way ideologically (equal power) but another way in practice (the larger contributor having more control). Sometimes the smaller contributor did not feel he or she had the right to as much control as her or his spouse, even when the larger contributor seemed willing to share financial control equally. The issue seemed to become especially salient when one partner (usually the wife), who was used to equal status as breadwinner and financial decision maker, stopped working outside the home temporarily or cut back to part-time work. Although the change in work schedule had been mutually agreed upon and may have been considered necessary for the family unit (for example, staying home to care for an infant or small child), the temptation was to revert to the more conventional way of viewing control of money. Caught between two conflicting sets of norms, the traditional and the egalitarian, these couples found the pull of the former to be very powerful indeed.

Values

Over and over again couples who pooled their incomes stated that this financial arrangement worked because they shared the same values regarding money. They saw agreement about expenditures as a sine qua non of combining money without major conflict. These couples did not mean that both spouses necessarily had to agree upon every single expenditure but rather that there were no serious disagreements about how the combined money was spent. Sometimes the agreement might involve some type of trade-off, such as purchasing a boat, which the husband wants but the wife does not, provided they also get new carpeting for the downstairs, which the wife wants but the husband is indifferent about. The safety valve in these joint financial arrangements seems to be each partner's having a reasonable amount of individual money in addition to spend as she or he chooses.

Unlike traditional families with only one breadwinner, dual-earner couples who do not share the same values regarding money have a feasible alternative—they can keep their incomes separate and devise a way of handling common expenses. Values concerning money are certainly less of an issue when spouses manage their incomes independently, but the issue may not disappear altogether. One partner may want something for the house or family to which the other is not willing to contribute. In addition to alternatives any couple might have in resolving this situation, each spouse may have enough individual money to purchase a wanted item by himself or herself. However, there is an economic factor to be considered here. It is much cheaper to purchase an item if one has to pay only half its cost; in effect, one can obtain a desired item for half price if one's spouse is willing, or can be persuaded, to go along with the purchase. Some items, like the new sports car the husband wants, may be affordable only if he can get his wife to see it as a common expense and agree to the purchase.

As previously indicated, sometimes when a spouse has financial obligations outside the present family unit, such as repayment of a college loan or support of an elderly parent or children by a previous marriage, the individual approach to money management may be chosen to minimize potential conflict in this area. Taking care of outside financial obligations out of individual money instead of family money may be preferred whether or not a difference in values between partners exists.

INDIVIDUAL AND COMMON EXPENSES

Although determining what is a common or an individual expense may be an issue for a couple who pool most of their money and view their incomes as family money, it looms larger as a potential issue for couples who have an individual orientation to money. For the latter couples, some expenses are not in question: for example, the mortgage payment and utility bills are clearly joint or family expenses while each spouse's clothing or separate vacations are almost always considered individual expenses. Some items and expenditures, however, fall in a grey area, and a decision must be agreed upon by the couple in each case or category of cases. Items that might be considered either individual or joint are those that benefit both spouses to some extent but are of far greater benefit to one spouse. Examples are expensive plants that the husband wants because gardening is his hobby but that the whole family will enjoy, special tools for the wife who loves carpentry but whose efforts add to the value of the house, or a car that the husband needs for transportation to and from work but that will be available to the one-car family nights and weekends. Although couples who pool their incomes may occasionally have to decide whether a purchase should come out of the family pot or a spouse's allowance, the expenses in question tend to be small ones and may not be discussed at all. The issue of what is a common expense and what is not and whose money bought what is one that pooling couples seek to avoid. Couples who opt for the more radical approach, that is, individual money, have to develop new principles and rules to make this approach workable.

UNEQUAL INCOMES

Other issues that are likely to be more salient for spouses who manage their money independently than for those who combine incomes as family money are those arising from the partners' having unequal incomes. In fact, some of our couples pooled their money as a way of preventing or resolving issues due to a disparity in incomes. As we have already seen, spouses with greatly unequal incomes who pool are more likely to be caught up in the power issue. However, if other issues to be discussed in this section were relevant for these couples, these issues seemed to stem from other factors rather than to be related to the disparity in their incomes.

The major financial decision that had to be made by couples with unequal incomes who worked full time and had an individual orientation to money was how to split up the common or family expenses. Dividing expenses equally seemed unfair to, and may even have posed a hardship for, the spouse with less income. It would also mean that the family's standard of living would be set at the level of the lower wage earner. On the other hand, if partners contributed to family expenses in proportion to their incomes, it is conceivable that the higher earning spouse might feel penalized for earning more and therefore perceive the arrangement as unfair. In such a case, the incentive for increasing his or her income may be dampened somewhat for the higher earning spouse. Most of the couples in our study with vastly unequal incomes took the position that it was not the lower wage earner's (usually the wife's) fault that she or he earned less. Usually they considered extenuating circumstances such as other contributions to the family unit (for example, more responsibility for child care) or discrimination against women in employment and salaries. Often they also pointed out that the lower wage earner worked just as hard as the better compensated spouse.

What emerges is a variety of compromises but no clear principles. If incomes are more or less equal, then an equal contribution to joint expenses seems to be a logical solution. As income disparity grows, the spouse with the lower income is likely to find the principle of "who earns more pays more" to become increasingly attractive. But there are no standards for guidance in this uncharted area of family finances. If the higher earner spouse contributes a larger share of his or her income toward joint expenses or is required to engage in mandatory treating, he or she is in effect being asked to pay a special "tax" on the margin of earnings exceeding those of his or her spouse. How much of a margin should there be before this tax takes effect? What should be the tax rate? That is, how much of this extra margin should the higher earning spouse contribute to common expenses? Further, what should the earnings base be? After-tax income? Income after alimony to an ex-wife? Should the tax apply to elective work such as overtime, consultation, and so on? As these questions multiply, the relationship begins to sound less like a marriage and more like one between an IRS auditor and a taxpayer. However, once partners commit themselves to an individual money orientation, such questions are likely to arise in one form or another.

The higher earning spouse may, of course, challenge the principle that he or she—usually he—should pay more. One rationale often presented is based on the equality of effort that full-time working spouses expend in the work market. "We work equally hard; it is only fair that the one making more should share the wealth." If the higher earner is the husband, as is usually the case, then one can add that the wife's income is lower because of inequities in the job market, sex discrimination, lower pay for jobs typically held by women, and so on. The husband owes it to his wife to compensate for such inequities.

Couples who accept such rationales appear to be influenced by the traditional notion that marriage means that "two persons become one." Even though they might scoff at this idea, they accept it in part if they sacrifice claims of financial autonomy. Still, their embrace of the notion is not so total that they conceive of their incomes as "family money." In matters of money we fall somewhere between being "two" and "one," they seem to say.

Other bases for adjusting income differences are more clear-cut. If discrepancies are very large, then the higher earning spouse may need to contribute more simply to attain the standard of living he or she wants. If the lower earning spouse has suffered a loss in his or her earning potential for the sake of the family, then that spouse can claim an "income credit." Thus, a husband and wife with individual-money orientations may share common expenses equally. After their first child is born, the wife quits her job to care for the infant and remains out of the labor market for a two-year period. When she reenters, her income may be less than her husband's simply because of his staying on the job. A reasonable adjustment would be for the husband to contribute his extra margin of income for common expenses to compensate for the wife's loss of earning power. Although the principle is straightforward, its implementation may not be. Loss of income potential may be difficult to determine. In some careers, even a short time on the sidelines can blunt one's competitive edge and have long-range effects on earning capacity that are difficult to calculate.

The adoption of the principle of contribution according to income is, as noted, a compromise between newer egalitarian ethics and more traditional values. The principle may bring with it other traditional orientations that may fit less well into a role-sharing marriage. For example, what does it mean to a woman who works full time and wants to be self-sufficient to be partially supported by her husband, as she may view his larger financial contribution to the household? Does either spouse, or do both spouses, perceive the larger contributor as having more decision-making power about their finances? How can couples maintain a sense of fairness and equality in their relationship when their individual opportunities and circumstances are unequal?

Although not confined to the area of financial management, the concept of flexibility is exceedingly important in trying to achieve and maintain equity concerning money. A financial arrangement that seems fair and is satisfactory to a couple at one time may seem grossly unfair at another stage of family development or under different circumstances. Not only must couples adapt to the changed circumstances by changing their behavior, (e.g., working out a more suitable financial agreement), they must also be able to modify their attitudes and perceptions accordingly. Couples in our study found the latter adjustment harder to make. A typical example is as follows. A couple who maintained an individual orientation to money after marriage decide to have a baby. They plan for the wife to stay home with the infant and later work part time until the child is in school for the full day. Because the wife, who is home more, will assume major child care and domestic responsibilities and the husband will be the principal breadwinner for a few years, the couple decide to pool all money, which will be considered family money. The couple readily shift into the agreed upon procedure for handling money and may even have little difficulty adjusting to the lowered income, but some issues concerning money may appear for the first time in their marriage. The wife may feel she is not entitled to as much say as her husband about large financial expenditures. The husband may also feel he should have a slight edge in power in this area. (At the same time, the couple would probably accord the wife more control in the child care and domestic areas). Although she may be aware that it is irrational, the wife may feel uncomfortable about her loss of financial independence and about being taken care of. The husband may be more acutely aware than a traditional husband would of the financial responsibility of a family since for the first time he is having to support his wife, in addition to the baby, and to be the sole breadwinner. Although this awareness may result in positive feelings on the part of the husband (e.g., closer knit family group), it may also result in ambivalence or negative feelings (e.g., feeling overwhelmed, burdened, or resentful).

As this example illustrates, attitudes and perceptions must be as adaptable to changed circumstances as behaviors are. Just as traditional couples can be very rigid and stereotypical in their thinking, so can egalitarian couples, and the result can be dysfunctional for both, though in different ways. Although it would seem easier for egalitarian couples to be flexible, since the attitudes and behavior that may be called for in situations like the illustration above are socially sanctioned, this sanction may exacerbate the conflict these couples feel. Some of these unorthodox couples may feel threatened by what they view as any relapse into conventional patterns. New roles that are not socially sanctioned are apt to be fragile. Although tragic, it is not surprising that some of these more radical couples feel they cannot let their guard down even temporarily or they may lose the gains they have made toward sex-role equality in the home.

5

Domestic Tasks

A general picture of how domestic tasks were shared has been presented (chapter 3). We begin the chapter with more detailed examination of how these tasks are actually divided. Against this factual backdrop we then consider aspects more related to issues and dynamics in achieving role sharing: the question of standards and the processes of initiating and maintaining patterns of dividing labor.

The tasks to be examined are the usual household chores (cooking, cleaning, laundry, and so on), plus other routine work necessary to maintain the tangible resources of the domicile (house repairs, outdoor work, and car maintenance). Excluded are other activities involved in managing a household or a family such as child care, money management, handling social obligations and leisure activities; these are dealt with in other chapters. The concept of domestic roles that we use here is broader than what is sometimes used in studies of dual-earner couples that include only those household tasks traditionally performed by women on a daily, or at least frequent, basis. Such studies are interested in ascertaining to what extent husbands are sharing in "women's work." We included three tasks traditionally performed by men because we think it is important to recognize that men have been traditionally involved in some family work and because we were interested in learning if wives were sharing in their husbands' family work, as well as in their provider role.

Task Division: Who Does What

From an initial question it became apparent that the great majority of couples took care of their own domestic labors. Only eight of the couples employed a person to do household tasks, invariably part-time help to do the cleaning. To ascertain how domestic work was allocated, we went over a list of tasks with the husband and wife in the joint interview. The task list, which was reasonably exhaustive, was constructed to include specific chores strongly associated with sex roles (e.g., mending and car maintenance) as an index of role sharing in the sample. The complete list consisted of cooking, cleaning up the kitchen afterward, planning meals, grocery shopping, ironing, vacuuming, dusting, scrubbing floors, laundry, mending, house repairs and maintenance, yard work, and car maintenance.

In telling us who did what in respect to each task, respondents indicated whether the task was carried out primarily or entirely by the husband or wife or if work on it was so closely divided that both spouses could be regarded as equal task performers. If one spouse usually performed a task but the other sometimes did it or participated in it in some way, this was noted. For example, the wife might do most of the cooking, but her husband might prepare the salad, fix the children's breakfast, cook on Sundays, or "fill in" as needed. In addition to task performance, we ascertained for each item on our list who was *responsible* for the planning and overseeing of the task regardless of who carried it out. We were interested here in determining to what extent one spouse might be simply *helping* the other with "his" or "her" work instead of actually *sharing* the chore, as discussed in chapter 1.

Since the sample had been purposely selected to include only role-sharing and transitional couples, it was not surprising that all of the couples reported sharing at least one domestic task in the traditionally female role set and many couples at least one in the traditionally male role set. The amount of sharing varied greatly among couples. Some shared all or almost all of the tasks, appeared interchangeable as the performer of the tasks, and divided household chores without regard to gender. At the other extreme of the continuum, some couples appeared to divide tasks in the traditional manner, the husband performing at times one or more of "his wife's" tasks on what looked suspiciously like a "helping" basis. Most couples fell between these two extremes. Although we report data on the entire sample, we concentrate on couples with more developed role-sharing patterns. In evaluating data on the full sample, the reader should keep in mind that the role sharing of some couples appeared to have been unbalanced at least temporarily by the wife's having reduced her outside employment while her husband did not in order for the wife to assume child care responsibilities in the home. Many of these women felt they should do more of the housework since they were home more than their husbands but indicated that they expected a more nearly equal division of the domestic tasks to resume when they returned to full-time jobs. Although these wives tended to view the current imbalance as temporary and perhaps even as fair under the circumstances, some indicated that this was a source of dissatisfaction for them. The most dissatisfied wives, however, were the few who believed their husbands had used this opportunity to revert to traditional roles (which these wives suspected they may have preferred anyway), leaving them "stuck" with the housework and child care. The husband's continued participation in these two roles, even though temporarily at a reduced level, plus an egalitarian attitude on his part, seemed related to less dissatisfaction on the part of the wife and less tension in the marriage.

INDIVIDUAL TASKS

Examination of the division of work on individual tasks indicated a great deal of role sharing on some tasks, but the traditional sex division was still in evidence. Responses to our inquiry about who performed each task could be readily grouped into the following categories: husband, husband mostly, both more or less equally, wife mostly, wife. In reporting the percentages in table 5.1, the "husband" and "husband mostly" were combined, as were "wife" and "wife mostly." Percentages are based only on couples who reported that they carried out the task; a minority of couples stated that some chores such as ironing, dusting, scrubbing floors, and mending were either done entirely by someone else or done by the couple so seldom that they did not count.

Because one could argue that a task is shared even if performed mostly by one spouse, we present in table 5.2 percentages of couples who did some sharing of each task (by combining "husband mostly" and "wife mostly" with "shared equally"). As their titles suggest, the tables present in turn strict and broad interpretations of role sharing.

Both tables present a picture of considerable sharing across most tasks but with the traditional mode of division of labor still in evidence. When sharing is viewed broadly (table 5.2), we find that the majority (often the great majority) of couples share most tasks to some extent. If

Table 5.1
Sharing Domestic Tasks: "Strict Interpretation"

Task	Wife/ Wife Mostly	Shared Equally	Husband Husband Mostly	N
Traditionally female:	%	%	%	
Cooking	49	39	13	64
After Meal Cleanup	21	52	27	63
Planning Meals	50	45	5	60
Grocery Shopping	38	42	20	64
Laundry	38	44	18	63
Vacuuming	26	46	29	59
Scrubbing Floors	33	37	30	54
Dusting	55	34	11	53
Ironing	47	45	9	47
Mending	62	35	4	52
Traditionally Male:				
House Repairs/				
Maintenance	5	20	75	60
Yard Work	7	21	72	58
Car Maintenance	10	43	47	61

we consider the first seven tasks listed, those defined in chapter 3, as the heavy-duty traditional female tasks, we can see (table 5.2) that a high degree of some sharing prevails. When done by one spouse, the wife is the major sole task performer in four (cooking, planning meals, grocery shopping, and laundry) while the husband is the major sole performer—although barely—in three (after-meal cleanup, vacuuming, and scrubbing floors). The wife appears to retain her edge on tasks that require greater skill and sophistication presumably acquired through socialization. Men are more likely to be sole performers with less skilled tasks. With the exception of floor scrubbing, the same picture is obtained from the stricter interpretation of role sharing (table 5.1). Note, however, that both tables show wives as still carrying a disproportionate share of the burden on this set of tasks.

The remaining tasks show a much more traditional division, men having made larger inroads in the typically female tasks of ironing and mending than women have made into the typically male domestic task domain (house repairs, etc.). This finding is consistent with results reported by Szinovacz (1979). The high percentage of wives who "share somewhat" yard work is accounted for largely by wives who garden, though a few wives made clear that they did help cut grass or shovel snow.

Table 5.2
Sharing Domestic Tasks: "Broad Interpretation"

Task	Wife Only %	Shared Somewhat %	Husband Only %	N
Percentages				
Traditionally female:				
Cooking	14	83	3	64
After Meal Cleanup	11	75	14	63
Planning Meals	37	62	2	60
Grocery Shopping	20	70	9	64
Laundry	21	67	13	63
Vacuuming	15	68	17	59
Scrubbing Floors	24	48	28	54
Dusting	40	51	9	53
Ironing	36	57	6	47
Mending	54	42	4	52
Traditionally Male:				
House Repairs/ Maintenance	2	47	50	60
Yard Work	2	71	28	58
Car Maintenance	5	39	56	61

The person who performed a task was generally reported by the couple to be responsible for it. Some differences between performance and responsibility occurred on those tasks performed by both equally: responsibility was more likely to fall toward the wife on after-meal cleanup, grocery shopping, vacuuming, dusting, and scrubbing floors; responsibility for meal planning shifted slightly to the husband. The differences between performance of a task and responsibility for it in our data were so small that they are not reported separately.

Also not reported here are comparisons between domestic role sharing according to wives' paid work effort—that is, whether they are employed full time, part time, or temporarily staying home full time. Task performance by spouse differs very little from the tables for couples in which wives have full-time paid work because these couples constitute by far the greater part of our sample. Compared with couples in which the wives were employed full time, couples with wives having less than full-time paid work were less likely to share housework and more likely to have these tasks performed by the wife (see chapter 3 for more comparisons).

Fairness and Standards

As is already apparent, these couples reflect a shift from one principle in allocation of domestic tasks to another—from a principle based on sex roles to one based on an equitable division. In this section we consider how the couples in our study struggled to put the ideal of equal sharing of domestic tasks into practice and some of the reasons why their success was less than complete. One issue in this struggle was the question of fairness in allocating tasks. Another arose from the remarkably consistent differences between husbands and wives in standards concerning traditionally female tasks. How these issues were dealt with appeared to determine other coping efforts.

FAIRNESS

When the sex-role principle is forsaken for an egalitarian norm, new rules must be developed for equitable task allocation. Who is to do what and on what basis? Some tasks are more onerous or disagreeable than others, and complete sharing through turn taking or some other device may not be practical or efficient. If each partner is to do somewhat different tasks, then how is the question of fairness to be decided? Is preparing a meal an even exchange for doing the dishes and cleaning up the kitchen afterward? What is the boundary between a task done for the common good and a hobby? Does a husband who spends hours on gourmet cooking (his hobby) get "credit" for all the time he spends in the kitchen (particularly if his wife prefers plain baked chicken to coq-au-vin)? Also, difficult judgments need to be made about effort and performance in doing a task in decisions about equity. Does the husband's whirlwind "no-corners" tour with the vacuum cleaner really discharge his designated task of vacuuming the house? He says it's all that is needed. His wife has another opinion. Or if a wife meticulously scrubs pots and pans by hand because the dishwasher does not in her mind (not in her husband's) get them clean enough, can she be faulted for making what should be a simple task into a complicated one and should her claims about all the time she spends with the dishes be discounted? Does the concept of equity leave room for altruism or is reciprocity the more appropriate norm in an effort to maintain balance?

For example, can a wife go on a cooking splurge and prepare dinner for several nights in a row when this is her husband's task, or can a husband with restless energy suddenly do a thorough spring housecleaning though cleaning is normally his wife's job without expecting anything in return or without the other spouse's feeling obligated in any way? How should partners handle the reluctance of one or the other to do chores because of "not feeling up to it?"

Such issues, which arose frequently among our couples, perhaps make the point that a commitment to share domestic tasks equally and an honest effort on the part of both partners to implement the commitment provide no guarantees that conflict will be avoided. Additional agreements may need to be worked out about what mix of tasks represents a fair exchange, what is "work" as opposed to "recreation," what constitutes an acceptable completion of a task, when is "sick leave" justified, among other matters. One way of solving such quandaries would be to mark out precise definitions and keep track of time spent on different tasks, all under a strict rule of reciprocity. Solutions of this kind were rarely in evidence in our sample. Not only did they strike couples as unweildy, but more importantly, they clashed with their sense of what a marriage should be like. Partners should be close, caring, willing to help each other. A difficult challenge for our couples was the integration of these altruistic sentiments with principles of fairness and reciprocity that were also central in their relationships.

The tension between altruism and reciprocity was revealed in a question asked of each spouse in the individual interviews: "If it were necessary for one spouse to do a task the other was supposed to do, how important would it be for the other to reciprocate?" Answers were categorized as either indicating or not indicating that the principle of reciprocity was of some importance. Indicators that it was important included qualifiers such as "it would depend on the task" or "it would matter if things continued that way." About a third of the respondents indicated that reciprocity considerations would apply in some form. Most who said it did apply did not qualify their answers and many commented on the importance of reciprocity as a way of "keeping things even" or "not falling back into traditional ways." Wives were somewhat more likely than husbands to express unqualified support of the principle. When the principle was not seen as important the elaborations included a rejection of the idea of "keeping score" or stress on showing appreciation for the other's effort.

When only individual responses are considered it appears as if the importance attached to reciprocity is a minor theme of these marriages. However, when the responses are analyzed in terms of couples, a much different picture emerges. The reason for the difference is a considerable amount of disagreement between partners when their responses (given, remember, in individual interviews) are compared. In about 10 percent of the couples, the spouses agreed on the importance of reciprocity and in 40 percent they concurred that it did not matter. In the remaining half of the couples, however, there was *disagreement* between the spouses. An examination of some of the typical disagreements is instructive (see table 5.3).

Our interpretation of many of the disagreements was that they reflected differences in emphasis and perception of rules of reciprocation that were operative in some form but were not explicit. Thus, some of the spouses just quoted appeared to be rejecting a scorekeeping concep-

Table 5.3
"If it were necessary for one spouse to do a task the other was supposed to do, how important would it be for the other to reciprocate?"

Couple	Wife	Husband
G	"fairly important, would try to find him something to do"	"try to avoid tradeoffs, balance sheets, mechanized marriage contracts"
H	"fairly important, but not right away"	"not important, don't like keeping tabs—too narrow and without trust but important for each to ask for what they want (e.g., if you want reciprocation, ask for it)"
K	"not important to reciprocate"	"depends; person who did extra chore would talk with other to find out reason for not doing task"
L	"necessary to reciprocate, make deals, important to maintain equal division of labor"	"not important, wouldn't even discuss doing same amount of work"
I	"don't operate on a this-for-that basis unless things really become unbalanced"	"is important—each calls it to the other's attention because there's so much to do, and things can slide"

tion of reciprocity while their mates were endorsing some other aspect of the principle. Disagreements here and elsewhere often seemed real but not in flat contradiction.

At any rate, in the *majority* of couples the importance of reciprocity was endorsed either by both or by one of the partners. If our interpretation of the disagreements is correct, reciprocity functions as an unspoken norm for the most part but becomes salient if one partner or the other perceives an imbalance. While a strict accounting is avoided, an eye is kept on the long-term balance. Thus, in their responses some spouses seemed to take our question literally and said it would not be important to respond "tit-for-tat" while their partners often seemed to react to the question in terms of its longer run implications. The notion of reciprocity as part of a couple's unspoken contract to be used to redress imbalances was well expressed by the separate responses of couple C. As the wife put it in her interview, "We used to keep score and remind each other. We do that less and less now, but we'll talk if one feels things are getting unequal." To his interviewer, the husband commented: "We don't keep score, but if I feel overloaded I keep a scorecard in my mind."

This kind of flexible or long-run reciprocity resembled the "bank-account" model of exchange found by Gottman et al. (1976) in their study of marital interaction. The bank-account metaphor is apt in the sense that "deposits" (such as willingness to do more than one's share at a particular time) are made without expectation of an immediate quid pro quo but accrue as a "credit" to be paid back sooner or later. However, with our couples, and perhaps generally, the accounts are kept without books.

By avoiding explicit quid pro quos most couples were able to keep reciprocity in the background as a tacit understanding while stressing more altruistic principles in explaining their behavior. Although reciprocity norms are often kept implicit in social groups, many spouses seemed reluctant even to recognize the existence of reciprocity, often at variance with their partners' perceptions. One wonders how much miscommunication and conflict might have resulted from such differences.

STANDARDS

Perhaps the most common flash point in negotiating equitable division of domestic tasks was the question of standards: a task not done adequately could not be fairly exchanged for one done well. But the standards problem involved more than matters of fairness since it was likely to provoke resentment and criticism of the other's work or expectations. It was also likely to raise issues about control.

Although partners may wish to share household tasks as "equals," they may be very unequal in respect to what they expect and what they are able to do. Because of prior socialization, wives may have different standards from their husbands about what constitutes acceptable performance of domestic tasks. A wife may feel it to be a reflection on her if they are not done according to her standards and she may have the skill to do them more efficiently. Problems of this sort also arise in task divisions along sex-role lines, but they assume a different and less complex form. In a traditional arrangement, a husband may complain that his wife is a sloppy housekeeper, and a wife may see her husband as derelict about house repairs, but neither is so likely to feel that the other's shortcomings reflect on themselves or to feel impelled, and able, to do the other's jobs and thereby unequalize the division of work.

As noted in the previous section, role sharing in domestic tasks was characterized largely by husbands' greater than usual involvement in traditionally female tasks. In effect, men were doing what women had been socialized and trained to do. As a group their wives had been well schooled by mothers, who, whether they had worked or not, generally assumed responsibility for these tasks and did them well.

Thus, it is not surprising that the wives' standards for these tasks were higher than their husbands' were in more than three fourths of the couples. By "standards" we refer not only to judgments about the end product but also to how the work is done and when. Thus, a wife might throw up her hands at how her husband minces onions and take over the task to do it "right" even though the final result would be pretty much the same. Or a wife might expect a cleaning job to be done well in advance of the arrival of company rather than at the last minute.

Whether a couple decided from the outset to share traditionally female domestic tasks or whether the husband began to do them later in the marriage, the "standards problem" needed to be dealt with. (Here we note but will discuss later the very different situation with the half dozen couples in our study in which the standards of the husband were higher than those of the wife. The few cases in which spouses seemed to have comparable standards to begin with were not problematic and consequently are not discussed in this chapter.)

We were able to discern at least four different methods couples used to handle the standards issue. A given couple might use any one or more of these methods; if more than one was used, as was generally the case, they might be used in combination or sequentially. They are discussed here roughly in the sequence used by a number of our couples.

Prodding. Frequently when wives discovered the difference in standards for domestic tasks, they tried to upgrade their husbands' performance of their tasks. A wife might call to her husband's attention the fact that he missed a spot, that something still was not clean, and so on. In addition to helpful criticism, the wife might employ other strategies such as suggestions, demonstrations, playful teasing, and even nagging. Some wives complained that their husbands seemed unaware of certain aspects of a chore such as dusting when cleaning the living room, or cleaning the toilet when the task was to do the bathroom. Some thought husbands simply did not see such things as cobwebs on the walls or dirt in the corners of rooms. Streaks left on mirrors, spots missed on the floor, or laundry folded haphazardly simply did not bother their husbands. Thus, it is not surprising that many wives tried to increase their husbands' awareness of the "correct" way to perform household tasks.

Reallocation. After the prodding had accomplished all it could or had failed, couples might engage in a process of problem solving and negotiation. The net result was often a readjustment in the division of household responsibilities. The wife might take over those tasks that were very important to her and in which her standards, and perhaps competency, were much greater than her husband's. The husband in turn might do things that were less important to his wife, that required less skill, or that were more suitable because of the husband's greater physical strength. This kind of task allocation explains in part why the wives gravitated toward cooking, grocery shopping, and the laundry, whereas husbands tended to take on cleaning up the kitchen after meals, vacuuming, and floor scrubbing.

Acceptance. When such a reallocation of tasks was made, the tacit agreement was that the standards of the person performing the task would prevail. In other words, the wife would accept her husband's lower standards for his tasks. Sometimes this acceptance was accompanied by misgivings with the wife's redoing or taking over her husband's chores—or at the very least giving his work a finishing touch—at critical points, for example, in preparation for company. A number of couples commented that when the wives lowered their expectations for their husband's tasks, the husbands raised their standards in an effort to please their wives.

Lowering Standards. Some wives, sooner or later, gave up trying to maintain their homes in the manner they would have liked. They realized that their high standards of cleanliness and order could be maintained only if one spouse did not work or if they were able to obtain good outside help on a sufficiently frequent basis. The latter was rarely an alternative: few of these couples felt they could afford it, and even if they could, they doubted that they could find a person or cleaning service that would meet their standards. Thus, with both spouses working full time, an immaculate house like the one they may have grown up in and had come to expect was a sheer impossibility. These women came to accept lower standards as simply realistic, often after an exhausting attempt to maintain them through sheer effort—the superwoman syndrome. When this realization occurred, the wives not only were more accepting of the way their husbands performed their chores but also became more relaxed about the performance of their own chores. Many got to the point that when they could squeeze the time to clean kitchen cabinets, polish furniture, and the like, they often would not do so but would use the time for other things they thought were more important. Generally this meant spending more time with one's spouse or children. With so little free time, these dual-career couples tended to put a premium on family time. In fact, having more time to enjoy their spouses and children seemed to be a major incentive for wives to relax housekeeping standards.

As indicated earlier, going through the stages of prodding, reallocation, acceptance, and lowering standards was only one pattern used by couples when the wife's housekeeping standards were noticeably higher than her husband's. Some couples used only one of these methods, two or more simultaneously or in another sequence, or went back and forth between methods. Although any number of ways may have been tried to resolve the standards issue, in the long run most couples ended up accepting the standards of the task performer. This does not mean that couples in which the wives with higher standards accepted their husband's lower standards from the beginning necessarily were better satisfied or came out ahead. The discussion and negotiation that couples engaged in around differences in standards often resulted in a clarification and mutual understanding of each spouse's standards, a more satisfactory and workable task division, and a movement toward more comparable standards.

Sometimes the process of trying to resolve the standards issue helped couples come to grips with related issues. For example, a few wives were reluctant to let husbands take over "their" jobs even when the husbands could do them adequately. The wives may have been hesitant to share control over the kitchen or other household matters. A few wives indicated that they felt guilty about their husbands' having to cook and do housework, believing that their husbands' involvement would reflect poorly upon them as wives. Some husbands were reluctant to participate in household responsibilities, and a few tried to keep their participation hidden from friends, co-workers, or their children's playmates. However, most husbands accepted their involvement in cooking, housecleaning, and child care tasks as fair or at least inevitable if their wives worked outside the home full time. Many also thought their standards for task performance had risen in response to expectations and pressures from their wives. They tended to acknowledge that upgrading their standards was reasonable and in their own interest.

Judging from the few couples in our study in which the husband had the higher standards for domestic responsibilities, we can say that this condition was as desirable and as problem-free as the one in which both spouses held very comparable standards. These wives appeared quite willing to raise their standards to meet their husbands' expectations for tasks that they did. Perhaps because they were so appreciative of the end result (excellent meals, a well-kept home, etc.) that came about in a relatively painless manner since no more than half the effort came from them, these wives seemed eager to encourage their husbands' participation by accommodating to their standards. Unlike wives in families with a traditional division of labor where the husband's higher domestic standards mean more work for the wife, wives in role-sharing families where the husband's standards are higher generally have less work to do since these husbands tend to take on more domestic responsibilities than other role-sharing husbands do. At the same time, there was a tendency for husbands with high housekeeping standards to lower their expectations in line with what was realistic for a dual-career couple.

Many wives felt the way the home was kept was a reflection on them as women, as was seen in responses to one question we asked. "If unexpected company comes and the house is in disorder, who is more likely to be embarrassed?" More than half of the wives admitted they would be. Nine couples thought either spouse would be as likely to be embarrassed as the other while five couples denied that either would be. A dozen husbands stated that they would be more likely to be embarrassed in the situation posed, but the reason was not clear. After all, some traditional husbands might respond in a similar manner for a variety of reasons: embarrassment on his wife's behalf, reflection on him for not having a better housekeeper for a wife, exposure of his living in an unkempt home, and so on. Thus, while it is not clear how many, if any, of these husbands have internalized the domestic role, it is certainly no more than a small minority. We did discover, however, that the company who count most, the people that each wants most to impress with their housekeeping standards, are their parents—hers, his, and each other's.

Pros and Cons of Sharing

On balance both wives and husbands in our sample thought the advantages of the way they shared domestic tasks far outweighed the disadvantages. As a matter of fact, most saw no disadvantages at all. When asked about compromises they had had to make in order to manage household tasks the way they do, women tended to see their compromises as being necessitated by the fact that they were working full time outside the home rather than by the role sharing, while men tended to think in terms of adjustments to living with another person rather than in terms of compromises. In this section, we look at how these couples evaluated their sharing of the domestic role.

ADVANTAGES

For most of our couples, the advantage of sharing household responsibilities that came to mind first was a very practical one: the work was done more quickly, efficiently, and easily since it was split between two

ıples found that meal preparation and housework not
ster when they worked together but also were often
ularly if talents and interests were criteria used for
cause most domestic responsibilities can be assigned
nd dislikes, many couples found that neither spouse
do much that she or he did not want to do.

Another practical advantage mentioned by a number of couples was
the competency and self-confidence each spouse develops in running a
household. This is particularly true for couples in which each spouse at
times participates in all domestic activities. Just as with the financial-
provider role when both spouses work, domestic role sharing allows
husbands to be self-sufficient in this area and relieves wives of the total
burden for the family. Many spouses become interchangeable in this
area, and this versatility provides a sense of security for the whole
family.

Many of the frequently mentioned advantages seemed to pertain to
the couple's relationship or to them personally. Above all, our sample
thought that sharing domestic tasks was fair. They strongly believed
that when both spouses were working outside the home, it was only fair
to share tasks and responsibilities in the home. As one couple put it,
"Since we both feel responsible for the way things are at home, neither
one of us has the full burden." The shared—and consequently lighter—
burden was appreciated greatly by wives, as one would expect, but also
by husbands, who felt a sense of personal responsibility and were not
expecting someone to take care of them (do their laundry, prepare their
meals, make their beds, and so on). By working together and participating more or less equally around the house, some husbands indicated
they felt a stronger sense of shared pride in their home than they would
have if their wives had most of the responsibility. They thought the
pride in helping to maintain their home made them enjoy it more.
Several husbands also mentioned that their involvement made them
feel like full partners at home and gave them a better understanding of
the various aspects of managing a household. One husband, for example, felt he was much more in tune with rising food prices and the
family's food budget since he does the grocery shopping instead of
"merely bringing home a paycheck."

Many couples stated that domestic tasks were less onerous—and
some tasks even fun—when they were done together. Because trying to

find more time to spend together is a high priority for most dual-career couples, these respondents thought their arrangement was ideal: they had time together while doing household chores and more leisure time together since the tasks were done in half the time it would have taken one spouse.

Some couples mentioned as an advantage the greater amount of communication between them that sharing the domestic role entails. Also cited was the attitude of cooperation. These couples thought these advantages carried over to other aspects of their relationship with the effect of enhancing the marriage. For example, many of these role-sharing couples believed they communicated more and better than most couples who divide family responsibilities in the traditional manner. They also thought if they could cooperate to get unpleasant tasks done such as scrubbing floors, cleaning toilets, and taking out garbage, they could cooperate on just about anything else.

Depending on how they viewed the domestic role, these working wives saw different advantages in their husbands' participation. For some wives, it meant they had help with the housework and consequently did not have to do it all; for some it meant that the couple did not have to go to the expense of hiring household help; for others, it meant that domestic chores were done better and more quickly than if the wife did them alone; and for still others, it meant that domestic chores were done at all. Regardless of how they saw it, wives were in unanimous agreement that it was clearly advantageous to them to have their husbands sharing household responsibilities.

Some husbands saw as an advantage the fact that their sharing the domestic role provided them with a tangible means of showing their wives the respect they felt for them as individuals whose time and effort were as important as their own. Others indicated that it allowed them to feel comfortable with themselves since they knew they were doing what was right; expressed differently, some husbands said it prevented them from feeling guilty. In addition to the personal gains, husbands generally believed the domestic role sharing enhanced their marital relationship primarily because their wives were better satisfied, not overworked, and had more time for themselves, their spouses, and their children.

A number of couples also commented on the more relaxed atmosphere in the home that flexible role sharing and less demanding standards provided. Since there were no rigid sex-role expectations, they felt freer to experiment with different ways of handling family responsibilities.

DISADVANTAGES AND COMPROMISES

As mentioned earlier, few couples saw any disadvantages to their way of handling domestic responsibilities. Perhaps this is to be expected since unsatisfactory methods are likely to be discarded. Yet a few couples were apparently still in the process of developing a mutually satisfactory method of sharing, and a minority were aware that their relaxed system was unstructured as well. Couples in the latter group commented that since no one person is responsible for tasks, some things do not get done. Yet they seemed to view in a matter-of-fact manner this consequence as a byproduct of a system that worked for them rather than as a real disadvantage. Wives in the first group mentioned such negatives as having to lower their standards, having to wait for their husbands to perform their tasks, and still having too much domestic responsibility.

Because their housekeeping standards were usually higher than their spouses', more wives than husbands felt they had to make compromises to manage the household tasks as they do. Having to accept lower standards for cooking and housework was by far the compromise wives cited most often. A satisfactory compromise for some wives desiring meticulous homes was what might be called the "public places principle." This meant that the couple agreed to keep living spaces that company would ordinarily see (for example, front hall, living room, dining area, and downstairs powder room) clean and orderly, with much more relaxed standards prevailing for the rest of the house.

A few wives mentioned nostalgically that by sharing the domestic role, they had relinquished the almost complete control over the home that wives in traditional families enjoy. Sharing control in the kitchen was often the hardest.

The compromises mentioned by the minority of husbands who reported having to make some were more diverse. They mentioned having to do more than they formerly did (either before the last reallocation of tasks or before the couple began sharing the domestic role) and the closely related circumstance of having less leisure time. They thought this was fair, however, and most indicated a desire for their wives to have less domestic work to do and more free time. A few mentioned having to arrange their work and business schedules in order to make time for their domestic responsibilities. Some indicated that they had had to lower their expectations for meals and household cleanliness, but more reported that they had had to raise their standards to meet their wives' expectations.

Most of the husbands took the view that their participation in domestic work was simply part of family life and rightfully their responsibility as well as their wives'. Some husbands commented that they were still doing only what they had done while they were single when they did their own cooking, laundry, and housework.

Origin and Evolution

The preceding sections have described how these role-sharing couples divide household tasks, how they handle major issues involved in the domestic role, and how they evaluate their domestic role sharing. In this section we take a step back to see how and why couples in our sample began sharing the domestic role. We also discuss strategies they use to maintain a mutually satisfactory division of tasks, which is no easy accomplishment when we consider factors such as differences in standards, changing circumstances, and the pull of the traditional.

As noted in the first chapter, role sharing can be based largely on practical considerations with little reference to values. Although most of our couples referenced their role sharing to egalitarian attitudes, the relation between these attitudes and behavior proved to be complex, as we shall see. Certainly, the presence of such attitudes on the part of both spouses did not automatically result in an equitable distribution of domestic tasks. Whether couples in our study had egalitarian ideals before marriage or developed them afterward, they found that translating these principles into specific behaviors was generally a very deliberate process requiring much communication, negotiation, bargaining, trial and error, and so on. It was not uncommon to find that couples who professed egalitarian ideals had rather conventional marriages in spite of having developed guiding principles and specific rules to put into practice their notions of fairness and equality. For example, couples in our study often divided domestic responsibilities according to preference, interest, ability, or, as some of them expressed it, "who holds the higher standards," "who it would bother more if it isn't done," or "who hates the task less." However, socialization, parental-role models, and societal attitudes are important determinants of these factors. Consequently, only very unorthodox couples managed to avoid traditional patterns in the division of household responsibilities. Even these couples often found that monitoring with frequent communication and adjustments as indicated were necessary to maintain mutually satisfactory sharing of domestic responsibilities. When drifts occurred, the tendency was almost always in the direction of the conventional division of responsibility, wives having the larger load.

FAMILY INFLUENCES

Like most couples of their generation, our respondents generally lacked role models for their role-sharing behavior. Virtually all described their parents' marriage as traditional or very traditional. Only five of the 128 respondents reported any sharing between their parents of housework or child care. Yet, two thirds of both wives and husbands had mothers who worked outside the home either full or part time while they were growing up. Some of our respondents whose mothers were full-time homemakers thought that their mothers would have preferred paid employment. Those who did have working mothers generally perceived them as wanting to work and liking their jobs. However, many perceived their fathers as less enthusiastic about their wives' employment. In fact, a third of those respondents thought their fathers either had not wanted their wives to work or at least had mixed feelings about it. Very few of the fathers were reported as proud or supportive of their wives' working; the majority were seen as simply accepting it, particularly if it did not inconvenience them (the fathers) in any way.

In considering how satisfied their parents seemed to be with their own marriages, the largest group of husbands and wives in our sample rated them as moderately satisfied. Less than a fourth believed their parents were very satisfied, and a third thought they were either dissatisfied (some were divorced by the time of our interviews) or ambivalent about their marriages.

Although only a small number of our respondents viewed their parents as role models for their own egalitarian marriages, almost all thought their marriages had been influenced by their parents or their parents' marriage. However, as many perceived this as a negative influence as a positive one. For example, a number of respondents indicated that their own marriage was a reaction against their parents' traditional one or against certain sex-stereotyped behaviors of their parents. Yet some were influenced positively by other qualities in their parents' marriage, such as the warmth and caring in their relationship, their respect for each other, their sense of fairness, and their joint decision making in family matters. Particularly mentioned by both husbands and wives, but especially the latter, were certain attributes of the mother, for example, her competence and independence.

How Role Sharing Began

The wives in our sample were more likely to voice egalitarian ideals than their husbands and before or during marriage had used these values as a basis for pressing for role sharing. Usually, however, these values began to affect (or rationalize) behavior when they were accepted by the husbands, that is, when they became jointly held.

According to our respondents, only a fourth shared egalitarian ideals about marriage before their current marriages. Another fourth indicated that their consciousness had been raised after marriage about the unfairness of traditional expectations concerning housework and child care when the wife had an outside job or career, and this led to the development of egalitarian ideals. The other half did not begin role sharing because of any ideology about equality between husbands and wives but rather for a variety of pragmatic reasons such as the wife's insistence on help with domestic (and child care) responsibilities when she had paid work or out of necessity in order to get the tasks done at all, to facilitate the wife's pursuing a career, or to enable them to take on the additional responsibility of having children when both spouses were employed.

Although few of these men initiated the sharing of domestic tasks, most cooperated with their wives in working out mutually satisfactory arrangements for handling domestic chores and conveyed to us their belief that this was the right and fair thing to do. This sense of equity seemed to permeate other aspects of the relationship as well. Thus, it seemed that role-sharing behavior often led to egalitarian attitudes, as well as the other way around.

The Vs are typical. They are a young professional couple who have been married for six years. They plan to have children but have not begun serious discussions about this yet. Although both were involved in careers on a full-time basis when they were first married, like most couples they divided chores around the home along traditional sex-role lines. Mrs. V did such things as planning and preparing meals, cleaning up the kitchen afterward, housecleaning, and laundry, while Mr. V took out the garbage and washed their cars. Both had simply assumed a traditional marriage as their parents had had and had not given the domestic role any conscious thought. It did not occur to them at that time that there was a major difference between their situation and their parents—Mrs. V worked outside the home while their mothers did not. Soon Mrs. V started commenting about all the things she did around the home. Later when her comments turned into complaints about the unfairness of her doing all the housework, the Vs began discussing their expectations, behavior, and needed changes. They began questioning their traditional sex-role behavior, realizing where it came from, how they had unthinkingly adopted it, and how inappropriate and unsatisfactory it was for them. They also realized that they had control over what they did at home: they could share or divide tasks any way they pleased. The Vs then began the process of working out ways of handling domestic tasks that they thought were fair. Although Mr. V carried out his agreed upon chores, he felt initially that he was doing his wife a favor by helping her with the housework. He soon became aware of how grandiose, unfair, inappropriate, and traditional such an attitude was. He felt ashamed of having seen himself as a benign husband who had the power to decide whether or not to help his wife with their housework. By the time of our interview, Mr. V was a full partner in managing the household, and both spouses were satisfied with what they considered a fair division of labor. In the interview Mr. V commented that it is a good feeling to have control over one's life and not be a slave to tradition.

Unlike the Vs, the Fs still maintain and value traditional attitudes about sex roles but find that they cannot live by them. For financial reasons, they believe they have no choice but to share the work-family roles. The Fs are a couple in their mid-thirties who have been married 14 years and have two school-age children. At the beginning of their marriage Mr. F was the breadwinner and his wife stayed home to take care of the home and later the children. While their younger child was still a toddler the Fs gave up the struggle of trying to live on Mr. F's salary as a postman. Mrs. F returned to school to complete her nurses training and has been working full time since then. The Fs have never had to pay for child care. They work different shifts in order to take care of the children themselves, and Mrs. F's mother is available as needed. Since Mr. F is the one home at dinnertime and evenings, he gives the children dinner, helps with homework, and sees to their getting to bed on time. Initially Mrs. F used to cook dinner before she went to work and Mr. F would heat and serve it. Gradually Mrs. F began cooking less and less, and Mr. F picked up the slack without complaining. In fact, he found he enjoyed cooking and felt rather competent at it. Although he did not like doing dishes, he gradually began cleaning up the kitchen after dinner rather than leaving it for his wife. In addition, when he was home for a few hours alone on weekends, he would clean the house "when he was looking for something to do." His mother had kept an immaculate house when he was growing up, and Mr. F had come to take a clean house for granted. Housecleaning standards had deteriorated in the F household after Mrs. F was no longer home full time. So without discussion, planning, or conscious decisions on the part of either spouse, the Fs found they were sharing domestic tasks, as well as child care responsibilities. Both indicated to us that assigning tasks would never work for them, because they "didn't like taking orders." Mrs. F is appreciative of her husband's help around the house and often thanks him for cleaning up. Mr. F says he would prefer to have his wife do all the domestic chores but he realizes that would not be fair. He sees his helping as making it easier for his wife and giving her more free time, though it cuts into his leisure time. On balance, however, he prefers to have his wife in paid work with his sharing household tasks and child care.

Some couples deliberately chose role sharing before marriage. For some, this was part of the planning of their lives together—making decisions about such things as where they will live, whether or not they will have children, whether or not the wife will continue with her career, and so on. If the couples lived together before marriage, the agreement to share household responsibilities may have grown out of that experience, and some of the details concerning who would do what may have been hammered out and put into practice before marriage. For some couples who lived together, the notion of role sharing was not fully implemented until after marriage, because of reluctance on the woman's part "to push" until she felt more secure in the relationship. Generally, this admission in the interview drew laughs from the couple, who were so used to role sharing by then that, in retrospect, they viewed the earlier hesitancy as immature and unwarranted. There were cases, however, in which the man had been resistant initially to sharing domestic tasks while living with the person he later married. Only the couples who were able to work out a role-sharing arrangement ended up in our sample, of course.

The decision made before marriage to share roles was sometimes the result of a previous traditional marriage, particularly on the part of the wife. Generally, the previous marriage was one in which the wife had been employed outside the home but still had most or all of the responsibility for the house and the children. Because they saw such arrangements as unfair and burdensome to them, these women were determined not to enter into another similar relationship.

The Ms are illustrative of a couple who consciously chose an egalitarian, role-sharing marriage after both had experienced more conventional relationships in their previous marriages. They are a professional couple in their early forties, who from the beginning of this marriage have shared the breadwinner and domestic roles and the child care responsibilities for Mrs. M's children from her previous marriage. Both feel very fortunate to have a marriage in which all of these roles are shared. Mrs. M explained that she had tried to be a superwoman in her previous marriage; then, as now, she worked full time outside the home, but during her first marriage she had all of the domestic and child care responsibilities, too. Her first husband's attitude had been that it was fine with him for her to have a career as long as it did not interfere with her home responsibilities. Although Mrs. M had felt burdened and overworked by having so much to do, she did not blame her former husband but rather the difficult situation they were in. She, too, was accepting of traditional sex roles and had not worked out a satisfactory solution to her family-career dilemma. Although the resulting stress and strain was not the sole reason for the marriage failure, Mrs. M later realized what a negative effect the unresolved dilemma had had on her. Through discussions with Mr. M before their marriage, she became much more aware of how unfair the situation had been and began to reevaluate the traditional values she held concerning sex roles. Mr. M, whose first marriage had ended years earlier, had given a great deal of thought to what he wanted and did not want in marriage, on the basis of his previous experience. He had certainly learned that the traditional model was not for him. He realized that he wanted a wife who was intelligent and independent and had interests of her own; he wanted to relate to her not only as a lover but also as a friend and as an equal. Before their marriage, the Ms discussed at length this egalitarian ideal that they found they shared and ways of putting it into practice in their relationship. Mr. M took the lead in suggesting novel methods of handling family roles, and much of their sharing behavior was agreed to before marriage.

For still other couples, role sharing was simply a continuation of their behavior before marriage (or living together for those who did before marriage), when each had lived independently and had been self-sufficient. Often these were couples in which both spouses had lived on their own in graduate school or at the beginning of their careers. The women in these couples were used to working and supporting themselves financially, and the men had gained a degree of proficiency in cooking, doing their own laundry, cleaning their apartments, and so on. Unlike some couples fitting this description who immediately fall into traditional sex roles concerning housework upon getting married, these men and women, for some reason, did not change. They seemed to assume that each would remain personally responsible for himself or herself and that sharing was a logical and efficient way of doing this when two people live together. Thus, in addition to taking for granted the sharing of financial responsibilities as most dual-earner couples do, spouses in these couples also automatically shared domestic tasks. Both the men and women seemed to view sharing the domestic roles as a welcome relief since it lightened the load for each of them; after marriage there were two people to do the domestic chores that each had done alone before. The exceptions to this sharing were cases in which each spouse continued to do his or her own laundry, ironing, mending, and in one case, cooking, since these two people liked different types of food. Even these couples shared the rest of the household tasks.

The Ws are one such couple. Their marriage seven years ago was from the beginning a role-sharing, egalitarian relationship—a natural outgrowth of their experiences and the relationship they had developed during their five-year dating period. During that time both had been independent as they worked to support themselves and both maintained their own apartments. Each respected the other's autonomy and competence. During their long dating period, they got to know each other's values and interests quite well. They discovered, for example, that Mr. W really enjoyed cooking. He liked cooking better than she did, was a better cook, and generally had more interest in the kitchen, including keeping it clean. On the other hand, Mrs. W was the better financial manager. Neither had much interest in or liked doing the rest of the domestic tasks, nor was one person regarded as being more competent at any of them. Both could do the laundry, housecleaning, and so on, but did them only because these tasks had to be done. Since they knew each other's likes and dislikes so well by the time they were married, it was not difficult for them to decide who should do what according to special interests and abilities or who disliked a task less—the two criteria they used. The system that resulted was a combination of each person's being responsible for certain tasks, doing some together, and taking turns with others. Both were satisfied with the way they handled home responsibilities since they viewed it as not only fair and balanced but also as less work for each of them compared with what they had to do while single.

MAINTAINING ROLE SHARING

As previously indicated, domestic role sharing is not a static phenomenon. Some couples described it as a constantly evolving process. Certainly most couples found that adjustments were needed from time to time whether these were due to changed circumstances or dissatisfaction on the part of one spouse, usually the wife. The latter might stem from a drift toward conventional sex roles with a resulting imbalance. According to our respondents, the guiding principles for maintaining a mutually satisfactory way of handling all family responsibilities were fairness and flexibility. Often frequent communication and negotiation were necessary in order to implement these principles. For example, a husband might be completely unaware that his wife felt she was unfairly burdened with domestic tasks unless she told him. The resolution to the imbalance might involve processes such as bargaining, negotiating, and compromising. Most of our couples engaged in such adjustment procedures only when one or both spouses felt a need to do so. A few couples, however, also set aside regular times, which might be as often as weekly or as infrequent as once or twice a year, in order to evaluate their role-sharing behavior and suggest desired changes. One purpose of the regular meetings, in addition to monitoring and providing a forum for counteracting the tendency to let things slide by, was an effort to guard against taking each other for granted. For example, some couples did not believe it should be assumed that the husband would do house repairs any more than it should be taken for granted that the wife would do the cooking.

From talking with these couples, we could see that certain attitudes and expectations on the part of the spouses ran counter to maintaining an equitable division of domestic tasks even when such a division had been instituted. Doubtless, what undermines domestic role sharing most is the belief, regardless of what they profess, on the part of one or both spouses that certain—and indeed most—household tasks are women's work. This attitude generally results in the husband's "helping" his wife rather than in his being *responsible* for some of the tasks. Although helping is better than not helping, it has certain attendant—some would also say, undesirable—features. As previously indicated, the husband can decide when to help or not, generally leaving the wife with having to perform the task if the husband decides not to. Because expectations about helping may be vague or differ between the spouses, conflict may result, especially if the husband refuses to help or does not help to the wife's satisfaction. When the husband does help, he may feel generous and benevolent, may see himself as doing a favor for his wife for which she should be thankful, may use it to bargain with his wife for something he wants, or any combination of similar attitudes and behavior may reflect an imbalance in marital power. The wife may feel grateful for what he does and lucky to have a husband who helps, or she may feel resentful and unhappy over the unfairness of such a situation, depending on how burdened she feels and how she sees sex roles.

Not only might traditional attitudes about sex roles lead to husbands' helping only when they choose to do so, it may also mean that the husband alone decides with which tasks he will help. It was rare for a woman in our study to indicate a specific household chore that she would not do, but several men did ("I don't do floors," "I don't clean bathrooms," etc.). Such attitudes not only influence the division of tasks in the first place but also can severely limit any attempted readjustments. Negotiations and compromises are restricted if the woman is bargaining from a relatively powerless position.

Another factor that has the potential of unbalancing agreed upon divisions of household responsibilities is differences in standards, a topic taken up earlier. Here we discuss only how higher housekeeping standards held by the wife can pose difficulties for the maintenance of domestic role sharing. We found a number of instances of husbands' not performing domestic tasks to their wives' satisfaction. Usually the husband's rationale was that the wife's standards were unnecessarily high, too high considering the relative importance of the task, or at least unrealistically high since both worked full time outside the home. Some wives concurred with their husbands' assessments, blaming socialization experiences and societal expectations. Other wives believed their standards were realistic and achievable, and a few wives implied that they suspected their husbands of trying to get out of a chore by their shoddy performance, hoping that their wives would take it over. One wife told us she silently accepted any level of performance of her husband's tasks because she had learned that if she complained he would stop doing the tasks altogether. In order to maintain domestic role sharing, many wives found they had to lower their housekeeping standards; some thought this was a small price to pay, particularly if they agreed that their standards were unrealistic for a dual-career couple and perhaps unnecessary for any couple.

One couple who thought they had exhausted all of the common remedies for inequalities in the performance of domestic tasks devised a novel system that worked for them. The problem was that no matter how they divided tasks or what they agreed to concerning standards of performance, the wife at times felt she was doing the larger share. She grew tired of having to bring this matter to her husband's attention ("nagging," they both called it), but she also disliked stewing over it in silence while feeling overburdened. Her husband, who was willing and creative if at times lacking in initiative and industry, suggested the "coupon system." Together, they developed a list of all the things they could think of that the wife might want the husband to do when she was feeling unfairly burdened. One or more coupons were made out for each of these tasks and given to the wife for use at her discretion, with the understanding that more coupons would be forthcoming as needed. With this system, whenever the wife felt her husband was not doing his fair share, she would decide what he could do to bring about a better balance and give him a coupon with that task written on it. Her husband was then obligated to perform the task without question.

Couples in which the spouses shared egalitarian ideals found the maintaining, like the developing, of mutually satisfactory divisions of domestic responsibilities easier to achieve. It was usually not without effort, however. The Ds are illustrative.

Mr. and Mrs. D are a childless professional couple in their mid-thirties. Both were thoroughly committed to equality in their relationship before their marriage nine years ago. Mrs. D stated that she would never have considered a traditional marriage, which she views as relegating the wife to the role of servant. Mr. D, who grew up in a home that strictly adhered to traditional sex roles, believes his egalitarian attitudes developed from his professional and personal contacts with independent women whom he admired and respected. At the time of their marriage, both of the Ds were well on their way to establishing their careers. Both were proficient in domestic tasks, for both had lived independently, doing their own cooking, laundry, housework, and so on.

In spite of their egalitarian attitudes and desire not to convert to traditional sex roles upon marriage, the Ds were surprised at first at the amount of time and effort needed to develop and maintain domestic role sharing on an equitable basis. At the beginning of their marriage, the Ds shared all of the household tasks. This seemed to them a logical and natural way of handling the domestic role since it meant a continuation of what both had been doing before marriage, and it certainly seemed equitable. However, problems soon arose when they discovered that different areas of responsibility were important to each of them and that they did not share the same housekeeping standards. Mrs. D, who was bothered by clutter and had the higher housekeeping standards, tended to prod Mr. D to perform his cleaning tasks better and to pitch in to see that they were done "right." Although a messy house did not bother Mr. D, a sinkful of dirty dishes did because he liked to cook. On balance, however, Mrs. D felt she was doing more than her share of the domestic work. Through a series of discussions in which dissatisfactions and grievances were aired, suggestions offered, negotiations made, and compromises agreed to, the Ds worked out a plan in which each spouse would take total responsibility for certain tasks that were important to him or her. With this principle, the routine housecleaning and laundry went to Mrs. D and the dishes to Mr. D. Because Mr. D did not have as many areas that were important to him, he also received some chores neither particularly wanted to do such as grocery shopping and scrubbing floors. They decided to take turns with things both enjoyed such as planning meals and cooking dinner, as well as with a few of the unpleasant chores. The Ds discovered that for them the principle of equal sharing refers to the role only, not the individual tasks and certainly not at the same time. Although some couples enjoy cooking, cleaning the house, or doing some other tasks together, the Ds found that the key to role sharing for them was to divide the work so that each person had complete responsibility for well-defined tasks. The other spouse then had to accept the standards of the person responsible for the task or had to reopen negotiations for reassignment of tasks.

Although the Ds stuck to their agreement about not trying to impose standards on the other regarding any task the other did, they soon discovered that Mr. D raised some of his standards while Mrs. D lowered some of hers. At the time of our interview, the Ds were still following the basic plan described here because it had resulted in a fairly equal division of responsibility and tasks and was still satisfactory to both of them, but they had made minor alterations and planned to continue doing so as necessary in order to prevent drift toward imbalance. They foresaw major adjustments and reallocation of responsibilities in the event of substantial changes in their lives such as having a baby or buying a house with the additional work each would entail.

Couples in our sample emphasized how important flexibility on the part of both spouses was in maintaining satisfactory ways of sharing family roles. Circumstances change and couples have to be able to adjust to these changes. What is fair under one set of conditions, for example, both spouses employed full time, may no longer be fair under another set, such as one partner staying home. Couples who are committed to equity and egalitarianism in their relationship, yet are flexible, appear to be able to maintain a sense of sharing—even a degree of sharing—regardless of the circumstances. An illustrative case (the Ps) in which the wife stays home to take care of their infant—a drastic change for a dual-career couple—is found in chapter 7 on the child care role.

Some couples found it desirable to shift from time to time tasks that were performed by only one spouse even when there was no apparent need to do so. They believed change for the sake of change not only helped maintain a modicum of interest in domestic tasks but also helped to ward off resentment. They were referring, of course, to the boring and repetitive nature of most household chores and to the negative feelings (e.g., feeling trapped or put upon) that can result from having sole responsibility for a task over a long period of time. Consequently, a reallocation in the division of tasks at points was viewed by these couples as functional. Although this kind of change could be—and was—effected on a spontaneous basis, it was done more systematically by those couples who set aside regular times to discuss how things were going.

6

The Childbearing Decision

Of the 64 couples in our study, 37 had children living with them. Of the remainder, neither spouse in 26 of the couples had ever had children. These latter couples were in their twenties and thirties, the prime childbearing years. And, indeed, 12 of these couples did plan to have children, and two other couples, though still undecided, were leaning toward starting a family. Five additional couples had not made a decision and did not seem to be veering in either direction; they were just plain undecided. Seven couples had decided not to have children.

With the possible exception of the seven couples who had been married for fewer than four years (all of whom were either planning to have children or were leaning in that direction), the couples seemed to be going through or had gone through a very deliberate decision-making process in which they reviewed the arguments for and against having children. Of paramount importance in their deliberations and decisions, if already made, were concerns about what having children would do to their lifestyle and what effect their dual careers would have upon the children.

The Undecideds

The Js are one of the couples who have not decided about having children. Every few months they have lengthy discussions in which they agonize over whether or not to have children. They have been married for five years and since both are in their early thirties, they are beginning to feel pressure to come to a decision within the next few years. On the one hand, they would like a child and believe that they would be good parents. They would want to be equally involved in all aspects of childrearing. The Js believe it would be very beneficial for a child to have both parents actively involved in his or her care and to have the model of role sharing that the parents would provide.

Given their present situation, however, they realize that their ideal of sharing equally in child care is not possible because of Mr. J's career. He teaches at a university and is working toward tenure. This places heavy time and energy demands upon Mr. J since he is under pressure to do research and publish while carrying a heavy teaching load and committee responsibilities. Mrs. J, whose job as a vice-principal in an elementary school does not pay as much as his, had considered working part time for a few years in order to carry the major responsibility for their child but decided not to because it would mean accepting a lesser position if she could obtain one at all. Consequently, the Js see their only options as maintaining their current egalitarian, role-sharing relationship with no children or having a child and becoming more traditional, Mrs. J staying home and Mr. J becoming the sole breadwinner. They do not like either alternative. Like many couples in our study, they do not see as a viable option having someone else care for their children during infancy and early preschool years in order to permit both parents to work full time. Although the Js want a child, they see the costs (the sacrifice Mrs. J would be making in terms of her career, the giving up of much of their role sharing, their reduced income, etc.) as being very high—thus, their indecision.

Other undecided couples struggled with similar dilemmas. For some, the issue of child vs. wife's career was even more salient, for these wives did not want their careers interrupted or slowed by working only part time, even if they could. Because their husbands felt they could not sacrifice their careers by staying home temporarily or working part time, an assessment with which their wives were inclined to agree, and because these couples did not feel they should have children unless one parent could stay home to take care of them, they saw no resolution to the dilemma. Some of these couples thought they probably would not have children.

It was clear that these couples intended that whatever children they might have would be the result of a very deliberate choice. They indicated that an agreed upon plan for child care would be integral to a decision to have children. Although day care was mentioned by an occasional respondent, it did not seem to be a serious option for these couples, perhaps because they were thinking of infants and very young children rather than older preschool-age and school-age children. At the beginning, at least, these couples felt strongly that they themselves wanted to take care of any child they had. As one respondent put it, the point of having children would be to take care of them, not to walk away and leave them. Consequently, if neither parent was willing, or felt she or he was able, to stay home, these couples did not believe they should have children.

Other factors they considered included ways having a child would affect them and their relationship. To them a child meant a great deal of responsibility and a much more structured lifestyle. It would mean giving up much of the freedom and flexibility that they enjoyed and took for granted. Both spouses anticipated having less time for themselves and with each other and less money because of the added expense of a child on a reduced income. The couples also believed their relationship with each other would change—as one couple put it, "We'd be going from a couple to a group"—but they were not sure just how. Consequently, there was ambivalence and apprehension, because they valued the relationship they had and did not want it to change, and anticipation, because they thought the change might be exciting and that their relationship was strong enough to withstand the strain a child would add to it.

In addition to the changes in their relationship that any couple contemplating having children might expect, most of our respondents were also concerned about possible changes in the egalitarian nature of their relationship. They thought their role-sharing marriages would be put to a test since they were skeptical about being able to share the child care role equally. Generally, they believed the wife would have the primary responsibility for child care, and this would necessitate a renegotiation of roles between the couple. They foresaw a shift to a more traditional division of work-family roles and possibly an imbalance between them in the performance of family roles, the wife having the greater responsibility when she returned to work. Although some of the undecideds felt more confident than others that the role shift and imbalance could be minimized, none of them seemed to feel they could avoid these changes entirely.

On the other hand, these undecided couples were afraid they might be missing something by not having children. They thought they might later regret a decision not to have children. Although none of these couples stressed the enjoyment parents might derive from children while they were growing up, one respondent did mention the pleasure her mother received from her relationship with her adult children. Perhaps the reason for the nonspecificity and sparsity of positives mentioned for having children was that the positives were simply taken for granted by these couples. Since these factors were not problematic, they may not have received the conscious attention that the factors mentioned earlier did. This is not to say that all the changes previously mentioned were regarded as negatives by all the couples. Although some couples did view them on the negative side of the ledger in weighing the decision about having children, other couples saw them as challenges or were ambivalent about them. Regardless of how they viewed the changes that having children would mean, the couples also varied in the degree to which they were accepting of these changes. At the time of our interviews, however, not one of these couples was at the point of making a commitment to having children.

No Children Planned

The Rs decided before marriage not to have children. It was not an agonizing decision for them since neither wanted children. They had married in their late twenties after both had started their professional careers and had lived independently for several years. Both have demanding and satisfying careers as university professors, he in biology and she in art history. The Rs spend almost all their time away from the university together but still feel they do not see as much of each other as they would like. After several years of marriage, they find they enjoy each other's company as much as when they were first married. They attribute part of this to the fact that they enjoy the same activities and share common values. For example, vacations are spent traveling throughout the United States and abroad to visit art museums and galleries. Both delight in tracking down and purchasing, when possible, obscure but valuable works of art. They admit that while their collection may be an investment, it is also a major extravagance on their part in view of their income. The Rs do not want the changes in their relationship and lifestyle that they believe a child would bring. Since they would not be able to spend as much time together as a couple if they had children, they believe their relationship is closer because they are childless. They also prefer to be "selfish," if that is society's label for people who choose to spend their time and money on activities and things other than children.

Unlike the Rs, who seem completely unconflicted about their decision not to have children, the Ss have made the same decision, but Mr. S seemed ambivalent about their choice. Like the Rs, they decided before their marriage not to have children. Mrs. S felt strongly about the matter while Mr. S was neutral. Mrs. S's reasons for not wanting children were both ideological and personal: in addition to her concern about overpopulation, she had no desire to go through pregnancy, childbirth, or childrearing. Now after several years of marriage with both well along in their careers (she is a social worker, he is an electrical engineer), she is as adamant as ever about not having children. Mr. S verbalizes the tradeoffs that he sees if they were to have children, and he is not sure that he wants these tradeoffs. While children would add more stress and strain to their relationship, they would also provide an additional bond, according to Mr. S. He believes not having children makes it harder to maintain a marital relationship because of the great amount of freedom. The Ss believe that some of their friends are staying married only because they have children. Thus, they view this additional bond as "golden handcuffs," to use their phrase. If they had decided to have children, Mr. S thought he would have been the one to stay home for a while and later work part time while using a day care arrangement in addition. Thus, the Ss believed they would be able to continue sharing work-family roles if they had children but for other reasons did not want children.

All the couples in our study who had decided not to have children were in their thirties and had been married for at least five years. Although generally the decision not to have children was made either before marriage or soon after marriage, a few couples had waivered at times in their decision. Possibly some of these couples will change their minds and have children at a later time. It was evident that all had given the matter a great deal of thought and had made considered decisions.

All expressed great satisfaction with their marital relationships and did not want their relationships changed, as they believed they would be by having children. They seemed to want to preserve not only the egalitarian, role-sharing aspect of their relationship but also the freedom they felt as individuals and as a couple to do what they wanted. They also voiced concern about the pressure and tension that they thought children would impose upon their relationship. Although most of the couples felt their marriages could withstand these changes, one couple stated bluntly that children would "blow the relationship." This couple was not referring to the fragility of the bond between them but rather to the fact that children would fundamentally alter their relationship, which was based on friendship and individual autonomy, as well as on love and intimacy.

Most of these couples did not seem to feel that the changes that children would bring about would be either desirable or exciting; in fact, they stated clearly that they did not want their lifestyle disrupted. Work was very important to these couples, and they did not want their careers hampered. One couple had had experience with a foster child, and this only confirmed their choice not to have children.

Few of these couples seemed to think that there were any disadvantages involved in their decision. In addition to the ambivalent Mr. S mentioned earlier, another husband regretted not having anyone to carry on the family line. Although our respondents did not think they would be missing positive experiences by not becoming parents, those who had thought about the issue believed that their type of marriage would be beneficial to children. The major advantage they cited for children being reared in role-sharing families was equal access to both parents. They believe shared parenting would be "healthier" for children. These couples were assuming that both parents would make the necessary work adjustments to participate equally in child care.

Children in the Future

The Ns have always wanted children. Two would be nice, three would be better. Although both recently turned thirty and they have been married for seven years, they have not decided when to start their family. They have thought through some of the issues involved in having children, but many more remain to be discussed. Although the Ns do not believe all details can be worked out in advance, they believe a great deal of planning and preparation are necessary before having children.

They are already resigned to the fact, for example, that having children will affect Mrs. N's career as a high school mathematics teacher. In their discussions of which parent will stay home, they keep arriving at the same decision because they cannot see how Mr. N can give up his higher paying executive position with a manufacturing company, though he says he would be willing to do so. A leave would be out of the question. Mr. N wistfully stated that he wished our country had a system like Sweden's which permits either the father or mother to take parental leave. He thought that not only would such a system be fairer to the parents and make it easier for them to plan, but also it would be better for the children to have both parents actively involved in child care from the beginning.

As it is, Mrs. N says she is still in the process of trying to "adjust her feelings" to having to stay home for a while. Although she wants to work after having children, she agrees with her husband that it is very important to have one parent home with the children while they are young. The Ns will have to decide later when it will be all right for her to return to work, leaving the children in the care of someone else. Their strong preference for this "someone else" would be a member of one of their families. At this time, Mr. N's father seems to be the best candidate because he loves children, is good with them, and plans to retire soon. The Ns realize how fortunate they are—particularly regarding child care—to be settled in the same community as both of their families. They admit that their decision about having children would be more complicated if this were not the case. Even so, the Ns are taking their time about starting their own family. They see children as an awesome responsibility, one not to be entered into lightly.

The Ns have agreed upon some general principles concerning childrearing, such as that discipline must be shared between them and both parents are to be very involved in the children's upbringing, but the specifics of childrearing are yet to be discussed. They believe their type of marriage will be beneficial to their children, for their egalitarian attitudes and behavior will convey to each child an awareness of his or her own importance as a person, instill self-respect, and foster the belief that they can do whatever their potential enables them to do. They believe that one of the most important things parents can do for children is to expose them to a wide variety of options regardless of their sex, encourage them to make their own choices, and support them in whatever choices they make. At the same time, they believe parents have a responsibility to ensure their children's awareness of society's attitudes about certain sex-linked behaviors. They think this will not be easy. For example, how can parents convey to a son that it is all right for him to play with dolls or want to be a kindergarten teacher, while having to tell him at the same time that other people may think he is an oddball for making these choices?

Few of the childless couples in our study who intended to have children were as far along in their planning as the Ns. This may be because they had been married for a relatively short period of time. Only five of the twelve couples planning to have children, and neither of the additional two couples leaning in that direction, had been married for as long as five years. It is possible, of course, that some of these young couples will change their minds about having children as they begin to evaluate seriously the tradeoffs involved.

Whether they viewed having a child as a distant event or were engaged in thoughtful consideration about starting a family, almost all these couples saw the solution to the child-career dilemma in the same way. They planned for the wife to stay home for a while, then work part time, at least until their child or children (most wanted only one or two) reached school age, possibly longer. They realized that this would mean a more traditional division of work-family roles for a while, but most saw this only as a temporary phenomenon. Some of these couples, particularly those seriously thinking about having children, had considered the possibility of taking turns staying home with young children or even having the husband stay home instead of the wife. These alternatives had generally been rejected—rather quickly by some couples—as not feasible given each spouse's job and salary, society's attitudes, and in some cases the couple's own feelings about what they would be comfortable doing. Only one father thought he might take a turn staying home with their child, and another said he would stay home instead of his wife if her salary was higher than his at that time. The latter couple, who were both clinical social workers, were earning equal salaries at the time of our interviews. All the couples indicated that both parents would be very involved in child care.

Like the undecided couples and the couples who planned not to have children, these couples weighed the advantages and disadvantages of having children. Their beliefs about how children would affect their marital relationship and lifestyle and about how their egalitarian attitudes would affect their children were similar to those couples in the other two groups. The difference seemed to be that these couples clearly wanted children and were willing to switch to more traditional work-family roles for a few years (that is, become transitional couples) in order to accomplish this more easily. It is impossible to predict whether or not this assessment will hold true for all the young couples married for a relatively short period of time. Some wives may increasingly find their jobs harder to give up, some couples may find it more difficult to change their lifestyles as they become more and more accustomed to them, and some couples who may now be taking for granted having children may later feel that children are a deliberate choice. Such changes may lead to a more agonizing—and possibly different—decision than appeared to be the case at the time of our interviews.

Components of the Decision

As this discussion indicates, not all the considerations involved in a role-sharing couple's decision about whether or not to have children were due to the egalitarian nature of the marital relationship. For many couples, however, this aspect adds another layer of issues to be dealt with in making the decision. One might think of four different groups of issues on the work-family dimension that might be involved in decisions about having children, perhaps only one or two groups being applicable to most couples. (We recognize that not all children are planned. Couples who do not make a conscious choice about having children obviously do not fit into the framework discussed here, though they must deal with some of these issues after the fact, so to speak.) These groups of issues are discussed here under the following rubrics: basic considerations, working wife, wife with a career, and couples committed to role sharing. Some of our respondents were dealing with issues in all four groups.

BASIC CONSIDERATIONS

Regardless of lifestyle, it is a major step to go from being a childless couple to being a couple with a child. Traditional couples with home-maker wives and dual-executive couples alike find their lives greatly changed by the addition of a child. The couples in our sample were well aware of this and reacted variously to these anticipated, but for the most part unknown, changes. Some found them exciting and looked for-ward to them, some were accepting or even resigned, and still others did not want the changes at all.

The additional responsibility of having a child was a salient consid-eration for these couples. Although some perceived it as awesome, none seemed to feel they were unable to handle it if they chose to do so. The financial costs of a child, the additional demands on their time and energy, the curtailment of freedom to come and go as they pleased, and the necessity for a more structured lifestyle were other factors consid-ered seriously by these couples.

Although the examples of basic considerations mentioned here are factors that might enter into any couple's decision about having chil-dren, some of these factors may be viewed differently by role-sharing couples. For example, while a child is a major responsibility for any couple, the child may be viewed more or less as an extension of the responsibility some spouses feel for each other. At least, the idea of family responsibility is already in place for many couples by virtue of their being married. This may not be so for many egalitarian couples, for these spouses are likely to perceive themselves and each other as autonomous—self-sufficient and responsible for herself or himself. Consequently, these spouses may not feel responsible for each other. Assuming the responsibility for a child may be the first time either of the spouses has taken on any responsibility for anyone besides himself or herself.

Another illustration of a basic consideration mentioned by a few of the couples in our sample that may not be a concern generally shared by prospective parents is the potential of abuse of power with children. These role-sharing couples were acutely aware that while they saw and treated each other as equals, this would not be the case with children. Although they viewed children as having rights—rights that often su-perseded the rights of their parents—children could not be equal to adults, because of their dependency. The fact is that parents have con-

heir children (when they are young, anyway), which may be
for them to accomplish childrearing tasks such as physical
urance, and socialization. At the same time, however, the
ability to exercise control over another person can be a rather heady
feeling. Parents can make children do something just because the parents want them to without regard for whether or not the child wants to
do it, how the child will experience it, or if it is truly "good for the
child." To these couples who see any attempt by one spouse to exert
power over the other as unfair, this is an abuse of parental control.

WORKING WIFE

In addition to factors that any couple may need to consider in deciding whether or not to have children, dual-earner couples must make
some arrangements for the care of the child. If the mother is to stay
home to care for the child, the couple might weigh such factors as the
family's income, her job seniority, her ability to reenter the labor market
at a future time, and the satisfaction she may derive from the job.
Although some women may be glad to give up their jobs, particularly
menial, low-paying ones, and some women with more traditional attitudes may have been planning to work only until they have children, the
reality is that many wives and mothers no longer have the option of
staying out of the labor market indefinitely.

If the mother plans to take only a paid or unpaid maternity leave,
some type of child care must be arranged. This might involve a host of
practical, perceptual, and attitudinal considerations, such as who is
available to care for the child, what kind of arrangement might be best
for the child and the family, what kind is feasible and affordable, the
couple's beliefs about the effect of the contemplated child care arrangement on the child, and the mother's feelings about being away from her
young child.

Generally, couples in our study who were contemplating having children gave these issues a great deal of thought. Since they were making a
deliberate choice about having children, they wanted to plan carefully
for the care of their children. On the one hand, they strongly believed
that one of the parents should stay home with small children, some
couples going so far as to say people should not have children unless

they themselves would provide the child care. On the other hand, this goal would often be difficult to achieve. Sometimes neither parent wanted to stay home. In other cases, they saw the financial sacrifice as being too great. The child care problem weighed heavily in some couples' decisions not to have children and in the indecision on the part of others. As previously indicated, most of the couples who planned to have children had resolved the issue in favor of the wife's staying home for a while, then returning to work part time when the children were older. An occasional couple counted on another family member or planned to get someone else to come to the home to provide child care.

WIFE WITH A CAREER

When the wife not only works but also has a career, another major consideration must be factored into the decision-making process: how having a child would affect the wife's career. Careers by definition involve commitment and may be in demanding professions. Compared with other working women, some of whom may be glad to give up outside jobs temporarily, career women may feel that they would be sacrificing more to stay home or even to cut back to part-time work in order to assume childrearing responsibilities. Even if she planned to continue with her career full time and use some form of child care, the competing demands on her time and energy from her career, child, husband, and home may be very stressful for her and her family. Since both rearing a child and having a career have been traditionally viewed as full-time occupations, it is not surprising that many career women wonder if they can do justice to both or if they must choose between them.

Most of the wives in our study had careers that they liked, were committed to, and were reluctant to set aside even temporarily. Husbands seemed to be understanding, supportive, and encouraging of their wives' careers. They verbalized the feeling that their wives' careers were as important as theirs and that their wives should not jeopardize their careers or slow down in pursuing them in order to have children unless the wives themselves wanted to. Although we have no way of knowing if there was subtle pressure from husbands who really wanted children, we saw no evidence of any. We did see evidence to the contrary, that is, where husbands seemed to want children but respected their wives' desire not to have their careers interrupted.

Couples Committed to Role Sharing

Couples who share the work-family roles as an expression of strong egalitarian ideals will not automatically assume that the wife will have the primary responsibility for the child. If the couple plans to share this role as equally as possible, they will consider how having a child would affect both their careers. Planning for the husband to stay home for a while or cut his work back to part time may be viewed equally as plausible an alternative for these couples as planning for the wife to do so. In other words, these couples may consider all possible options with the childrearing role as they do with other family roles.

Indeed, some of our couples did consider the possibility of the husband's staying home with their child or having the parents take turns staying home. Although only one or two couples planning to have children considered these options feasible, many other couples had seriously considered them. In most cases, they were ruled out because the husband either did not want to or could not make the career sacrifice. Some husbands indicated that they would like to share child care equally with their wives and expressed regret that the world of work and our society are not supportive of, and in fact discourage, such efforts. (In the next chapter, examples will be given of husbands who did cut back on their work to participate equally in child care). Some couples who were undecided about having children or did not plan to have children seemed to weigh the husband's and wife's careers equally in terms of sacrifices that would need to be made in order to have children.

All the couples who thought they might have children planned to share childrearing responsibilities. They felt strongly about this both because of their egalitarian ideals and because they believe children need both parents actively involved in their care. Although in most cases the mother would have the lion's share of responsibility when the child was small because she would be the one at home during the day, the couples thought child care responsibilities would be more nearly equally divided when the child was older. Some couples planned for the husband to be the primary caretaker for the young child evenings and weekends to relieve the wife and to help redress the imbalance during the time the wife was home during the day. Husbands generally felt they had more to learn about the care of infants and children than their wives did, but they were willing to learn. Both spouses believed the husbands could attain the same degree of proficiency in child care as their wives.

Changes and Choices

The changing attitudes and behavior about childbearing in this country are reflected in our role-sharing couples, who like other highly educated, career-oriented couples, are in the vanguard of these changes. They are certainly exercising their ability to make choices, increasingly made easier by more widespread availability of reliable contraceptives and of abortion, about having children—whether to have, when, and how many. A comparison of the fertility behavior of these couples with that of their parents, together with some information about their families of origin, might help to highlight some of these changes.

As the description of our couples in chapter 3 indicated, the 37 couples who did have children had very small families, mostly only one or two children. This is in sharp contrast to their families of origin, in which four, five, and six children were not uncommon. Only six of our 128 respondents were only children. Approximately half of our respondents came from working-class families, and almost half grew up in Catholic homes. Their mothers were not all full-time housewives, however. Two-thirds of the husbands and of the wives in our sample had mothers who had paid work, divided roughly equally between full time and part time, while they were growing up. However, few of these mothers, most of whom were in clerical, professional, or technical occupations, began working before our respondents reached school age.

Like the trend of very small families, the trends of indecision, childlessness, and delayed first births—phenomena considered in this chapter—are recent among married couples. These trends are not unrelated (Wilkie 1981). For example, Veevers (1973) found that most of the voluntarily childless couples in her study had planned to have children but for various reasons had postponed their first child. And, of course, some couples who decide not to have children later change their minds. But as Sweet (1982) observes, "later means fewer," whether one is referring to increasing age at marriage or the postponement of having the first child (both of which are more typical of better educated, dual-career couples). The trends mentioned here are at variance with what our society considers normative behavior. "Social norms in the United States, at least until recently, have pressed people into a preference for marriage over nonmarriage, parenthood over nonparenthood, and at least two children rather than only one—with the provision that one should be in a position to fulfill one's parental obligations" (Ryder 1979:361).

Although many couples in our study exhibit normative behavior, attitudes, and expectations regarding childbearing, there is also evidence that many others consider parenthood a matter of choice, not an obligation or simply a concomitant of marriage. With some couples, the choice involves the weighing of costs and benefits—to the marital relationship, to their careers, to each spouse, and to the child. A major consideration is what Sweet (1982) calls "lifestyle opportunity costs." The couples without children have developed a lifestyle that they know would have to change in many ways if they had a child. Unlike conventional couples with the traditional sex-role division of labor who have a family structure that readily accommodates children and possibly was developed for precisely this reason, role-sharing couples do not have such a family structure. Alterations must be made in their lifestyle if children are to fit in. Perhaps it is not surprising that in their review of research on parenting decisions, Rosen and Benson (1982) found that studies showed that childless couples, compared with parents, have relatively egalitarian interactions with each other.

7

Child Care

In this chapter we focus on those couples who already had children. Although there were 37 couples altogether, the 33 with children under twelve years of age are our chief concern. Not only is child care less of a burden when children are older, but also older children can help with household tasks. The younger children are the ones who pose the greatest threat to a role-sharing marriage, according to our respondents.

Most couples with children had either one or two. Some of these couples planned to have another child. The few couples who had three or more children were generally older. They had started role sharing after the children were older, when the wife either began her career or resumed the career she had started before having children. Although the ages of the children ranged from one month upward, the vast majority were under eleven years of age. Few of these children were unplanned; most were the result of a conscious joint decision. Generally the couples had made the decision to have children before the marriage, and the decision about when to have them some time after marriage. For many of these couples, the latter decision was the problematic one. For others, the timing was dependent on having attained a particular goal, such as the wife's finishing a graduate program, the husband's reaching a certain point in his career, or the couple's having bought a home. Usually a great deal of planning concerning child care and childrearing took place before they decided to have the first child. The children these couples referred to as "unplanned" were likely to be a second or third child that they had decided to have but whose timing had not been planned. Some of the couples referred to themselves as "over ready" in terms of planning by the time they finally had a child.

By this they meant that they had discussed the pros and cons of having a child at length, were committed to having a baby, had a definite plan for child care, and had hammered out agreements on as many anticipated childrearing issues as they could think of.

The Caretaker Role

The large majority of the couples with children under twelve years of age had worked out arrangements that permitted the parents to take care of the children themselves. Often this was accomplished by the wife's cutting back to part-time work (13 couples) or temporarily not working at all (four couples; two additional mothers were on short maternity leaves at the time of our data collection). A few couples managed such an arrangement by having the father or both parents cut down on their work hours or by working different shifts or different seasons (for example, one parent working during the school year and the other doing free-lance work summers and weekends during the school year). Sometimes sitters or family members were needed for short uncovered periods of time such as an hour per day or a morning each week owing to an overlap in the parents' paid work hours. Obviously, parental child care was easier to work out if the children were in school all day. Few of our couples used other family members or day care centers for supplementary child care.

If the mothers worked full time, as twelve of these 33 mothers of preadolescent children did, the family generally relied on a sitter for child care. However, four of these families managed without outside help, but in each case, at least one spouse was a teacher with shorter work days and summers off. Two of these couples had only school-age children whose hours roughly coincided with one parent's. Spouses in the other two couples with preschool-age children worked different hours.

Most of the fathers in our sample were very involved in the caretaker role, but their involvement varied greatly by family and by child care activity. A few transitional families looked very traditional, at least at the time of our interviews, in terms of how they handled the parental roles, especially if the mother was staying home to care for the children or working only part time. However, the majority of these couples in which the mother was the primary caretaker because she was home more made a special effort to have the father involved in the care of the children when he was home. A few couples accomplished this goal by the father's simply assuming the role of primary caretaker evenings and weekends. For example, one father of an infant, whose wife was temporarily staying home to care for their child, insisted on taking over child care duties when he was home. Although this undertaking was rather strenuous for him, he felt it was worth it for both him and his child; he did not want to miss out on the pleasures in taking care of his child, and he enjoyed the close father–infant relationship. His wife was happy about the sharing of their infant's care and was better rested and relaxed because of it. The couple felt the entire family benefited from this arrangement, which they saw as continuing the role-sharing pattern established early in their marriage.

A more common pattern was for both parents to participate more or less equally in child care when both were home. Often the care of the children was split up between the couple along with domestic tasks: that is, one spouse might be involved with the children while the other performed a necessary chore around the house.

We specifically asked parents about four types of child care activities or concerns: routine care, child's development, emotional support, and child's entertainment. By routine care, we meant such activities as bathing, feeding, and responding to crying at night for a very young child or seeing that an older child eats breakfast or does her or his homework. Parental concerns regarding the child's development would include, for example, noticing the child's readiness for toilet training or for learning to tie his or her shoe laces. For older children it might involve taking the initiative around decisions such as if and when to start music lessons or how late a child should be allowed to stay up. Emotional support was illustrated by comforting a child when she or he does not feel well or listening when the child wants to discuss a problem. Entertainment would include playing with the child or supervising his or her other recreational activities, such as playing with friends or watching television.

The large majority of parents said both were equally likely to perform the tasks associated with each of the four aspects of child care. However, if one parent was more likely to perform the activities, it was usually the mother. The child care role shifted even more to the mothers when the couples were asked who assumed the primary responsibility for the children in each of the four areas. Yet two thirds of the couples believed the responsibility was shared equally. A number of the couples who admitted unequal sharing in performing (and assuming responsibility for) the child care role explained the imbalance on the basis of the wife's being home with the children more. Some indicated that they expected more nearly equal participation when the wives returned to work full time. Again, probably because many wives were staying home full time or part time to take care of the children, more than half of the parents indicated that the mother, as opposed to the father or both parents equally, devoted the most time, energy, and effort to child care. Although more than half the couples thought the mother took more responsibility for learning more about a child care issue that neither knew much about, most of the couples believed that the fathers knew as much about child care as the mothers.

Thus the major patterns that evolved concerning the performance of the child care role were more or less equal participation of both parents or for the mother to assume primary responsibility. Because it is still very uncommon, the cases in which the father assumed primary responsibility were of particular interest. Two fathers had the major responsibility for each of the following aspects: routine care, emotional support, and the child's entertainment. In addition, two fathers knew the most about child care, two took responsibility for learning about new child care issues, one devoted the most effort and energy in child care, and three spent the most time with the child. In all, this involves a total of 12 fathers who assumed primary responsibility in at least one of these areas. Two additional couples would be included if we also counted cases in which the father was reported to perform the tasks in an area more often than the mother.

One area that seems to remain almost exclusively the wife's domain is arranging for and dealing with the sitter when this arrangement is used either on a part-time or full-time basis. The husband's role in almost every case was limited to joint discussion and decision making with his wife about this type of child care arrangement in general, approving the wife's choice of a particular sitter, and helping in transporting the sitter or the children. Husbands indicated that they preferred to have their wives make the arrangements, talk with the sitters about the children, and pay the sitters. That the sitters in every case were female was largely the reason for the sex-role distinction in handling these arrangements. According to the husbands, the sitters preferred dealing with their wives because they were the mothers and mothers are responsible for children in our society. As one husband put it, it was simply easier for his wife to have the contact, because the sitter could not accept his status as a full parent. More subtle, but still conveyed by some of the couples, was the impression that the wife was a better judge of prospective child caretakers (because she was the mother?) and that it was more important for her than for her husband to be satisfied with the arrangement, possibly because otherwise she would stay home to take care of the child herself.

CASE EXAMPLES

A few examples may be helpful in understanding how some couples managed to share the child care role more or less equally. The cases selected illustrate four different ways of combining work and family roles: both of the As work part time outside the home, both of the Es are employed full time, Mr. P has full-time employment while Mrs. P stays home, and both Mrs. V and Mrs. O work full time outside the home while their husbands work part time on a free-lance basis. Each case illustrates the flexibility of the couples to make the necessary modifications in their lifestyles in order for both parents to participate fully in child care.

The As. Dr. A, a dentist, and Mrs. A, a social worker, had both worked full time before the birth of their two-year-old son. Dr. A had entered the marriage twelve years ago with the expectation that the housework would be divided in the traditional manner as in his parent's home. In other words, he did not expect to do anything that was not "his job," and very little around the house was. Mrs. A did not think this arrangement was fair, and many discussions and arguments ensued. Over the years, they evolved a relationship of sharing domestic tasks, starting first with Dr. A's helping his wife and later assuming full responsibility for certain tasks.

The As waited ten years before having a child. At first they could not decide if they wanted a child, and later, after making a tentative decision to have a baby, they vacillated for years. By the time they made a firm decision, they were also committed to sharing child care. They planned to do so by each working part time, on alternate half-days, so that one parent would always be home with the baby. It was not a decision without consequences because it entailed a great financial sacrifice, particularly by cutting Dr. A's income in half. In addition, Mrs. A felt somewhat guilty about not wanting to be a full-time mother. After a three-month maternity leave for Mrs. A, the plan went into effect. By the time of the interview, the part-time work arrangement had been in effect for two years. The As had found that it had worked better than they had anticipated. Dr. A feels he would be missing a wonderful part of his life if he did not stay home part time and be actively involved in caring for his son. Mrs. A no longer feels guilty about working part time because she finds she can share fully the parenting role. Both believe their son has benefited from the arrangement.

Contrary to many dual-career couples with children, their marriage did not become more traditional since the birth of their son. In fact, many of the problems they had had earlier over a fair division of labor have been resolved by their child care arrangement. The spouse who is home simply does everything for their son and around the house that needs to be done without putting anything off. Both of the As find that they each do more than is necessary during their separate time at home so that there will be less to do and more time for leisure when together as a family. The arrangement is so successful that the As plan to continue it at least until their son is in school all day and possibly even longer, because it would give each spouse more time to pursue hobbies he or she enjoys.

The Es. Mr. and Mrs. E are another professional couple who share the child care responsibilities for their ten-year-old daughter. Unlike the As, both of the Es work full time. Mrs. E's hours as a public defender are longer than her husband's as a high school teacher. In addition, he has summers off while she does not. Since the father's time at work and the daughter's school hours and days coincide, the Es do not need outside help with child care. If their daughter becomes ill when both parents are working, the Es take turns staying home with her. Mrs. E has some ambivalence about this arrangement since it is harder for her to take time off than for her husband; at the same time, she feels guilty about being away from her daughter so much. Although both parents feel they participate fully in the care of their daughter, the reality is that Mr. E does more than his wife in this area because he is home with the daughter more.

Role sharing for the Es began with the birth of their daughter. Before that, Mrs. E had worked outside the home, sometimes part time, sometimes full time, but she had always done the housework. Both of the Es, having been reared in traditional families, assumed that that was the way it should be and did not question the fairness of the arrangement. However, when their daughter was born after eight years of marriage, Mr. E took a very active role in child care from the beginning because it appealed to him and seemed an interesting challenge. Mrs. E, who had given up her employment when the baby was born, was impressed by her husband's competence in caring for their daughter. She decided if he could do that, he could also do housework. Mr. E cooperated by beginning to help with domestic chores. When their child was sixteen months old, Mrs. E entered law school to prepare for a career. During that time and until their daughter started school, the Es used a sitter, the parents' sharing the transporting of their daughter to and from the sitter's home, in addition to sharing other child care and household responsibilities. By this time, Mr. E was no longer helping his wife with domestic tasks but was a full partner in their homemaking, as well as in childrearing.

The Es are very satisfied with their pattern of sharing the work-family roles and believe it is a much better arrangement for them than the one they had at the beginning of their marriage. Household tasks and responsibilities are divided fairly equally, Mrs. E being responsible for food preparation and Mr. E for the care of the house. However, most of the domestic tasks fall to Mr. E during the summer when he is home. Both participate in all aspects of child care. Mr. E provides more of their daughter's emotional support because he is with her more, while Mrs. E takes more responsibility for their child's entertainment. Although Mrs. E is still experiencing some conflict between the demands of her career and her role as a mother, she does not think her daughter is being shortchanged because of Mr. E's active role as a father. In order to manage their two careers, both admit that their housekeeping suffers. They have had to adjust to a more "lived-in" appearing home that bears little resemblance to the immaculate homes of their childhoods. Mr. E is aware that by sharing the domestic and child care roles as he does, he is more confined to the house and has less freedom than more conventional husbands and fathers. He believes this sacrifice is more than compensated for by the feeling of fairness he and his wife have and by the close father-daughter relationship he enjoys.

The Ps. On the surface, the Ps look like a typical, traditional American family. He supports the family by working as a speech therapist in the public schools during the school year and by working summers as a park supervisor. She stays home to care for their nine-month-old son. Before their son's birth, she had worked as an administrative assistant at the local college. Although she liked working, she considered her work more of a job than a career. Because she is not strongly committed to a career yet (she anticipates developing one later), Mrs. P has no conflict about staying home until their son is two or three years of age and can go to nursery school. She then plans to return to work part time for a few years and then increase her outside employment to full time.

Yet, the Ps are far from typical or traditional. From the beginning of their marriage seven years ago, the Ps have shared the domestic role. He does the cooking, she manages their money, and they both pitch in to do whatever else needs to be done to run their household. They worked out a mutually agreeable modification to their role-sharing pattern in order to have a much wanted baby. Both strongly wanted one parent home to provide child care for the first few years. Because Mr. P earned twice as much as his wife and would have had to interrupt his career, it did not take them long to decide that Mrs. P should be the one to stay home.

However, Mr. P has been actively involved in child care throughout. In order to share the parenting role with his wife—a role that both enjoy and find very meaningful—Mr. P takes over the primary care of their son when he is home, including getting up at night when the baby cries. Although both would rather take care of the baby than do anything else around the house, Mrs. P does most of the evening and weekend chores in order to give her husband undisturbed time with the baby. She also thinks its only fair to take on more of the housekeeping tasks since she is home during the day. Even so, some chores are not done as well or at all, and the meals Mr. P prepares now are quicker and simpler than the ones he cooked before the baby came. Even though Mr. P assumes major responsibility for the baby outside of his working hours, the Ps in fact often do things with the baby together, such as playing with him or feeding and bathing him. They spend a great deal of time discussing the baby, his care, and childrearing methods. Mrs. P has more time to read about child care, and she shares this information with her husband. As a result of their shared knowledge and experience, both feel equally competent in taking care of their baby. They believe the baby benefits from the care and attention he receives from two parents. They see the extra holding and touching from two actively involved parents as not only good for the baby but also conducive to close, warm parent-child relationships. Mr. P said sadly that most fathers in our society "are not aware of the satisfactions to be gained from close involvement with their infants and children."

The Us. The Us' son has been cared for primarily by his father since his mother returned to work as a chemist when he was a month old. At that time, Mr. U gave up his job as a landscaper with a large nursery in order to stay home to provide child care. This arrangement had been worked out by the Us for several reasons. Both perceived Mrs. U as more career oriented than her husband, and Mr. U as more family oriented than his wife. In addition Mrs. U, who loved her job and the social contact she and her husband had with her co-workers, earned as much as her husband and had the potential for earning more than he. Although Mr. U liked landscaping, he considered his job far from ideal. It was located at quite a distance from his home, and his boss was cantankerous and difficult to get along with. Mr. U was not surprised to find that he enjoyed taking care of his son, and Mrs. U thought he did an excellent job. However, the satisfaction that the Us derived from this arrangement was gradually undermined by the reaction of significant others, specifically of males, to Mr. U: teasing from friends and flak from relatives, as Mr. U put it. Although Mrs. U was very supportive of her husband and urged him to ignore these reactions, she also understood the strong traditional attitudes held by her husband's working-class family and friends. In spite of his growing discomfort, Mr. U had not given up on his role as primary caretaker by the time of our interviews with the family when his son was 14 months old, but he had begun doing free-lance landscaping evenings and weekends and was talking about starting his own landscaping business. If he followed through on the latter, the Us would need to find a

suitable child care arrangement, which they thought would probably involve a sitter's coming to their home.

As Mrs. U sees it, she has always been a feminist. She grew up
feeling self-confident and competent at whatever she attempted,
whether it was sewing, driving a truck, arranging flowers, or
fixing the plumbing. She ignored sex-role stereotyping and felt
constrained not at all by her sex. Although her independence,
competence, and nonconforming behavior were traits that Mr. U
found attractive and admirable, they were not viewed positively by
his family and friends. Essentially, they saw Mrs. U as too powerful, bossy, and strong willed. They also saw the Us' role-sharing
marriage, which Mrs. U had made clear to Mr. U before their
marriage was the only kind she would have, as strange and de-
viant. Although Mrs. U simply shrugged off their opinions and
comments, Mr. U could not always do so. He particularly found
their traditional attitudes and disapproval of the Us' egalitarian
sex-role orientation difficult to ignore after the birth of their son.
The major source of his intermittent but gnawing discomfort was
their attitude, which he admitted that he shared to some extent,
that a man should not let his wife support him but should be the
provider for the family.

The Os.   Like Mr. U, Mr. O was the primary child care provider
for his young children, but the arrangement was not at all problematic for the Os. This couple, who were slightly older than the
Us, had more support from their immediate families and seemed
more impervious to the reactions of others. The Os had timed the
births of their two children for the summer months when Mrs. O,
a high school teacher, was not working. The children, now two
.and four years old, have always been cared for by their father while
their mother worked. Mrs. O assumes major child care responsibilities afternoons when she comes home from work, weekends,
school holidays, and summer vacations. This frees Mr. O, currently a self-employed carpenter, to take outside jobs when his
services are most in demand. He finds that he is able to do very
little carpentry work at home while he is taking care of the two
active preschoolers; that time is spent with the children and on
domestic work. This arrangement also works well financially for
the family since they keep all necessary expenses within Mrs. O's
salary, which they view as stable and secure. Thus, the money Mr.
O earns is used for "extras" and savings. From what we could

discern, none of the Os seemed to have any qualms about this arrangement, which seems to be working well for all of them.

Role sharing for the Os developed gradually during their first few years of marriage before the children came. Both were from very traditional, working-class backgrounds, and neither perceived their parents' marriage as happy. Mrs. O had been influenced by the women's movement and saw her older sister's role-sharing marriage as the way to go. Mr. O had to be convinced, but he was open minded and wanted his wife to be happy. By the time they decided to start their family (the children had been planned before the marriage), the Os had worked out a mutually satisfactory egalitarian relationship. Although both wanted to stay home with the children, they agreed that it made more sense financially for Mr. O to do so. Mrs. O, with a master's degree in French, earned more as a high school teacher than her husband did as a shoe salesman in a department store with his bachelor's degree in history. In addition, Mrs. O felt settled in a career while Mr. O was still trying to find the right job. Also considered was the fact that Mrs. O worked shorter hours and had summers off, which would give her time to be with the children. Soon after quitting his job to stay home with their first child, Mr. O parlayed his hobby (carpentry) into part-time work.

At first, both of their families had been surprised—his even flabbergasted, according to Mr. O—at their child care arrangement, but after seeing how well it worked and how comfortable the Os were with it, they soon accepted it and became verbally supportive of it. By the time of our interviews with the family, Mr. O had decided to continue with his carpentry business but on a full-time basis, rather than take another job, after both children were in school.

Effects of Children on Role Sharing

These examples illustrate that role sharing is not behavior that only childless couples can indulge in. Having children may simply add another family role to share. Although many transitional couples moved toward a more traditional pattern of handling family roles, only a few couples gave up the notion of sharing when they had children and shifted to a typical sex-linked allocation of family responsibilities. Almost all couples saw the adoption of more conventional practices as temporary. In any case, the effects of children on a role-sharing relationship are profound, as the couples made clear.

A sizable group of couples thought having children enhanced their role sharing; a few couples even reported that their role sharing started with the birth of their child. A number of other couples, however, said that having children made sharing harder. One wife bluntly stated that it made an egalitarian marriage impossible. Whether they found they shared more or less than formerly, many couples agreed that having children challenged their egalitarian attitudes and role-sharing behavior. As one husband put it, it brought the notion of equal sharing to the forefront. For many of our couples, this was the crucial test. Sharing the child care role represented for them the greatest break with tradition.

Many of the problems and issues in caring for children mentioned by these couples might be expected in any type of marital relationship. For example, children are a great responsibility, are expensive, take up a great deal of time, and curtail their parents' freedom. However, because of their egalitarian attitudes, the couples we interviewed appeared to perceive, react to, and be affected by some of these problems and issues differently. A case in point is the temporary loss of income that any dual-earner family would have to adjust to if one parent (almost always the mother) gives up her job to stay home to provide child care. As discussed in the chapter on the provider role, this circumstance may represent more than a tightened budget for some egalitarian couples; it may involve a shift, or perceived shift, in power regarding financial decisions. Such an imbalance could be expected to be more devastating to a wife committed to a relationship based on the premise of equality.

The amount of time children take was mentioned over and over by these couples. Again, the time factor itself may be no different from what it is in any family, but with our couples it was salient for fathers, as well as for mothers. Since almost all these fathers shared the child care role, albeit to different degrees, they, as well as the mothers, had less time for other activities and less freedom of movement. Although both parents mentioned the limits on time and freedom for them as individuals, they seemed even more concerned about how these limits affected them as couples. Generally, these were couples who spent most of their free time together. Often they cooked together and cleaned the house together; they spent most of their leisure time together. For many, one's spouse was one's best friend. They spent a great deal of time conversing. The addition of a child altered this quality of closeness. Time together now revolved around the baby or was "family time." For some, a child meant more to share and more to communicate about; other couples perceived the arrangements they had to work out to share the child care role as separating them and limiting their time together. For example, one parent might take care of the baby while the other did a household chore. Because at least one parent had to be with an infant or small child almost constantly, such divisions in the performance of roles often occurred, usually shifting back and forth between the spouses. If both parents had outside employment, often work hours were scheduled at different times so that one could be home with the children. A number of couples mentioned this separateness as a negative consequence, and some even stated wistfully that they missed cleaning the house together.

Children are, of course, a great deal of responsibility in any family, regardless of its structure or method of handling family roles. Unlike housework, which can be left undone for a period of time, or cooking, which can be circumvented at times by eating out, snacking, or fasting, child care must be given by someone at all times. And not just any child care; most parents in our society insist on good child care, however they define it. As has been made quite apparent, our role-sharing couples did not take on this responsibility lightly. Yet, the idea of having a completely dependent person in the household may require a little more getting used to for role-sharing couples than for traditional couples. In traditional marriages, child care roles are largely present waiting to be filled by the arrival of the first child. It is clear that the mother will be the primary caregiver. The major questions to be settled concern the extent and specifics of whatever subsidiary helping role the father is to perform. With a couple committed to a role-sharing marriage, the shape and detail of who is to do what needs to be worked out. No amount of advance planning can anticipate the myriad of changing realities that will arrive with the infant. Not only must child care tasks be sorted out and divided up but also the existing allocations of domestic chores may need to be restructured. Moreover, larger questions concerning the mother's and father's child care and paid work responsibilities may need to be reconsidered in the light of the actual demands of parenthood. It is little wonder that some of our couples seemed awestruck when discussing the ramifications of having children.

A number of couples mentioned the stress that having children causes for any family. Some thought that a major advantage of role sharing was that this stress was easier to handle since it was shared rather than imposed mostly on the wife as in conventional marriages. One couple—one of the few who said their children were not planned—commented that their egalitarian marriage was actually a response to the stress involved in parenting since neither was really "into having kids," as they put it. It was obvious from observing the family that their children were happy "accidents" and that role sharing was really working for this couple.

As indicated earlier, a sizable group of husbands took on more domestic, as well as child care, responsibilities to help lessen the stress on their wives and, consequently, on their marriages. Frequently, the results were positive; in a few cases they did not seem to be. Sometimes, it appeared that the stress, though shared, was still very difficult for the couple for one reason or another: a crucial resource might be inadequate (e.g., not enough money or a problematic child care arrangement); the parents might work different shifts in order to provide child care themselves; the father might be sharing the child care role reluctantly; or one spouse had not really wanted a child. Such problems seldom occurred in isolation but usually in a constellation.

Another type of situation proved very stressful for some of the couples in our sample—the change to a more traditional pattern than the wife wanted during this transitional period. In one case, the conventional pattern of dividing work-family roles was nearly complete: the husband supported the family financially and expected his wife to assume full responsibility for their child and house since she was home. More typical, however, was the husband's not doing what his wife thought was his fair share of the housework and child care. In these cases, the husband generally agreed with his wife's assessment of the situation but attributed his behavior (including unsuccessful attempts to reform) to such things as the pull of the traditional, lack of outside supports, and general laziness. These wives seemed to feel let down by their husbands, overworked, and dissatisfied with their circumstances. In describing their feelings, they used words such as dumped on and angry. Fortunately, there were not many such cases. It is possible, even probable, that these husbands were still participating in the domestic and child care roles far more than the average husband. Apparently, what was important to these wives was not a comparison to a general norm of behavior but to the norm these couples had established for themselves.

A number of mothers and a few fathers mentioned conflict between their careers and parent roles. Mothers who had temporarily given up their careers and both mothers and fathers who had cut back on their work hours in order to provide child care were likely to have some ambivalence about their career sacrifice. Obviously, their parenting role took precedence. These parents believed it was very important to them and to their children for the parents themselves to care for their children during their early years. Yet they were aware of their financial sacrifice, their curtailed career development, and the relatively low regard that society holds for child care. In addition, the fathers knew that most people today, including family and friends, saw them as odd. However, the husbands and wives in our sample seemed to be self-confident, independent individuals who were not readily influenced by what others thought of them.

Some of the mothers who worked outside the home full time (occasionally even part time if their children were very young) had conflicts about not performing the traditional mother role by staying home with their children. As other studies have found, guilt was particularly likely if the mother really liked her job. In the families in which the father shared the child care role and no outside help was needed with the children, the mother generally seemed to have less guilt about working since the child was still being taken care of by a parent, on the assumption that the father was participating willingly.

We found it interesting that not one role-sharing father employed full time felt guilty about not staying home with his children. Some fathers indicated they would not mind staying home with the children or that they would like to have more time with them, but that is different. These fathers knew they were not expected to stay home with their children; child care is not a part of the father's traditional role. The sharing of the child care role is generally voluntary on the father's part and is still unusual. It is certainly not the norm.

Effects of Role Sharing on Children

We wondered how parents who were committed to egalitarianism and role sharing in their marriages thought their lifestyle was affecting or would affect their children. The effects these couples mentioned were overwhelmingly positive. Yet there were some concerns, particularly among parents of school-age children.

First, the positives. The advantage parents cited most often (mentioned by two thirds of the couples) was that the children would not be limited by sex-role stereotypes. They will not grow up as their parents did believing and expecting men to work outside the home while women work inside the home. From the role model that the parents present, their children will know from the beginning that women can have careers, men can cook and do housework, both can take care of children, and neither dominates the other. Consequently, these couples believe their lifestyle will open up options to their children of both sexes. They think their children's behavior, activities, careers, and so on will be determined by such factors as interests, preferences, and talents rather than by gender. Many of these parents are encouraging their children to broaden their horizons by exposing their daughters to activities generally reserved for boys, such as all types of sports, and talking with them about majors and careers seldom chosen by women, such as mathematics, the physical sciences, and engineering. Although many of these parents also verbalize the importance of not restricting boys in their interests and careers, they do not appear to make a special effort to expose their sons to traditionally feminine pursuits, such as sewing or nursing. Instead, they tend to concentrate on helping their sons develop egalitarian attitudes toward girls, teaching them that role-sharing behavior is desirable in families and helping them gain competence in performing age-appropriate domestic chores. Perhaps the different approaches with sons and daughters is due to the parents' perceptions of where the most salient sex role constraints lie—outside the home with girls and inside the home with boys.

Other interpretations of the parents' handling of sex-role stereotyping differently with their sons and daughters are possible. Two that come to mind are the deeply imbedded cultural attitudes about the superiority of traditional masculine roles over traditional feminine roles and the widespread fear of homosexuality. A few parents in our sample admitted some uncertainty about how far in the direction of androgyny it was wise to go with their sons. Other researchers have also found reluctance on the part of parents to translate their attitudes about non-stereotyped gender roles into behavior in rearing their sons. For example, Farrell (1974) found that fathers were more likely to consider a baseball bat an appropriate gift for their daughters than they were to consider a doll an appropriate gift for their sons. The author concluded that although fathers thought it was all right for daughters to adopt the traditional masculine value system, they did not feel the same way about preparing their sons for parenthood (the feminine value system) by playing with dolls. "Most men, in fact, were blocked from even considering that possibility by their fear that it might encourage homosexuality—probably the single biggest fear that fathers have about their sons" (Farrell 1974:219). Although fathers seem to be more concerned than mothers with the traditional sex-role development of their children, especially their sons (Goodenough 1957; Heilbrun 1965; Lansky 1967; Langlois and Downs 1980), mothers are not immune to the impact of society's evaluation of sex roles and sexual preferences.

Another major advantage that accrued to children from their parents' role sharing, according to our couples, was the close father–child relationship that resulted from the father's sharing the child care role. They thought the father's active involvement with the children was highly beneficial for both sons and daughters. Among other things, they believed it provided a good role model for sons to emulate and a foundation for good relationships with men for their daughters. Generally, these parents thought the image their children would get of fathers as warm, loving, nurturant, competent, and involved parents would be a great improvement over the way fathers generally appear. Implicit in this is not only the better quality of father-child relationship but also the increased quantity; by definition, fathers who share the child care role spend more time with their children than the typical father does. Better physical and emotional care for children as a result of role sharing was mentioned by some couples. For example, with the double dose of parenting, infants were likely to get more touching and attention. With fathers competent in the domestic role, children could get good meals even when the mother was not home to cook. Having two good parent-child relationships was viewed as providing additional security for children because they would not be totally dependent on one parent. Also cited was the lessened opportunity for children to play off one parent against the other when both parents are actively involved in child care and communicating frequently with each other about the children and childrearing issues. Thus, such sharing was seen as resulting in more consistent parental behavior.

Some couples thought children of role-sharing couples benefited from better family relationships generally. They were referring to the fact that the father's sharing child care responsibilities alleviated some of the stress involved in this role. Better mother–child and marital relationships could be expected if the mother does not feel burdened with the total responsibility for the children.

These parents believed that providing good role models for their children would increase the likelihood of their children's having egalitarian, sharing relationships, which they saw as desirable. They thought both their sons and daughters might want and expect this type of relationship. On the other hand, they were aware that traditional sex-role models were dominant outside the home and that their children would get more support outside the family for relating to the opposite sex in the conventional manner (sex-differentiated roles and behaviors). They saw their own attitudes and behavior as being the best hope of circumventing sex-stereotyped ones in their children. They thought their children would learn from their example to respect other people as individuals and not to take them for granted as a stereotyped role occupant (e.g., mother or wife). They also believed their role sharing would teach their children such helpful skills as good communication, cooperation, negotiation, and flexibility. These would stand them in good stead regardless of the type of relationship they chose.

Parents in our study thought there were few, if any, disadvantages of their role-sharing marriages for their children. When negatives were cited, they seemed to stem from a common cause—not the parents' relationship, but the values, attitudes, and expectations of the larger society. Some parents worried that when their children grew up, they might expect their relationships to be like their parents' and be disappointed. A couple in our study with several older children (in their teens and early twenties) told us, with amusement, that their children were consciously trying to develop egalitarian relationships with members of the opposite sex in whom they were interested. They were winning some but losing more. However, they were undaunted, so firmly held were their egalitarian ideals.

Parents of very young children were concerned about potential pressure from their children's peers and their families, who in all probability would be more traditional. Among the concerns were that their children might feel out of place around their friends' parents, that they would be teased by peers for their nontraditional attitudes or behavior, and that they might be criticized by their friends' parents (and others) for interests and activities atypical of their gender. These parents hoped that their role modeling, family relationships, and childrearing methods would help their children develop enough self-confidence to be able to take such things in stride.

While the concerns mentioned here had not come to fruition yet for most parents in our study because their children were still infants and preschoolers, some parents of school-age children were experiencing problems with their children because of peer pressure. The parents of a six-year-old reported that their daughter wanted the mother to stay home, rather than work, like some of her friends' mothers. Although this couple make a wide range of toys and activities available to their child, the daughter currently plays exclusively with typically girls' toys and engages in typically female activities, which the parents attribute to the strong peer influence. Another couple shared that their nine-year-old daughter is envious of a friend whose parents have a traditional marriage since the friend's mother does not work outside the home. Their daughter complains that because her mother is employed, she is not available at times when the daughter wants her.

The father of another nine-year-old daughter is concerned because of the negative feelings, including enbarrassment, that their daughter has begun experiencing recently because of her parents' role sharing. In this case, the father's work schedule is more flexible than the mother's; consequently, he is the parent who provides transportation for their daughter and her friends, the one who goes to school for parent-teacher conferences, and so on. But it is her classmates' mothers, not their fathers, who perform these functions, for they are the available parents. The daughter, who does not like being different, is hurt and embarrassed by her father's involvement instead of her mother's. She recently blurted out angrily, "Why are you the only father coming up to the school?" Obviously, she does not appreciate the wisdom and merits of role sharing at this time. Her parents are trying to be as understanding and supportive as possible, but they cannot—and believe they should not—change the way they are sharing the child care role.

Parents of infants mentioned one other possible disadvantage of sharing the child care role: the effect on an infant of having more than one primary caregiver. These parents were not convinced that the effect would be harmful for a child. In fact, their experience in sharing the parental role so far seemed to indicate exactly the opposite: their babies seemed to be enjoying and thriving under the care of two involved parents. In spite of what they were observing, they were willing to concede good naturedly that if the theory about a child's needing one constant caregiver for the first year of her or his life proved to be correct, then their child will have missed out on this.

Recent research on the role of the father in child development generally supports the views of the role-sharing parents in our study. In a review of this research, Lamb (1976b:23) concluded that "one of the best established findings is that masculinity of sons and femininity of daughters are greatest when fathers are nurturant and participate extensively in childrearing. Thus, the father's similarity to a caricatured stereotype of masculinity is far less influential than his involvement in what are often portrayed as feminine activities." At the same time, Baruch and Barnett's (1981) study suggests that the greater the involvement by the father in the parent role, the less extreme are the sex-role stereotypes held by the children. Among other influences, fathers contribute to sex-role, moral, and cognitive development of their children. One implication that Lamb (1976b) sees is the fostering of more egalitarian sex roles by fathers who favor such and whose behavior indicates no incompatibility between egalitarian sex roles and the father's own gender identification.

Any concern about possible negative effects on an infant of having more than one primary caregiver should be allayed by the accumulating body of research that shows that most infants become attached to both parents during infancy anyway (e.g., Cohen and Campos 1974, Kotelchuck 1972, Lamb 1976a). Mead (1962), among others, considers it advantageous for infants to form attachments to more than one person.

8

Work and Role Sharing

We are becoming increasingly aware of how intertwined work and family are. If this is true for the traditional male breadwinner families, it is even more so for dual-earner families. The connection between work and family reaches its ultimate when both spouses have careers and attempt to share family roles. This chapter discusses how work and the specific jobs held by our respondents were seen as both facilitators and constraints to their role sharing and family life. It also looks at the effects, if any, they think their egalitarian marriage may have on their work and on their involvement in each other's jobs. The chapter concludes by describing the couples' experiences with and views on relocating because of jobs.

In this study, we were not interested in all aspects of the work-family relationship, nor did we approach the topic from the standpoint of working mothers or dual-career families. Our interest was more narrowly defined as the relationship between role sharing in the home and employment conditions. We were particularly interested in the effect the jobs held by these couples had on their sharing of domestic and child care responsibilities. Although our query was framed in terms of role sharing, couples sometimes indicated the effects of their jobs on their family life more generally. Information presented in this chapter was obtained in the individual interviews.

Facilitators and Constraints

FACILITATORS

Flexibility on the job emerged as the single most important factor that positively influenced family life and husbands' sharing in domestic and child care responsibilities. Included here are flexible work hours (e.g., flexitime), ability to choose one's work shift, having few set hours (such as university professors), ability to choose one's own working hours (such as free-lance work and some types of self-employment), and ability to take off hours or days from work as needed. The last not only included short amounts of time such as might be needed for errands or appointments and time needed to take care of emergencies but also referred to more formal work policies such as sick days, personal and family days, maternity (regrettably, not parental yet) leaves, and other paid and unpaid leaves.

Flexible work hours, particularly if both spouses had them, made it much easier for couples to handle family responsibilities such as staying home with a sick child, attending school conferences and functions, being home to let in servicemen, and taking care of personal or family business that can be done only during certain hours. Parents with pre-adolescent children were especially apt to find a flexible work schedule beneficial since it often permitted them to take care of their children without outside help. Sometimes child care was accomplished by the parents' working different shifts and sometimes by a combination of flexible working conditions, e.g., part-time work, working at home, and taking children to work at times.

As noted in the chapter on child care, the ability of the wife to work part time was a frequent solution to the problem of child care in dual-career families. Some mothers were able to do their work (editing, artwork, writing, and so on) at home and take care of the children at the same time. While such arrangements facilitated the provision of child care, they often proved to be constraints as far as the wives' careers and role sharing between husbands and wives were concerned. As indicated earlier, wives who were home full or part time found that their husbands—with or without their wives' approval—participated less in child care and domestic tasks than when the wives worked full time. In general, job flexibility for the wife or husband made family life easier by facilitating the handling of family roles, but only the husband's flexible working conditions were conducive to role sharing. One husband stated flatly that flexibility on a man's job was imperative for family role sharing.

In addition to flexibility on the job (flexible work hours, being able to take time off as needed, ability to work part time or at home, to take children to work at times, and so on), couples also found proximity to their jobs and telephone accessibility at work helpful in managing family responsibilities. Again whether or not these factors were conducive to role sharing depended on whether or not they were characteristic of the husband's job. Having one's place of employment closer to home not only meant less time and energy expended in traveling to and from the job—which was very helpful in itself—but also meant being more accessible in case of home emergencies or in order to handle other family responsibilities (e.g., going home to let in a serviceman or picking up something at the grocery and taking it home on a lunch hour). Being available by telephone and able to use the phone at work as needed were facilitators most of these couples took for granted. However, some did mention the advantages of being able to communicate with each other by phone (e.g., deciding who can take off to pick up a sick child at school, checking to see if the meat for dinner was taken out of the freezer, or asking one's spouse to pick up the cleaning on the way home); to be able to check on children just getting home from school; or to make necessary calls that can be done only during the day (e.g., making dental appointments or speaking with the school principal).

In addition to the employment policies and work conditions mentioned here, men in our sample mentioned two other work factors that they found supportive of an egalitarian marital relationship. One was understanding by superiors and co-workers that employees also had family responsibilities. This atmosphere seemed to be the result of working with women who thought husbands should help at home or with other men who did participate in housework or child care. Unfortunately, relatively few of the husbands in our sample worked in a family-tolerant environment, but those who did seemed greatly encouraged by it in their role-sharing behavior. The other factor some men found helpful in their egalitarian marital relationships was working with people in a therapeutic or counseling capacity, as social workers, psychologists, psychiatrists, etc. Husbands in these occupations were required to understand other people's feelings and to accept them as individuals. Several of these husbands found their work reinforced egalitarian attitudes and role sharing in their own marriages. Some commented that they believed being aware and accepting of emotions and able to relate to one's spouse on an emotional level—assets in any type of marital relationship—were particularly important in a nontraditional marriage like theirs for which there were few guidelines and little outside support.

Women in our sample saw their full-time employment away from home, the personal benefits they received from their work, and the equality of their and their husbands' jobs—when these existed—as being conducive to family role sharing. Working full time has already been discussed. The personal benefits from working and having one's own career (stronger self-identity, enhanced self-image, independence, feelings of competency, being respected and treated as an equal at work, and so on) were seen as being carried over into the marital relationship. (Such benefits are possible from part-time employment but were reported more often by women employed full time.) These wives believed that the way they viewed themselves and their expectations of their marital relationships greatly influenced their behavior at home and in turn their husbands' attitudes. Although few spouses in our sample had comparable jobs in terms of status, pay, work hours and effort, those who did perceived the job parity as a facilitator of marital equality and the equal sharing of all major family roles.

MIXED EFFECTS

Some work factors were seen both as facilitators and constraints to role sharing, depending on which spouse the condition applied to, on the couple in question, and sometimes on which spouse was doing the perceiving. Some of these, such as part-time work and working at home, have already been discussed; they were facilitators if they applied to the husbands or both spouses but constraints if they were true only of the wife. Other factors mentioned that were variously viewed as pro or con include both spouses having the same work schedule and one or both spouses having to travel on their jobs.

A few couples found that when both worked the same hours outside the home, the husband was less likely to participate in housework and child care, apparently because he felt his wife was there to do it. More commonly, however, couples having the same work schedules reported that this facilitated their role sharing, for they enjoyed performing domestic tasks together. In fact, one of the major complaints couples in our sample had generally was not having enough time together, though they thought they probably spend far more time together than the average couple does. We have already noted in this chapter and in previous ones that role sharing, particularly of child care, is enhanced by the spouses' working different hours outside the home. Thus, whether sharing a common work schedule acts as an inducement or an inhibitor to sharing family roles depends not only on the particular couple but also on other factors in their situation at the time. Since circumstances may change over time (e.g., need for child care or other demands on one spouse's time), it is not surprising that couples value having some control over work schedules, as well as other kinds of job flexibility.

The way in which travel connected with one's job affected the amount of family role sharing depended largely on how much traveling there was and which spouse was required to travel. Frequent trips by the husband tended to reduce role sharing, while those made by the wife or by both spouses at different times tended to increase the sharing. As with working different hours, husbands who were home at times when the wife was not tended to be more involved in housework and child care, often out of necessity.

CONSTRAINTS

Many of the aspects of work that are problematic for family life and for role sharing are the converse of the aspects mentioned as inducements. For example, inflexible job conditions of either spouse are stressful for family life, and the husband's job inflexibility does not augur well for role sharing at home. Long work hours and stressful, demanding, exhausting jobs seem to have similar effects. A number of husbands cited these two reasons for not being as involved in domestic and child care responsibilities as they felt they should be or wanted to be. Some husbands also mentioned as constraints to role sharing long commutes to work, having to work some nights or weekends, and, as mentioned earlier, having to travel. Whenever one or more of these conditions characterized the husband's job but not the wife's, the wife picked up the slack at home on domestic tasks and child care. If it was the other way around (i.e., the wife's having to travel, work long hours, or having a high pressured, exhausting job while the husband does not), the husband assumed more responsibility in some families, but the house "just went to hell" in others. In such cases, husbands were much more likely to provide necessary child care than to do much housework. Two very demanding jobs generally resulted in more balance between the spouses in the performance of family roles, frequently with less being done by either and possibly with outside help.

Effects on Work

The other side of the coin is how role-sharing marriages might affect the outside work or careers of the marital partners. We asked about this somewhat hesitantly since we expected little response. We were wrong. The query seemed to strike a responsive chord in the participants of our study. Only a small minority, mostly men, saw no connection between the type of marriage they had and their attitudes about work and their job performance; they believed they were able to keep these two areas of their lives separate. On the other hand, a number of women and men saw no disharmony in the way they carried out their family and work roles since both were influenced by their egalitarian attitudes. Others spoke only of the practical consequences of their role-sharing marriages.

Both husbands and wives thought the type of marriage they had made their outside jobs easier, less stressful, and more enjoyable. Although the end results were the same for women and men, the reasons for these effects differed according to sex. Essentially, women felt freer to work more and men to work less. Husbands felt relief from not having to shoulder the total burden of supporting the family financially, which enabled them to consider their own needs and preferences at work and not just their family's needs. For example, some men mentioned the freedom they felt by not having to be constantly concerned about earning more money and trying for promotions in which they were not really interested. Some men felt freer to take risks in business, to change jobs, to return to school for advanced degrees, and so on. Apparently, it was not only the sharing of the breadwinner role that took some of the pressure off of husbands but also their wives' understanding, encouragement, and support stemming from the fact that they had careers themselves.

By the same token, wives felt freer to pursue their careers. As one woman put it, she thought her egalitarian marriage elevated her work to career status from the job it would have been if her marriage were more traditional. By this she meant she could be fully committed to her work and attempt to advance as far as she could. Because their husbands shared the responsibility for the home and children and because they encouraged and supported them in their careers, these wives thought their work was made much easier and less stressful for them. They commented on such things as being able to devote as much time as they needed and wanted to the job, including working overtime or traveling, since they did not have to do such things as rush home to cook their husbands' dinner. They found it easier to concentrate on the job since they did not have to worry about the children if their father was home with them or about a lot of domestic tasks awaiting them when they got home.

While wives felt they could be more career oriented, husbands felt they could be more family oriented. Several husbands mentioned their attempts to control the number of hours they worked, and when they put in these hours, in order to have more time with their wives and children. Some husbands had rearranged work schedules to be able to assume their family responsibilities, and some felt guilty or resentful (depending on whether or not it was mandatory) about working long hours, evenings, or weekends. One father, who attributed his very close relationship with his young children to his role-sharing marriage, sometimes took the children to work with him so that they could see what he does and where he spends a large part of his time. He thinks that their seeing him in his work role will enable his children to know him better as a person.

Husbands often were more sensitive to their co-workers', subordinates', or clients' family needs. Some mentioned treating women at work as equals when this was not the prevailing organizational norm and of making special efforts at affirmative action when they were in a position to do so. Wives in our sample expected to be treated as equals at work and were sensitive to—and incensed over—having their ideas or preferences ignored by men with whom they worked.

Since there were a number of therapists, counselors, and educators in our sample, their egalitarian values frequently had a direct application in their work with clients and students. When appropriate, one form this took was encouraging the people they worked with to question traditional sex roles and to explore alternatives. Teachers, for example, would discuss sex-role stereotyping with their students in order to make them aware of how pervasive and dysfunctional it was. They treated the students as individuals and urged them to perceive and treat others in the same manner, without preconceived notions about them based on sex. Sometimes they told them about their role-sharing marriages in order to present another role model to them. They encouraged girls to prepare for careers and consider a wide range of career options. Some high school teachers commented that they found disconcerting the fact that so many female and male students held so firmly to traditional attitudes about sex roles. Educators and counselors working with parents found that they expected fathers to be as involved with their children as the mothers were. When possible, they encouraged the fathers' involvement.

Counselors were generally open with their clients about their own values. They thought their own nontraditional marriages made them more accepting of other lifestyles. However, they encouraged clients to question patterns of behavior that were problematic for them and to explore and choose options that might be more functional. Sometimes, they used their own marriage as a model of an alternative way of relating and behaving in an intimate relationship. Some counselors commented that they thought their own marriage made them more empathic with both single mothers who have all of the family responsibility and with working wives in traditional families. They found egalitarian issues in marriages easy to detect.

One wife, a social worker, gave an example of a strategy she used in a case; she thought her egalitarian values had prompted her to do what she did. She was providing follow-up supportive service to a young unmarried mother who had recently undergone major surgery. Living in the home with the mother and her three young children were the mother's two adult brothers and one of their male friends. It was a traditional household in that the men were providing the financial support and the woman did all of the cooking and housework in addition to taking care of her children. This pattern had resumed immediately upon the young woman's return home from the hospital, and the social worker was incensed to learn about it on her first home visit. She thought her client was physically unable to do all her brothers and their friend expected her to do. Instead of just pointing out this reality to her client and exploring alternatives with her, the social worker went further by gathering the three men together to discuss what she considered to be an intolerable situation. She clarified the facts of the situation with them, let them know how she saw the situation (as unfair and as harmful to their sister), and asked what they could—and would—do about it. When they expressed concern but helplessness because they were men and did not know how to cook and do other household tasks, the social worker suggested—with conviction—that they could learn. Although they seemed rather amused that a woman would talk to them as the social worker did, they promised to try, and the worker later learned that they did.

Spouse Involvement

Since most of these couples seemed to spend a great deal of time together at home, whether involved in domestic tasks or in leisure activities, we wondered if they might also be involved in some way with each other's work. We do not know if their behavior in this area was any different from other dual-career couples; we have no reason to believe it was.

As expected, the extent and nature of involvement depended primarily on how closely related the two spouses' occupations or fields were and on the requirements of the specific jobs. For example, two university professors in the same or similar fields might engage in any number of activities together such as discussing professional topics, doing research, writing and publishing, attending professional meetings, sharing professional literature, and guest lecturing in each other's classes. In such situations, work and home overlapped maximally with one almost an extension of the other. However, two high school teachers of the same subject or two elementary school teachers might share much less at home because the major part of their work is done at school during the day.

Sometimes similar occupations were viewed as a two-edged sword. On the one hand, because of the common knowledge and experience base, there was more to talk about with the possibility of a mutual exchange of helpful ideas and suggestions; on the other hand, some spouses found that they needed a complete break from work, particularly if it was emotionally draining, such as teaching or counseling. Tension might develop if one spouse wanted to use his or her work-exhausted mate as a consultant for ideas about how to help a client, handle a classroom situation, or resolve some other problem or issue at work.

Most couples, regardless of the similarity of their fields or the kind of work they did, seemed to enjoy sharing with each other things of a general nature that occurred at work—an interesting incident that happened, news about a co-worker the other spouse knew, or something similar. But the more disparate and technical the two occupations were, the less the spouses discussed the actual work itself. In fact, some spouses were not even interested in specific details of the other's work because they would not understand what the other was talking about.

Although a few couples made it a point not to bring anything concerning their jobs home, the large majority did talk about their work, colleagues, things that happened at work, etc. Sometimes they just shared information or related an amusing incident. Sometimes they ventilated frustrations, possibly to obtain support from their spouses. Frequently one used the other as a sounding board or source of suggestions for a work-related problem.

Occasionally one spouse might be able to accompany the other on an out-of-town business trip such as professional conference, but generally this was difficult to arrange if they were in different fields or if they had children. Very frequently, however, spouses did entertain together or socialize with each other's business associates, co-workers, customers, or others from work. Possibly because work is such a major part of the lives of dual-career couples and because of similar interests, colleagues and co-workers are often friends as well.

Few couples mentioned serious problems with this aspect of their lives. Since any type of involvement in the other's work is probably considered voluntary, spouses are likely to participate only in activities that are enjoyable to them or at least about which they feel indifferent. If spouses are in the same field, they may collaborate successfully on some activities or be very helpful to each other professionally in a number of ways. Yet, there is also the potential for competition between such couples. Although this potential exists for any dual-career couple in the same profession or occupation, it may be more likely to occur with role-sharing couples who are used to relating to each other as equals in their personal lives. At the same time, role-sharing couples may be more likely to have suitable mechanisms for resolving the conflict and behavior that might result from competitive feelings. To illustrate, one of the couples in our study worked together as co-therapists with groups of clients. Since it was difficult, if not impossible, for them to coordinate their roles without a hierarchical flavor to their positions and since neither was willing to take what they considered the subordinate position, conflict ensued. Taking their cue from the way they worked out the allocation of household tasks, the couple resolved the power issue in their work together by having one assume the role of primary therapist for the first half of the group sessions and the other for the second half. The following week, they reverse the time slots, the person who was primary therapist in the second half assuming that role in the first half.

Relocation

More than a third of the couples had been faced with the possibility of relocation because of a better job opportunity for one of the partners. Sometimes the job offers were accepted and the family moved, sometimes not. The processes in making the decision, the factors weighed pro and con, and the final decision reached were probably identical for most of these role-sharing couples to those of dual-career couples generally. We thought we detected some nuances with couples most committed to egalitarianism.

For most of the couples who had considered relocation because of a job, the situation came about either because the couples wanted to move to a specific area, resulting in the partners' looking for jobs there, or because the husband was offered a transfer or new job in another location; seldom was the wife the spouse offered a transfer or new job. The latter was probably due in large part to the differences in occupations between the sexes in our sample: men were more likely than their spouses to be university professors, in other assorted professions, or in business, while women were more likely to be social workers, teachers, and nurses—professions in which individuals are seldom transferred or sought after by out-of-town employers.

Almost always when the husband had an out-of-town job offer, the couple would discuss it pro and con and arrive at a mutual decision. Generally both spouses had an equal say in the decision, though there were instances of one spouse's deferring to the other for a variety of reasons such as the wife's not wanting to move away from her family of origin and her friends, the husband's greater earning power, or either's wanting very much to take the new job.

Depending on the couple, any number of factors might be influential in a decision to relocate. (Here we consider not only the couples who had had to make such a decision but also the other couples whom we asked to speculate about what would happen if the wife or husband had a job offer that would involve relocation.) Mentioned most often was the need to have something in the move for both spouses. By this, they often meant a job for the other that would be satisfactory to her or him or perhaps the opportunity to acquire further education. Many couples stated that family considerations—whether the other spouse could get a job in the new location and wanted to move, and if there were children, whether the parents thought the new location would be good for the children, and if the children, particularly older ones, had definite feelings about the move—would take precedence over the merits of the new job. The specific location (the climate, how far away it was, etc.) was another important factor. Occasionally, money considerations were said to be influential, but most couples indicated this would have relatively low priority. Possibly because of the areas from which we drew our sample, family ties and roots in the community were major considerations. (A large proportion of the families in these areas had lived there for generations, and their young were reluctant to leave.) Often one or both of the partners stated that they would not consider moving from the area, because they liked it, it was a good place to rear children, and their families and friends were there.

Some couples, who seemed to have more egalitarian attitudes than the others, put more emphasis on the other spouse's having found a job in the new community before making the decision to relocate. Not only would this job need to be satisfactory for the other partner, but some insisted that it would need to be at least equivalent to the one that partner currently held. If the new job would pay less than the old one or if living expenses would be appreciably higher in the new location, some couples indicated that the spouse for whom the move was being made would be expected to pick up the slack; that is, a readjustment would be made in terms of how much each partner contributed financially to the family unit. These more egalitarian couples also seemed more likely than the others to insist that both partners have an equal voice in the decision about relocating. They were also more likely to consider a move for the wife's career advancement, to take turns moving for the benefit of each spouse, and to consider commuting by one or both spouses as a temporary solution.

Both the Bs and the Ts, professional couples in their early thirties, have relocated because of job or educational opportunities for one of the spouses. The Bs, both of whom are in higher education, made their first move because of a job offer the wife received. It turned out to be a good move for both. Their second move was to take advantage of an excellent opportunity Mr. B was offered. Both were in complete agreement that Mr. B should take the one-year offer that would advance his career, whether or not Mrs. B would be able to go with him. As it turned out, Mrs. B was able to get a leave of absence from her job and was able to find a job in the area where her husband was going. Before the year was up, it was clear that both could remain in their positions for an indefinite period of time. Mr. B wanted to stay, but Mrs. B did not, because she was unhappy with her job. In talking over the job situation, they decided to move because Mrs. B wanted to but to have Mr. B hit the job market first because they thought a position for him would be harder to find. The Bs weighed the several good offers Mr. B received and decided together which he should take. Their decision was based in large part on where they thought Mrs. B would have the easiest time finding a job. Thus, the move was made without Mrs. B's having a job in the new location; both found this a scary position to be in. However, Mrs. B was soon offered a job, but it was clear that she was being taken advantage of because of her situation, that is, having to work in that particular area. She refused the offer and later found a satisfactory position. At the time of our interview, the Bs were currently in the position of Mr. B's having received a one-year fellowship that he had applied for in another city. Mrs. B had also applied for one but did not get it. Again, the joint decision was that Mr. B should take the offer, and Mrs. B was looking for another fellowship or job in the new city. Again, she planned to move with her husband if she found something satisfactory but to remain behind if she did not. Although they were not looking forward to commuting for a year, they found this preferable to either's having to pass up a good career opportunity.

At the beginning of their marriage the Ts lived in a large urban area where Mrs. T was employed as a nurse while her husband finished his residency in psychiatry. Upon graduation, Dr. T was offered an excellent position in a veterans administration hospital in a neighboring state. At that time, he could not understand his wife's refusal to move, particularly since his salary would be so much higher than her current one. Mrs. T very much liked her job, knew her husband could work where they were living, and had no desire to move to the new community about which they knew very little. It was at this point that she realized how career oriented she really was and how strong her egalitarian attitudes were. In keeping with the latter, she believed her husband should also work where he wanted to. After much discussion, they worked out a compromise that involved moving for one year to a city halfway between their two jobs, from which both would commute. That would give Dr. T a chance to find out if he liked his new job and for both to get to know more about the city it was located in. Both found the commuting difficult but stuck it out. At the end of the year, because Dr. T liked his job so well, Mrs. T agreed to move with him on a trial basis to the city where the hospital was located. Their agreement was that if she did not like it, they would move elsewhere. As it turned out, Mrs. T grew to like the new location, helped, no doubt, by the superior position she was able to obtain there.

9

Personal and Social Aspects

The kind of role-sharing marriage that we are considering is more than the sum of its roles. As we have seen, its configuration of values and behaviors may influence various aspects of family and work life. In this chapter, we examine the consequences of this configuration for the more personal and social sides of the marital relationship. At the same time, we also consider how personal and social factors may in turn affect role sharing.

Data reported here were in response to our query of each of the spouses in the individual interviews about the effect she or he thought their role-sharing marriage had on their self-image, sense of masculinity (asked of husbands) or femininity (asked of wives), way of expressing affection in the marriage, and their sexual relationship. In each case we asked them to think of their marriage as compared with a more traditional marriage. Of course, the ideal research design for gathering the kind of data we wanted here would have included also a sample of couples who had conventional marriages. The same questions would have been asked of people in the two samples and the responses compared to see what, if any, differences existed between the two marriage patterns. Since such direct comparisons were not possible in our study, we were limited to the perceptions about such comparisons of spouses in our role-sharing sample.

The other two sections cover information obtained in the joint interviews. One section deals with leisure time and social life. The other reports the couples' perceptions of the way relevant others (their families of origin, friends, and co-workers) view their role-sharing marriages. Areas of support are identified and a sense of the extent of the couples' nonconformity to their immediate social environment is obtained.

Self-Image

The majority of wives and husbands thought their type of marriage had a positive effect on their self-image. None reported a negative effect, but some believed it had no effect. Included in the "no effect" group were several men and women who thought the relationship went in the other direction; they believed their positive self-image had resulted in their egalitarian, role-sharing marital relationship. Qualities that both women and men identified as contributing to their choice of relationship included their feeling self-confident and independent, being open minded and not rigid, feeling competent and secure, having a great deal of self-respect and respect for others as individuals, and viewing men and women as equals. These men had no need to be dominant or controlling in relationships with women, and the women saw no need to be subservient to or passive with men. Both indicated that traditional marriages would not have worked for them.

Also in the "no effect" group were a few women who thought their type of marital relationship had no direct effect, for they saw the most influential factor contributing to their positive self-image as their professions, careers, or jobs. To the extent that role sharing permitted or encouraged them to work, their marriages may have had an indirect effect.

Several men indicated that their marriages had "no negative effects" on their self-image, and this response suggested a more cautious appraisal. Not one woman used this terminology. These men seemed to feel that they "had not lost control of the marriage" but were only sharing it with their wives.

Wives were only slightly more effusive than husbands were in citing beneficial aspects of their marital relationship and the resulting positive effects on their self-image. Both referred to the equal partnership and sharing as improving their self-image. In discussing some beneficial aspects, men were more likely to refer to the qualities in a reciprocal manner and women more on a personal level. For example, men spoke of the spouses' viewing each other as competent and as equals, valuing and respecting each other, being proud of each other's accomplishments, and sharing family responsibilities and decision making. Women were more likely to speak of being viewed as competent and intelligent, being treated as equals, having their opinions sought and respected, and having equal decision-making power.

Regardless of how they phrased the attributes of their relationship, both women and men saw the result as an enhanced self-concept. Both spoke of feeling more self-confident as a result of demonstrated competence in so many areas (pertaining to work and family roles) and more comfortable because of their satisfaction with the sharing relationship. Women liked themselves better, respected themselves more, and felt more important and worthwhile because of the sharing and the way they were perceived and treated by their husbands. Men also felt good about themselves and had more self-respect for the very same reasons. Their willingness to share the domestic and child care roles made them feel more responsible, fair, and generally better about themselves because they felt they were carrying their load and did not have to feel guilty about their wives' having to work too hard. Their respect for their wives and treating them as equal partners enhanced the men's own self-respect.

Among other positives wives mentioned were their feelings of independence, self-sufficiency, security, and general happiness that resulted from the type of marital relationship they had. In describing themselves they used terms such as strong, powerful, autonomous, and a whole person, "not half of a joint personality." Some women indicated they felt well rounded and fulfilled because of their broad range of interests and capabilities. They liked the assumption that they could make a solid contribution to all parts of family life but did not have to be a superperson, since family responsibilities were shared. Some women mentioned the absence of what they considered negatives, for example, not feeling owned by their husbands, not being treated as if they were weak or feebleminded, not expected to be dependent and passive, and not feeling they had to please someone else (their husbands in this case) all the time.

Husbands also indicated additional positive effects. Men spoke often not only of feeling good about themselves but also of feeling good about the relationship. Some felt reassured that their wives wanted to be with them as much as they wanted to be with their wives since their partners were not tied to them by financial dependency. Some expressed relief at being able to share family decision making and not having to feel they must "know it all." They said they felt more comfortable at home and enjoyed their homes more because they were more involved in them. Contributing in a major way to their children's development was especially a self-image booster. Role-sharing husbands said they liked being a full partner in the family. Some husbands thought their type of marital relationship encouraged them to be more rational, objective, tolerant, liberal, flexible, and open to new ideas. Generally, they felt more well rounded, competent, and secure. They liked being able to give and get support and affection easily. They saw themselves as being more expressive and freer to show emotions—a welcome relief from the restricted traditional male stance. Men said they felt a greater sense of freedom, independence, and being able "just to be themselves." As one husband and father put it, he "felt lovable and nurturing as well as strong." These husbands viewed wives with high self-esteem, competent and intelligent wives, professional wives, and so on as ego-enhancers. The fact that such accomplished wives who were held in such high regard by their husbands also recognized and valued their husbands' achievements was an additional self-image booster. Some husbands used a word that seemed rather interesting (and somewhat puzzling) to us in this context: successful. They said their kind of marriage made them feel successful.

Masculinity/Femininity

Our question asking these wives and husbands if their role-sharing marriages affected their sense of femininity (of wives) or masculinity (of husbands) seemed to take most of our respondents by surprise. They found the question difficult to answer; they seemed to find it necessary to "shift gears" first. Apparently a number of our respondents either did not think in such terms or did not see the relationship between these concepts and role sharing. They could see how there might be a problem (cognitive dissonance) if one defined masculinity and femininity in the narrow, rigid, traditional manner. However, most of our respondents either had never completely accepted this traditional view or had made a shift in their definition before or after marriage.

In order not to experience cognitive dissonance, men and women in role-sharing marriages have to incorporate in their images of masculinity and femininity the roles they perform that are traditionally associated with the other sex and the traits and skills they possess or develop (many of which are also associated with the opposite sex) that may be necessary for the successful performance of those new roles and for equality in their marital relationships. Conversely, they must relinquish exclusive performance in their families of roles traditionally performed by their gender, as well as attributes that are no longer functional, if they ever were, in their modern lifestyle. Some respondents found this much easier to do than others. It was least problematic for those women and men who had grown up with the least stereotyped notions of how each sex should be or behave. Usually this resulted from the role models their parents provided them or from the attributes and behavior they themselves were encouraged in or rewarded for while growing up. Others who were brought up with traditional sex stereotypes later questioned the usefulness of such notions or found them constraining and dysfunctional. For some this happened before their marriage and thus facilitated the choice of their type of marriage, but for others it occurred after the role sharing in marriage began. The shift from traditional sex stereotypes about what men and women are like is still in process for some of the respondents in our study. At a fairly early stage of this process is the husband who stated that he "still makes enough decisions [in his marriage] to feel masculine." This young husband felt good about role sharing around his wife and others supportive of such behavior but admitted doubts about it when around "the boys," who prided themselves on their sex-stereotyped behavior.

If one of the spouses in this type of marriage feels insecure or uncomfortable about the role-sharing or egalitarian nature of the relationship, he or she is likely to be more sensitive to the attitudes and opinions of others about sex roles. For some, like the young husband just mentioned, the support of others is crucial. While assuming far less importance for most people in our sample, the support of others was helpful and almost always welcomed. Even spouses who were generally secure and confident in their roles could be taken aback at times and perhaps shaken temporarily by overt disapproval. To illustrate, Mrs. Q, who had been married a relatively short time but who had consciously worked out with her spouse during their long courtship the type of relationship they would have, found the attitude of a female co-worker unsettling. Upon learning that Mrs. Q and her husband do the laundry together, this woman conveyed her disapproval. "She thought I was a 'rotten wife' not to be able to handle 'my' responsibilities alone," as Mrs. Q put it. In this case, the husband, who was more comfortable and secure about the role sharing than his wife, provided her with the support she needed. Even more so than with the role of "wife," women can be made to feel guilty about their role as "mother," especially when they work full time. Satisfactory child care arrangements and support from relevant others appear to be crucial here.

Most of the women in our study did not believe their type of marriage had affected their view of themselves as feminine; they felt they were as feminine as they had always been. However, their concept of femininity did not include such attributes as helplessness, dependency, cuteness, sweetness, incompetence in the job market, and staying at home. Many seemed secure enough to feel that whatever they were or did was feminine because they were women. They thought it was feminine to do what they wanted to do, whether it was sharing family roles with their husbands or doing traditionally male or female chores out of choice. A number of these women indicated that they had never believed in the traditional stereotype of femininity but had always thought of themselves as persons with whatever attributes they had and with the freedom to develop functional and desirable characteristics and behaviors for the performance of adult roles such as spouse, parent, and worker.

Some women stated that they no longer thought in terms of masculinity or femininity but simply in terms of humanness. Some emphasized that masculinity and femininity were defined not by the tasks one does, but simply by one's gender.

Some women felt their sense of femininity had been enhanced by their type of marriage. Again these were women who did not adhere to traditional sex stereotypes but believed femininity included attributes such as intelligence, competence, and independence. The enhancement they mentioned appeared to be the result primarily of their husband's reinforcement through their attitudes and behavior toward them, e.g. their admiration and respect for them as capable women.

There were women who admitted their concepts of femininity had broadened, with much overlapping with what they considered masculine. These women tended to think that there were some essential differences that should not be lost between what was feminine and what was masculine (such as manner of dress), but that most things were neither. They did not believe women should be restricted by having only stereotyped feminine characteristics, because realistically the options are much broader than that. Yet they emphasized women should feel free to perform roles and tasks that have traditionally been considered "women's work."

Like the women in our study, none of the men felt their role-sharing marriages had had a negative effect on their sense of masculinity. A few commented that this type of marriage had not threatened their masculinity. Many simply did not define masculinity by the roles or chores performed. They tended to see the traditional assignment of sex roles as artificial and inhumane under certain circumstances (for example, the wife's having sole responsibility for the domestic and child care roles when she also works outside the home).

Few of these men valued the traditional definition of masculinity. They did not share a concept of masculinity that meant having dominance and control over their wives, being aggressive and using physical force, being unable to express emotions, and refusing to do certain tasks around the house. They tended to view "macho men" as fearful and insecure and the "macho" role as limiting and undesirable. Some thought that the traditional views of masculinity and femininity had neglected the many traits and behaviors appropriate to both sexes. A number of men expressed their belief that the qualities they possessed, a mixture of what is traditionally regarded as masculine and feminine— being sensitive, perceptive, gentle, competent, strong, and so on— made them complete human beings. They felt freer not being constrained by the conventional definition. For example, as one man expressed it, "I do not feel that I always have to be the strong, brave one in the relationship; I don't feel less of a man when I am not. Society can pressure me only as much as I let it. I intend to control my own behavior."

A number of these men indicated that they seldom thought in terms of masculinity as such but rather considered being masculine simply a quality of being male. Frequently, these were men who had been reared in homes where the traditional view of male and female roles was not strictly adhered to. As with women, sometimes their concepts shifted at a later time—some before and some after marriage. Some broadened their concepts of masculinity to include attributes they thought desirable for either sex. Many recognized that some things were skills or abilities—not masculine or feminine traits. Wives often helped their husbands to develop characteristics associated with being feminine; for example, several men indicated that their wives encouraged them to be more open and freer to experience emotions. By the time of our interviews, most of the men in our study viewed sex roles as flexible and overlapping and were secure in their own sense of masculinity. Some felt more masculine as a result of the role sharing and equality in the marriage. For example, they thought having a subservient wife would detract from their positive self-image as males. They seemed to value the freedom of not being stuck in a given role; at the same time they saw this freedom as permitting them to perform traditional roles if they chose to do so.

Some men indicated that there still might be areas of strain between their sense of masculinity and the requirements of role sharing. This theme emerged in such two-edged comments as, "I feel I make enough decisions to maintain my masculinity," or "It's okay not to be 'macho' all the time," or "I would feel upset if my wife earned more than I." It seemed likely to us that such men still held some fairly conventional attitudes toward masculinity that their relationships permitted them to preserve or perhaps that limited the extent of their commitment to egalitarianism. Role sharing did not seriously threaten their feelings of masculinity, because they had struck a compromise between their masculine ideals and role sharing or, to put it differently, they felt their core sense of manhood, old fashioned as it may be, was still intact despite role sharing around the perimeter. This position seemed to be echoed in such terse unelaborated comments as "role sharing has had no negative effect on my sense of masculinity." One wonders how many had retained the illusion of being masculine in the traditional sense despite daily behavior to the contrary, as if waiting for their big moment of assertiveness, decisiveness, cool-headedness, or whatever. Be that as it may, their guarded position seemed quite different from the more open stance of men who clearly renounced conventional definitions of masculinity.

Expression of Affection

Traditionally, men have been expected to provide the instrumental functions in a family, and women, the expressive functions. There is ample evidence that the instrumental role is no longer sex linked in role-sharing marriages, and there is growing evidence that fathers in such marriages share in the expressive role when it comes to their children. To what extent the sex-linked pattern regarding the emotional or affectional aspect of the marital relationship has broken down was also of interest to us. One way of exploring this with wives and husbands in our sample was to ask if their way of expressing affection had changed in any way as they developed their egalitarian relationship. Regardless of whether or not it had changed, we wanted them to compare their expression of affection with what they perceived as the more traditional pattern.

Most of the women and men in our study thought they and their spouses had changed in the emotional-affective area. Sometimes they were not sure how much of the change would have occurred over time regardless of the kind of marriage they had, but more often they seemed confident that the changes were due to their type of marriage. They pointed out that the changes that occurred in the emotional area were consistent with the way their role-sharing relationship was evolving in other areas. For example, the extensive communication engaged in to work out role-sharing patterns and egalitarian issues carried over to the affective area, too. They communicated openly and honestly about their wants and needs for affection and emotional support, including the specific ways these could be shown that would be most meaningful to them. They let each other know when affection or support was wanted if it was not automatically forthcoming. In this area, as in others, they did not expect their partners to be mind readers and consequently did not blame the other if she or he did not sense when they wanted a hug or needed to be comforted or reassured about something. They emphasized that each person had the responsibility for making his or her own needs and wants known to the other.

At the same time, many found that both became more sensitive to the other's feelings and needs, and both became more spontaneous and freer in expressing their emotions and their affection to each other. Since men and women were encouraged by the other spouse to be themselves, not a sex stereotype, both felt freer to express a range of feelings. The greatest change here occurred in men—a change appreciated by both wives and husbands. As noted earlier, men felt freer to express their tenderness toward their wives, to be openly affectionate, to indicate when they were scared or needed comforting, and so on.

They did not have to keep up a "tough guy" front and suffer in silence, nor did they have to worry about "exposing different parts of themselves" for fear that their wives would think less of them or that their vulnerabilities would be taken advantage of or used against them at some later time. Many husbands put it in just those terms: being able to take risks. Such genuineness and openness on the part of both spouses, they thought, tended to reinforce the basic mutual trust existing between them and to result in a more intense and enjoyable relationship.

Some of the spouses commented on the fact that the amount of open communication in their marriages and their sharing and doing so many things together resulted in their knowing each other much better. Even if the communication was sometimes argumentative, it led to deeper friendships with each other, as well as more intense emotional relationships. Some wives commented that working and cooperating together made them feel more affectionate toward their partners.

Most of the spouses who saw no change in the emotional part of their marriage said that their marriages had started out on an egalitarian, role-sharing basis. These were the people who saw the type of marriage they chose as the result of who they were and what they believed. According to them, the spouses related to each other from the beginning of the marriage the way the "evolving" couples say they relate now.

Spouses in a few couples admitted that this was an aspect of their relationship that had not "progressed" far enough for their satisfaction. For example, one husband said he was more traditional, which he defined as emotionally aloof and nonapproachable regarding expressions of affection, than he would like to be. One wife (in another couple) thought that, in spite of her attempts to change the affective part of their relationship to a more openly expressive one, this aspect of their relationship was quite traditional. She described her husband as shy and undemonstrative emotionally and affectionately. Although they were able to communicate well about other aspects of their marriage, so far they were unable to do so about this part. She thought they, but particularly her husband, were not able to move away from the emotionally stoic role models their parents had provided them.

The trend seemed to be the absorption of such typically "feminine" attributes as readiness to share feelings and emotional expressiveness by the men. These characteristics tended to be seen as more desirable than the reserve and stiff upper lips associated with masculinity in our culture. In a similar vein, men attempted to help their wives acquire desirable "masculine" attributes, such as assertiveness in the work place. This kind of cultural diffusion seemed to arise from the emphasis these couples placed on uncoupling gender from roles and other attributes. If being nurturing is no longer typed as feminine and is considered to be a valuable human trait, then why should not men be helped to acquire it?

Herein perhaps lies one of the special advantages of the role-sharing marriage, as our couples made clear, but the down side of this advantage was also in evidence. Whatever their origins, such attributes as reserve and detachment were still valued by some husbands. Some expressed misgivings about what they saw as the expectancy in a role-sharing marriage to be open about feelings, to admit to feeling weak or scared, and so on. Their intellectual recognition that it was all right, in fact "good," to do so only sharpened their dilemma since they could not rationalize their behavior on the basis that it was masculine. Rather it had to be defended as a personal idiosyncracy.

The Sexual Relationship

As expected, responses to our query about the effect, if any, of their type of marriage on their sexual relationship were very similar to, and consistent with, responses about the emotional and affective area. However, both husbands and wives candidly admitted that if any one aspect of their marital relationship lagged behind the others in terms of becoming egalitarian, it was the sexual aspect.

The majority of our respondents seemed relatively free from viewing themselves and each other in sex-stereotyped roles in their sexual relationship. As one wife put it, she and her husband were a long way from viewing sex as "men's pleasure and women's duty." This group of spouses said they related to each other as equals sexually: either felt free to initiate sex, both felt free to enjoy it fully, and either felt free to say "no" to the other without fear that the other would feel rejected. They saw sex, like other parts of their relationship, as being determined by mutual decisions and as the responsibility of both partners equally. Being responsible, they thought, involved openly and honestly communicating to each other their needs, wants, likes, and dislikes; not making assumptions about the other but yet being sensitive to and considerate of the other's needs and feelings; recognizing that the sexual satisfaction of both partners is equally important; and not placing blame on the other at any point the sexual relationship is less than desired.

Many of these spouses emphasized that their attitudes and behavior in other parts of their relationship were carried over to and expressed in the sexual relationship. According to one husband, "If you're comfortable with other aspects of the relationship, all areas of the relationship blend." Another husband stated that "the increased level of freedom, flexibility, and communication results in a very creative and exciting sexual relationship, as it does in other parts of the marital relationship." Men especially seemed to appreciate the more relaxed nature of the sexual relationship, which they attributed to the lack of sex stereotyping and other qualities in their marital relationship. Women were more likely to mention the positive carryover to the sexual relationship from their enhanced self-image, increased self-respect, and greater freedom to express themselves as equal partners.

An issue emerged, however, over refusing sex in an egalitarian relationship. As one wife commented, "I feel free to say no. We probably would have sex more often if we had a traditional marriage." In his individual interview, her husband agreed somewhat unhappily: "My wife is less interested in sex than I would like. In an egalitarian marriage, you have to respect this." Another husband lamented the loss of the "script for sexual relations provided by the traditional marriage." Some respondents (usually wives) thought the frequency of sex may be less in an egalitarian relationship since either can refuse but that the quality was better because sex, when it happened, was more likely to be mutually desired and satisfactory to both.

The couples seemed to be grappling here with some intriguing nuances. Certainly wives in traditional marriages can refuse sex, as well as initiate it. Still, in such marriages, there is the convention of the husband's initiating sex and the wife's acquiescing. By setting the pace, husbands are better able to control the frequency of sex than in relationships in which these gender-linked expectations are attenuated, if not absent altogether. From the traditional husband's perspective the sexual relationship may be quite satisfying, though the wife may want less sex, or even more. With an increased sense of freedom to say "no, not now" or "come on, let's," the egalitarian wife has equal say about sexual frequency, requiring her husband to adjust accordingly.

Several husbands and wives indicated that this is the hardest part of the marriage to free from traditional sex-role expectations. Some husbands were struggling with trying to be more expressive and to communicate openly with their wives about sex. A few were described by their wives as "reserved," "shy," "prim and proper"; these husbands were very uncomfortable whenever their wives wanted to talk about sex. On the other hand, several wives seemed to have difficulty living up to the newer expectations of them; essentially, they were reluctant to assume half of the responsibility for the sexual relationship. They found it hard to initiate sex or to let their husbands know what they wanted. Consequently, they forced their husbands to play the traditional role of pursuer.

Leisure Time and Vacations

With so little time for leisure, it is not surprising that almost all of these role-sharing couples spend most of their free time together and with their children if they have any. Rarely did a couple mention a wife's or a husband's night out. Yet, except for constraints posed by children or having to work evenings or weekends, both spouses in most of these couples seemed to feel free to go out alone or with friends. The independence and role sharing that characterized their marital relationships were the underpinnings of this freedom. For example, one wife called her husband at work to tell him she was going to stop by a friend's house after work to have dinner with her. Neither she nor her husband had any qualms about it because the husband knew she had not seen this friend in a long time and there was no expectation that the wife had to go home to cook the husband's dinner. Perhaps it was because the marital partners felt free to have time apart when they wanted or needed it that they did not need a rigidly scheduled night out for the sake of having time apart. Of course, regularly scheduled activities (work, leisure, or volunteer activities) often dictated specific evening or weekend times away from home for one or both of the spouses. Generally, our respondents complained, not about the lack of time for themselves as individuals, but about not having enough time together as a couple or as a family, that is, with the children.

The kind of leisure activities these couples participated in together or with their children ran the usual gamut of middle-class recreational pursuits such as going out to dinner and having friends over for dinner; going to concerts, theater, ballet, movies, and museums; and taking walks, hiking, biking, and skiing. As in most families, the amount of leisure time and the way it was spent was greatly influenced by whether or not there were children and by the ages of the children. Not surprisingly, interests overlapped considerably between marital partners; no doubt this was one of the factors that brought them together in the first place and was one of the reasons many considered their spouse their best friend. When interests did not coincide, this situation was handled in the manner typical of these relationships: talking it over and arriving at a mutually agreeable solution. Each partner might pursue her or his separate interests alone or with other friends or relatives, the other might voluntarily decide to participate so that the couple could be together, the spouses might take turns pursuing together each other's interests, or some other arrangement might be made. Different arrangements might be used by the same couple at different times or for different activities.

Much of the leisure time that was spent separately consisted of reading and pursuing hobbies such as sewing, gardening, and assorted home projects. Husbands also spent separate time engaging in or watching sports activities, often on television. Frequently, these separate leisure activities were engaged in at home at the same time by the spouses. For example, both might be reading in the same room or one might be working on the car while the other did gardening chores. (One person's work may be another person's leisure.)

Vacations were almost always taken together, but in almost half the couples at least one spouse had taken a separate vacation. Some couples took separate vacations, in addition to those together, on a regular basis, and some couples who had never taken separate vacations thought they might do so in the future. Although a number of the separate vacations turned out to be visits to their families of origin or were connected with business trips, a few were trips with friends or relatives. Almost invariably both spouses reported that these separate vacations, which frequently were only weekends or a few days in length, worked out well for both. This was true whether both partners took separate trips at the same time or whether one stayed at home. They enjoyed the time apart, missed each other, and were glad to be back together again when the trip was over. Whether or not it was considered a vacation, most spouses who had families of origin in another location visited them alone, or with the children, at least at times because they thought this made sense.

Very likely, the way these couples handled separate leisure time and vacations differed little, if at all, in most respects from the way any considerate married couple would handle them. Two aspects may be different, however. One is the basic premise underlying the decision to spend the time separately: for egalitarian couples, there is no question about the right of *either* spouse to make this choice. Each views himself or herself as an autonomous person who makes his or her own decisions. This ensures personal freedom and guards against expectations on either partner's part that they will tell one another what to do. These marital partners discuss these matters and negotiate or compromise, if necessary, in order to try to arrive at decisions satisfactory to both, not because they feel they have to, but because they choose to. They choose to probably for a mixture of reasons such as respect and consideration for the other, to get input or ideas from the other spouse, desire or need for mutual planning and coordination, and so on. Although the behavior of these couples may not look any different from that of most couples in the same circumstances, the psychological effect may well be a distinction.

The other aspect that may be different with the role-sharing couples stems from their assumption that each spouse is responsible for himself or herself and is self-sufficient. Each is capable of—and generally does—her or his own packing for a trip and making other necessary arrangements. By the same token, each is capable of doing whatever needs to be done at home while the other is away. For example, wives do not have to worry about what their husbands will eat while they are away or make sure they leave the house clean, nor do husbands have to make sure all the monthly bills are paid or that the car is in tip-top shape before they take off. Even if children are being left at home with the husband, wives do not have to prepare meals in advance to be reheated by the husband, do the laundry just before leaving, and so on. This provides another type of freedom that may have psychological effects but most definitely has pragmatic implications.

Social Life and Friends

The responsibility for the couple's or family's social life is shared equally by roughly half of the couples in our sample. When one spouse assumes more of the responsibility, it is almost twice as likely to be the wife as the husband. Yet nine husbands were reported as taking primary responsibility for the family's social planning, engagements, and activities.

Most of the friends of these couples were friends of both spouses and often were couples with a similar lifestyle. The latter was explained on the basis that they generally felt more comfortable around other role-sharing couples because they had more in common with them. Many of the people they saw socially, whether they considered them friends or acquaintances, were colleagues or co-workers. Generally, people they socialized with often, whether these were one spouse's colleagues or friends from before the marriage, became friends of both partners.

Although they might seldom see them, almost all of our respondents had some friends separate from their partner. Again these were generally people met through work or known before the relationship with their spouse. About three fourths of both the wives and husbands who had separate friends had at least one who was of the opposite sex. Maintaining contact with a friend of the opposite sex who was not also one's spouse's friend presented the opportunity for some couples to come to grips with and define the limits of personal freedom.

At the time of our interviews, the large majority of couples told us that opposite-sex friends posed no problem for their relationship. Although very few couples were currently struggling with this issue, a number of other couples had done so in the past. With some couples, the problem occurred early in the marriage when feelings of security about the marital relationship and of mutual trust were still tentative. With others, it occurred after the relationship was well established. In either case, the process used to resolve the difficulty was the same: open communication about it. Solutions varied, but the goal in almost every case seemed to be to maximize the comfort level for both spouses and not jeopardize the marital relationship. Obviously, what spouses were concerned about were romantic involvements since they used words like "jealous," "feeling threatened," and "fear of too much closeness." Since they were used to communicating with each other about their feelings, concerns, and so on, they found it not too difficult to let each know when they felt uncomfortable about a relationship or specific behavior in the relationship. Couples who had experienced problems in this area often developed rules to cover potential future problems of a similar nature. Some were as simple as letting each other know right away if there was any discomfort or "opposite sex associations for business only." One was as elaborate as setting up a procedure for negotiating when one person is uncomfortable, each spouse having ultimate veto power over the other's opposite-sex relationships if no mutually satisfactory solution could be reached.

It was clear that very few spouses were interested in the kind of open marriage in which partners are free to have affairs. With one couple a sexually open marriage was apparently more satisfying to the husband than to the wife. Although they both had sexual partners outside the marriage, the wife seemed threatened by this part of their marriage and ready to give it up. The husband was not. Although the wife saw "an open marriage as an extension of an egalitarian relationship," she felt herself to be in a position of having to "go along" with her husband's sexual preferences. In that sense the sexual openness of their marriage seemed like the most traditional, least egalitarian part.

Normally, it seems that the limit of personal freedom is reached for these couples at the point beyond which the resulting behavior would have negative effects on the other spouse or the children. Generally, the exercise of personal freedom was voluntarily curtailed far short of this limit owing to consideration for one's spouse or children, or feelings of responsibility to the relationship, children, or family unit. As far as we could tell, both wives and husbands felt they maintained as much independence and personal freedom as they wanted. They did not seem to feel they were giving these up when they got married since they chose to embrace other values that the relationship entailed (concern for the other, cooperation, sharing, etc.). They did feel that they were sacrificing much of their autonomy and freedom when they had children— perhaps one of the reasons the decision about having children was often so agonizing. But again, if they freely chose to make this sacrifice that the responsibility of having children exacted, there was no issue. Of the many things we asked about in these interviews, the only one that seemed to hit a nerve concerning personal freedom was the issue of opposite-sex friends.

The Perceptions of Others

We wondered what these couples' families of origin, friends, and co-workers thought about this unorthodox marital form. We asked each of these couples about their perceptions of the reactions to their marriage of these relevant others. From their responses, it was clear that there were reactions to various components of these marriages (not all present in every marriage in our sample)—the sharing of the work-family roles, the spouses' being equal partners, and more generally, the feminist ideas held by the spouses.

PARENTS

The large majority of parents were at least accepting of their children's role-sharing marriages, though they seldom understood this type of relationship, according to our respondents. Almost all the parents had traditional marriages and had expected—most also wanted—their children to have the same. They did not understand this modern way of doing things, but since their children were happy, it was all right with them. About half even viewed their children's choice of relationship in a positive manner and were supportive of it. Husbands' mothers were reported to be the most positive of the four parents, while the wives' mothers apparently had the most reservations about the marital style. Fathers tended to say little, and so our respondents often did not know what they thought. Generally, when they hazarded guesses, they viewed their fathers as positive or at least accepting.

Husbands seemed less aware of their parents' opinions about their style of marriage than their wives were. According to the husbands, their parents seldom commented, but most seemed pleased. Some parents who were puzzled by the way they did things (ran their household, made decisions, communicated, etc.) seemed accepting, but others did not. On the negative side, a few parents were reported as thinking their son should have more authority than he does at home, that is, should be firmer and make more of the decisions. In these cases, their son's wife may be perceived as being too dominant. Occasionally, parents seemed threatened by the couple's free and open communication style, especially if it resulted in an argument or one person's stating that she or he was angry. Parents also sometimes reacted negatively to the couple's not having children, to the wife's working and using day care for the children, or to the wife's keeping her maiden name. (They were apt to feel hurt over the wife's not taking their son's—and their—name.)

On the positive side, some husbands reported their parents as being very supportive, accepting of their wives' careers, happy about the way they do things, and so on. A few parents were approving because they also shared roles and thought this was the way it should be. Fathers, but more often mothers, sometimes conveyed to their sons that they should "help out" even more than they do at home. Mothers were particularly apt to be pleased, although often surprised, that their sons "helped" their working wives with the housework and the children. Occasionally a mother, who had reared her children with attitudes and skills conducive to role sharing, expected no less.

As indicated, wives in our sample were much more attuned to their parents' views about their type of marital relationship than husbands were. Wives especially knew what their mothers thought. This set of parents had—or, at least, were perceived by their daughters as having—stronger opinions and reactions (both positive and negative) than the husbands' parents did.

When the wives' parents were critical, and more than a third of their mothers were, this criticism might be aimed at their daughter, her husband, or the relationship. For example, some parents were reported as believing their daughter was too pushy, too aggressive, and expecting too much by wanting her husband to help with the children and the housework. The daughter's husband might then be described as "henpecked" or as "a saint." Familiar only with marriages where wives and husbands play traditional sex roles and believing this is the way relationships should be, some of these parents were upset by any deviance. These parents disapproved of their daughters' working outside the home, particularly if there were children, believed their sons-in-law should earn enough so they could fulfill the breadwinner role alone, and saw their daughters' husbands' involvement with the housework and child care as "unmanly." One father was embarrassed that his son-in-law cooked, feeling that he was being compromised as a result. According to these parents, their daughters should be home taking care of the house, their children, and their husbands. Remarks referring to their grandchildren's being left alone or lacking proper care seemed to their daughters designed to try to make them feel guilty about their jobs or careers. As one respondent put it, marriage to her mother simply meant sacrificing for the family and keeping some order to the house; consequently, these "newer notions" seemed foreign and suspicious to her.

On the other hand, many parents were perceived by our respondents as being very supportive of their daughters and admiring of their life-styles. Some did not understand the relationship but approved of it because the couple was happy. Some who at first had not viewed positively the way the couple did things had learned to appreciate the relationship and thought it made sense, especially for a working couple. According to several wives in our study, their mothers were frankly envious of their careers and type of marriage, for they would have wanted a similar lifestyle for themselves. In fact, a few parents were reported to be beginning to question their own sex-role behavior, using their daughters' marriages as models.

Some parents had expected and wanted their daughters to be career oriented and independent. Others had been surprised at their daughters' and their husbands' ideas, found them curious or amusing, but were readily accepting of them. Some mothers openly expressed their approval of the husbands' helping with domestic responsibilities and being so involved with the children. They referred to their daughters as "lucky" and "fortunate" to have such "good" husbands.

It is difficult to say why some parents, particularly mothers, reacted so strongly, according to our respondents' perceptions, in such opposite directions to their daughters' lifestyles. Possibly many of these mothers identified with their daughters, either causing them to be envious but happy for their daughters who had the kind of lifestyle they would have wanted if circumstances had been different for them earlier or invoking their disapproval since their daughters had not followed the expected traditional path. Some of our respondents thought perhaps mothers in the latter group felt threatened by this new lifestyle, which seemed to be working, because it made them question—with the discomfort this can cause—their own traditional sex roles. This may be. Other explanations are also possible. For example, these mothers may feel like failures, because they failed to socialize their daughters into their proper sex roles, or alternatively, the mothers may be afraid for their daughters' sake, feeling these new attitudes and behavior are risky since they may lead to unforeseen undesirable consequences for their children at some future time.

OTHER FAMILY MEMBERS

When our query was extended to other members of their families of origin, our respondents overwhelmingly thought of brothers and sisters. Only occasionally was a grandmother, aunt, or uncle mentioned, and when they were it was almost always by wives in our sample. The reactions of these relatives (other than siblings) that were reported to us were very positive, with the exception of one grandmother who tried to make her granddaughter feel guilty over not doing traditional "housewife" chores. Other grandmothers were thought to be approving of the sharing of domestic and child care responsibilities. One had even influenced her granddaughter to be nontraditional in reaction against her own marriage, which she had considered too traditional. Aunts seemed to approve and to be impressed with the husbands' culinary skills; one aunt had a similar marriage herself.

Most of the wives' and husbands' siblings were positive or at least accepting of these role-sharing, egalitarian marriages, but three of ten respondents reported negative or mixed reactions from them. When siblings disapproved it was generally because they felt threatened by this type of marriage or simply felt marriages should follow the traditional pattern. Husbands' brothers and wives' sisters were the siblings most likely to be negative. Husbands' brothers, some of whom were described as "chauvinistic" or "very macho," had difficulty understanding a marriage where the husband did not dominate and the wife had so much freedom and independence. These notions of equality, in addition to husbands' helping with housework and child care, were foreign and threatening to them. They were often afraid their wives would get ideas. Wives' sisters who disapproved were generally in traditional marriages and thought that was the way any marriage should be. A few of the wives reported that their brothers shared such beliefs, often feeling that their sisters had too much power in their marriages. One wife was particularly irritated with her brothers, who felt she should wait on them hand and foot because she was a woman. Her brothers' attitude made it frustrating and difficult for her to be gracious to them when they visited in her home because there were certain things she wanted to do for them because they were her guests, not because they were men.

Most of the siblings, however, ranged from being tolerant or accepting to being very approving and supportive of our couples' marriages. Some of them had similar marriages themselves, and a few were reported to feel that our respondents were not egalitarian enough or that the husband should be doing even more of the housework. A number of their younger siblings were using them as role models: unmarried sisters and brothers wanted to have similar marriages, and the married ones were trying to develop this type of relationship. Whether married or not, siblings were reported variously as being curious about, intrigued by, amused at, admiring of, and open minded about the respondents' lifestyle. Some siblings sought their advice about how to make their own marriages more sharing and egalitarian. Some wives' sisters who were in traditional marriages were reported to be envious, especially wishing their husbands would help out more at home, but other sisters, apparently content with their own traditional marriages, nevertheless appreciated and were supportive of their sisters' different lifestyle. A few of the sisters' husbands were thought to be threatened, fearing their wives would be influenced by their nontraditional sisters. One senses that there may have been some basis for such fears. For example, one wife commented that her brother-in-law could "ground" her sister, that is, tell her she could not go out and have her obey.

FRIENDS

Seldom were there negative reactions from friends, primarily because of self-selection. Couples tended to select, gravitate toward, and maintain friends who had similar values and were supportive of them. Many of their friends had the same type of marriage or were working toward it. Some looked to the couples as role models, perhaps asking for advice about role sharing. Some of their friends who had traditional marriages were accepting of their lifestyle and a few were thought to be envious. Several married female friends were interested in their suggestions about getting husbands to help at home. Husbands in our sample occasionally had to endure good-natured teasing from some of the more traditional husbands, who accused them of making it rough for the rest of them. Friends who were not married generally admired the relationship and were impressed by the fact that both spouses could maintain so much autonomy after marriage. Some thought these couples had the best of both worlds: the world of the marrieds and of the singles. As far as sharing work-family roles was concerned, many of these single friends simply assumed the wife would work and that the husband would participate in the domestic and child care responsibilities.

Occasionally, a married female friend, perhaps envious, would make a slighting comment about the role-sharing wife's independence, or a male friend would think the egalitarian husband should keep a tighter rein on his wife. Unlike their single friends, a few of the married ones found it difficult to understand how the couple could maintain a close relationship when each had so much freedom and independence. Some wives in our sample found it easier to relate to their unmarried female friends than to women friends in traditional marriages, feeling that they had more in common with the former. For example, they felt alienated from women who always wondered aloud what their husbands would prefer when making even minor decisions or who referred to things that their husbands would not let them do.

CO-WORKERS

As with their parents, siblings, and friends, most of the colleagues and co-workers of these respondents were viewed as being positive and supportive of their type of marital relationship if they knew about it, and some did, particularly those who were also friends. Not only were our respondents more likely to be aware of the perceptions of their colleagues who were also friends than of those who were not, they were also more likely to choose as friends those colleagues who had a similar lifestyle and were supportive or who were at least accepting of and open-minded about their lifestyle.

Generally, these respondents tried to avoid discussing aspects of their marriages or family life at work, primarily because of what co-workers might think. They tried not to flaunt their lifestyle at work, or anywhere else for that matter, but occasionally someone could not resist a temptation to make a point. An example was a woman with mostly male colleagues who told them, when they were planning a party in which their wives (presumably housewives) would prepare the refreshments, that she could not bring anything, because she had no wife to prepare it. A man in our sample takes perverse pleasure in his co-workers' amused interest tinged with horror when he mentions some domestic chore he does as he pictures them thinking his wife leads him around by a ring in his nose.

Among co-workers who knew about the respondents' lifestyle, there were some who simply did not understand this type of marriage, some who were negative and disapproving, some with mixed reactions, and some with no reaction at all as far as our respondents could determine. For men the negative reactions arose, not only because of the unconventional behavior such as involvement in housework, but probably even more so because of the husband's ordering of priorities, that is, putting his family before his work. For this reason, men who worked only part time in order to share child care, who had to go straight home from work to take care of the children, or who had to take time off from work to care for a sick child or something similar often tried to keep people at work from knowing about this behavior or the reasons for it. Negative reactions for women were usually in response to their not staying home with small children, their not fulfilling the "housewife" role without their husbands' help, and their "radical" feminist ideas.

10

Issues in Role Sharing

We began the initial chapter with several vignettes of married life that one or two generations ago might have been regarded as evidence of strange, if not pathological, relationships but today provide examples of a new style of marriage that is growing in popularity. We introduce the final chapter will another set of vignettes.

- Steve, an engineer who works for a construction company, is taking a six-month paternity leave so that his wife Janice can return at once to her job as a buyer for a department store chain. (She had taken a maternity leave following the birth of their first child.) George, Steve's boss, said that Steve would be missed, particularly since the firm was about ready to start on a major project but that the leave should not interfere with his pending promotion. Shortly before his leave started, Steve's colleagues gave him a send-off party and a car seat for the new baby.
- Six-year-old Tony seemed to take a lot of interest in the dolls of a female playmate. His parents, especially his father, were very pleased at this budding paternal behavior. They bought him a doll set for Christmas.
- Although Madge and Jack had a close, happy marital relationship with many common interests, they differed on how they liked to spend their vacations. Madge loved a beach holiday while Jack's passion was canoeing in the wilderness. They decided to take separate vacations and for this purpose both found partners who shared their interests. Madge spent a week in Acapulco with a male colleague from work while Jack went off to Minnesota with a former girlfriend.

Whereas the vignettes that began the book reflect values and practices currently accepted by role-sharing couples and tolerated by most other groups in society, the vignettes just introduced would probably strike many role-sharing couples as farfetched. If our sample is typical, most couples would welcome the arrival of the first, many would have qualms about the second, and most would reject the third. The American public today would probably take a dim view of all of the examples. Yet, the vignettes reflect a plausible development in the egalitarian marriage if values concerning equality and autonomy are pushed far enough. New choices mean not only new freedom but also new problems. Without the guidance of traditional norms, choices may be more difficult to make. The new ideology may lead to developments that may be viewed as going too far and may give rise to expectations that may match the older tradition in their rigidity.

As we have argued in this book, the role-sharing couples in our study, and generally, can be viewed as distributed along a continuum of departure from traditional norms and values concerning marriage. We have considered the nature of these departures, how these departures create issues, and possible ways of resolving these issues. This has been done separately for different areas of married life—breadwinning, household chores, child care, and so on. We endeavored to be comprehensive in covering the wide range of issues revealed in the marriages we studied.

In this final chapter we present a synthesis of what emerged as the focal issues, together with some thoughts about their ramifications and ways they may be dealt with. These issues are framed from the standpoint of couples who are role sharing or who are interested in doing so. What do such couples need to be concerned about, given typical socialization histories and current job market realities?

Role Differentiation and Balance

In its ideal conception a role-sharing marriage should contain a minimum of differentiation in respect to major work-family roles. Both partners should share all of them. Also, the effort in carrying out these roles should be balanced with each partner doing his or her fair share with weight given to such factors as time spent and the desirability of specific tasks.

Issues in this area may be relatively minor for couples who do not plan to have children. For childless couples who wish to adopt role sharing as a lifestyle, issues around role differentiation and balance, while not unimportant or uninteresting, are usually relatively minor compared with other problems in their lives. Issues about childless wives' working are long dead. Although issues concerning their husbands' contribution to domestic chores are still very much alive, they appear manageable by prospective role-sharing couples. Husbands who take responsibility for a fair share of household tasks and do them are no longer oddities. In fact, such sharing is becoming increasingly expected on the part of wives and increasingly accepted by husbands. The major issue that arises, if we can generalize from the couples in our study, does not concern whether husbands should take on these tasks but rather whose criteria should be used in evaluating their performance. Thus, the issue is not so much one of role differentiation and balance but rather one of control, which we take up subsequently.

Critical issues in role differentiation and balance frequently arise from differences in skill and orientation related to prior socialization. For example, women are more likely to have better developed domestic skills, and this circumstance may lead to an unplanned drift toward the wife's doing more, because she can do it faster and better. When time is short or skill is demanded, such as preparing for company, the wife takes over. This creeping traditionalism may cause imbalance and eventually resentment on the wife's part.

As husbands get into the swing of sharing domestic tasks, a drift in the opposite direction may occur, as we saw in a few of our couples. Husbands in some cases may do more than their wives because of any of a wide variety of individual differences that may cause one person to do more than another in a two-person work situation. Again persistent imbalances and resentments may occur.

Problems of this sort can be corrected through two devices, both of which were used by couples in the study. One is for both partners to be alert to imbalances as they occur. One partner may take over a larger share of a joint task to repay the other for his or her extra efforts. This process of maintaining balance is probably best done if the partner does not make matters explicit and thereby avoids overt quid pro quos on a constant basis—a pattern most of our couples eschewed. The other device is a periodic review of who is doing what. Here the division of labor is made very explicit and may include estimating time spent in different tasks, challenging the other's estimate and justifying one's own, and driving bargains about task allocations. While some couples may find dealing with reciprocity in the raw rather distasteful, it may be preferable to allowing resentment to accumulate over work debts that may become so massive that they can never be paid back. The saving grace of this device is that it need not be used very often, especially if the first device is kept in good working order.

Issues of role differentiation and balance may become monumental when children appear on the scene. As Jessie Bernard (1973:282) has said, "When or if there are no children, role sharing is not too much of a problem. It is when there are preschool children that the real test comes, because sharing roles also means sharing the child-care and the child-rearing function as well as the work of the household."

In our study the magnitude of this issue was often seen in the tortuous decision making about whether or not to have a child and in the massive effects of child care on role sharing itself. Having a child brings to the forefront a coalition of strong traditional pulls. It is the woman who bears the child, the biological cornerstone of traditional differentiation of roles. Since most couples refuse to consider the purchase of full-time infant care arrangements, one partner must give up or reduce outside work commitments. The "logical" partner is the wife. It is expected by employers, relatives, and our social institutions. Maternity (but not paternity) leave is often available. Typically she earns less than her husband and is likely to be in an occupation in which future prospects would be damaged less by a leave or cutback in hours. Finally, given prior socialization and the effects of social expectations, both partners are more likely to see the wife rather than the husband as having the greater capacity and skill to care for the infant. For couples committed to role sharing, the decision to differentiate at this juncture places them in what has been referred to as a transitional status that, in our sample and typically, appears to resemble a traditional division of labor—the wife at home or working part time and the husband in the work place full time. As we have seen, however, the pattern differs from the traditional or quasi-traditional in that role sharing is still much in evidence.

Nevertheless, a transitional status of this kind sets up a structure that makes role sharing difficult and that may lead to a drift toward purely traditional or quasi-traditional arrangements, especially if a second child appears before the wife has reestablished her career. The short-run solution—the wife's leaving employment—may make sense at the time, but it may result in adverse long-term consequences for role sharing. The wife's career development may be impaired, or she may see it that way. Her husband may gain an even greater advantage in income without a career disruption, which would make the wife all the more the "logical choice" to subordinate her career to his in case of another child or a move.

Thus, a spiraling cause-effect sequence may be set in motion by the couple's once earlier, seemingly rational, decision. The family may begin to look more traditional. The husband becomes the primary breadwinner (with the edge in family power that generally accompanies this role); the wife's career becomes secondary to her husband's and to her roles as mother and homemaker, and so on. Even if the couple can adjust well to this shift in roles, which seemed more difficult for wives in our study than for the husbands, the return to more nearly equal role sharing at a later time is seriously jeopardized. The wife is now at a considerable disadvantage in terms of her career and her income. She would be penalized, for example, if she were expected to meet half of the family expenses or, in case of divorce, to contribute half of the children's support.

The wife is used as the example of the spouse who stays home because it usually turns out that way. The same considerations could apply to the husband, though with some important differences. Because the husband usually has an edge over the wife in the market place, a temporary hiatus in his career might not put him "behind" his wife (but probably would put him behind his colleagues) in terms of advancement and income. Moreover, there is probably less danger that the husband would drift into becoming a full-time "househusband" than of the wife's drifting into the role of housewife. It is also less likely that the wife would forgo participating as a full partner in the parenting role.

A solution that may be the most attainable for many couples currently and the kind used by a number in our study was to keep the transitional period short, with the stay-at-home spouse returning to work first on a part-time basis, then on a full-time basis as soon as possible. Some combination of parental leave, adjustment in work schedules of at least one but preferably both parents, child care by relatives (if available), and purchased care can be employed. As we implied earlier, if the spouse who cuts back on paid employment to provide major child care is the father—an arrangement harder to attain and considered less desirable by many couples—this solution would probably help maintain role sharing at a higher level than if the mother becomes the primary caretaker.

As far as we are concerned, however, the ideal arrangement is for both parents to cut back on their paid employment to share the child care role beginning with the young infant. In this way the role-sharing pattern could continue uninterrupted, except for a short time around the infant's birth. There seems to be little question now that the welfare of young children is best served by the active participation in their care of two willing parents. As Bernard (1972:243) states, child care and socialization are "far too important to entrust to one sex alone; both parents should participate." In order to make this possible, she calls for industry to accommodate to the family by making part-time work available for both men and women.

While we could not agree more about the need for this and other structural changes in the work world (e.g., flexitime, paid and unpaid leaves, family days), we also believe it possible for some determined role-sharing couples to make career and financial sacrifices to share the child care role in lieu of outside supports or until outside supports become available. Good child care (whether provided by the parents or someone else) is costly. So what else is new? Our suggestion that role-sharing couples who choose to become parents make such a financial sacrifice may appear punitive to some readers (akin to a "blame-the-victim" notion) and completely unrealistic to others. We can only point out that parents would need to want to make this arrangement and agree that some families could not afford it financially no matter how much they wanted it. The latter, however, is not the only reason many egalitarian couples do not share the parenting role fully. As Haas's (1980a, 1981) research on Swedish dual-earner couples shows, even when the national government has an egalitarian ideology and has tried to implement it by providing the necessary structural supports to encourage parents to share the child care role equally, only a minority of parents have taken advantage of these liberal provisions. Consequently, we believe our emphasis on parents' considering (and implementing when at all possible) arrangements to permit them to share the child care role from infancy on is not misplaced.

There is evidence (Moen 1982) that a significant proportion of fathers of preschool children may in fact welcome such an arrangement. If part-time employment for both parents is not feasible, flexitime, doing some work at home, bringing the baby to the work place, and use of vacation and accrued leave time are among other devices that may be employed to avoid excessive role differentiation or imbalance, while enabling parents to care for the infant.

Whereas not all of these devices may be feasible, enough of them may to put together a strategy that would enable both parents to avoid serious career disruption, ensure adequate income, and involve both parents in child care. Such arrangement "packages" may be complicated and subject to breakdown but may offer the best available compromises for couples who wish to ensure the continuance of a role-sharing relationship when children arrive.

Autonomy

Issues concerning autonomy are a part of any form of marriage, but they take on particular characteristics in role-sharing relationships. As discussed in the initial chapter, the notion that two partners are equal, in the sense of sameness of function, rights, and obligation, puts the partners in autonomous positions. They come together as equals or at some point decide they are. As equals they choose to limit their freedom of action for their common benefit. Autonomy may be reinforced by the development of independent resources as with the spouses in our study with an individual orientation toward money, by the creation of independent social networks related to the work place, by maintaining domiciles in separate locations to pursue career interests, and by such symbolic, but important, gestures as having separate last names.

In the sharing of family roles (i.e., domestic and child care), the role-sharing marriage promotes independence in some ways, but it also provides the opportunity for closeness and interdependence. How this gets played out in the performance of roles depends largely on how the tasks in the roles are shared. Spouses can operate quite independently by arrangements such as taking turns performing tasks, dividing tasks in such a way that little or no interaction is required, each doing his own laundry or mending, and so on. These independent methods may be used as a way of maintaining balance, achieving efficiency, minimizing conflict over standards, or simply acting from preference. The partners in one of our couples even cooked their own individual meals because of their different food preferences (but they ate together).

Another way of sharing roles is to perform virtually all tasks involved together. There were many examples of this kind of togetherness in our study. Generally, most couples used some combination of these methods of sharing tasks.

It might be said that the notion of equality that underlies ideological role sharing requires a certain measure of autonomy in the partners— that which is needed for each to operate with self-sufficiency in breadwinning, domestic, and parenting roles. Further, an orientation and structure are provided that set the stage for further autonomous development, but the extent to which this occurs are individual and couple decisions. A couple may decide to forgo any more autonomy than is necessary. Perhaps the major issue here can be put as follows: Do the "autonomy requirements" of the role-sharing marriage constitute a threat to the emotional bonds and sense of commitment that have long been regarded as central to successful marriages? Or can the autonomy brought about by role sharing be fitted into these traditional foundations of marriage? Some impressions from our data may be informative.

First, the range of behaviors displayed by couples in our study had no discernible negative effects on their emotional attachment to one another. Regardless of how autonomously they functioned in other important areas of their lives or how business-like their arrangements with each other regarding the carrying out of family roles, handling money, and so on, their independence did not carry over to the emotional area. The capacity of the couples to separate role sharing from intimacy belies notions often encountered that an egalitarian relationship, with its emphasis on reciprocation and self-sufficiency, would make it hard to attain that cozy sense of closeness that presumably makes for marital bliss.

The role-sharing marriage promotes autonomy in some ways, but as our couples demonstrate, the selfish sentiments sometimes feared need not be a part of the partners' independence. In fact, it can be argued that smoothly functioning role sharing can enhance cohesion. Many of our couples thought it did.

If partners can maintain a mutually satisfying reciprocation in roles and tasks, there is less likelihood of creating tension that would interfere with the emotional side of their interaction. Thus a business-like balancing of accounts in matters of breadwinning, household work, and child care can free a couple to enjoy a caring, intimate relationship.

A somewhat different aspect of the autonomy issue arises around questions of commitment, obligation, and self-sacrifice. For example, Elshtain (1982) questions the idea of marriages based on "unbinding commitments" between partners who are motivated by "possessive individualism." Their marriages become "starkly contractual," each partner seeking to maximize his or her own self-interest. Where is the sense of commitment to the idea of marriage as a bond between people that may require subordination of self-interest for the sake of the marriage, the children, the family? Thus, a marriage in which two people are autonomous yet close may not suffice if it is built on nothing more than short-run gratification. This point of view, which is shared by family traditionalists of the right and certain feminists of the left, may well apply to some egalitarian marriages that place great value on autonomy.

A young wife in a couple that functioned very autonomously told us in response to our question that she was not sure whether their marriage could survive if one of the spouses became permanently unable to perform any of the work-family roles. Her husband did not share her doubts about the continuation of the marriage but thought instead that such a situation would be handled by making the necessary adjustments. Another example of a couple for whom this may well have been an issue was the Zs, the criminal lawyer and his secretary wife, who insisted on equal financial contributions to the household from their very disparate incomes.

These are exceptions, however. Most of the partners in the couples we studied seemed strongly committed to their marriages and families. Although many told us they felt no financial responsibility for their partners, since their partners were self-sufficient, they felt a financial responsibility to the family unit and a potential responsibility to their mates if the mates could no longer work. It appeared that in our sample the nurturing and protective functions were shared by the partners, wives often performing more of the former and husbands more of the latter. (Tradition dies hard.) The role-sharing parents seemed to feel a keen sense of responsibility for their children. Most were not interested in paid child care arrangements, for they thought one or both parents should be home with the children. That many of these couples, particularly those with children, were more family oriented than career ori-

ented is borne out by behaviors on their part such as cutting back on
work hours to have more time for the family and refusing some assign-
ments, promotions, or jobs that they feared would not have been in the
family's best interest, though they would have benefited personally.
There were also examples of spouses' doing more than their share of
domestic and child care tasks to help their partners and to have more
time together as a family.

Perhaps commitments that are freely chosen are no less binding than
those entered into by way of following tradition. Whether and how well
people carry out the functions and responsibilities traditionally assigned to families depends to a large extent on the willingness of the
individuals to do so. The dependencies that exist in conventional marriages because of role differentiation do not negate this. However, it is
clear in the traditional family who is responsible for what and where the
blame can be placed if something goes wrong in a particular area. This
is minimized—if not eliminated—in the role-sharing marriage since
both partners are responsible for family functioning in all areas. The
risk is that when both are responsible, neither is. Alternatively, this type
of marital arrangement may be seen as providing a backup—if one
partner does not or cannot assume a responsibility, the other can. This
would appear to be a safeguard for children.

A number of couples stated the overarching principle of their relationship as "family first." Because of the characteristics of the role-
sharing marriage, particularly autonomy, interchangeability, and lack of
role differentiation, a great deal of communication was often necessary
to arrive at clear understandings and to solve problems in order to help
the family function smoothly. The ability to choose ways of managing
the family, rather than follow the prescribed sex-linked pattern, was
viewed by them as a major asset of the role-sharing marriage.

We would argue that the role-sharing marriage is not incompatible
with traditional values placed on emotional attachments and commitments in family life. The autonomy required of the partners in this kind
of marriage, or that may be assumed, need not threaten—in fact, may
strengthen—cohesiveness. For example, in one study, themes of intimacy and couple identity were found to be *more* characteristic of role-
sharing than non-role-sharing partners (Reitz 1982).

We use the term "cohesive role sharing" to describe marriages in
which the autonomous behavior of both egalitarian partners is subordi-

nated to the welfare of the family. Cohesive role-sharing marriages are characterized not only by the sharing of work-family roles but also by the emotional attachments and bonding, the sense of caring and commitment that exist between the partners and their children.

Disengaged role-sharing couples, each protecting his or her own interest in "starkly contractual" relationships, doubtless exist, but such couples may represent a small fraction of role-sharing marriages. Although we could find no clear prototype of this kind of role-sharing relationship in our sample, some of our couples had characteristics that might be associated with this type. In contrast to cohesive role sharing, we refer to this type of marriage, in which the individual interests of the partners take precedence over family interests, as "autonomous role sharing."

From couples who possessed some of the autonomous characteristics, it is possible to develop a profile of what such a marriage might look like in pure form. Autonomous role-sharing couples would be more likely than their cohesive counterparts to place their careers in a superordinate position. Temporary separations or indefinite long-distance commuting arrangements may be preferred to forgoing opportunities for career development. Orientation to family finances would be clearly individual. Each partner would have a social network and leisure pursuits in which the other did not participate. Extramarital sexual activity would probably still not be the norm but would be more likely to occur and be tolerated than in cohesive marriages. The attachment of the partners to one another would be less all consuming than in the cohesive couple, and their commitments to one another and to the family would be more likely to be cast in the form of limited, renegotiable contracts with self-protective clauses. Division of tasks would emphasize separateness. Purchased child care arrangements would be preferred, and children would be given impetus to develop their interests and social relationships outside the family.

In developing this simple dichotomy, we have, of course, passed over such mixed types as the couple who may have a highly cohesive marital relationship but see their own interests as a unit as superordinate to their children's (a variant we discuss subsequently). More generally, couples may fit the profile of autonomous role sharing in some respects but not in others. We do not know as yet how well the various characteristics we have posited for this type are correlated. Our guess is that there will be an increase in autonomous role-sharing marriages but that typically they will not become as autonomous as the pure form we have described.

Currently, most role-sharing marriages quite likely fall on the cohesive end of the spectrum and probably are as cohesive as more traditional forms. As suggested earlier, however, autonomy issues may differ between forms of marriage. In traditional marriages, these issues may concern tensions between the husband's freedom of action to pursue his career and the needs of his wife and children; the dangers in the partners' withdrawing into their own separate spheres of operation; and the wife's desires, when the children become older, to develop a life outside the home. In the role-sharing marriage the autonomy issues are more symmetrical. The partners have similar orbits of independent activity in their careers and similar responsibilities in the home, in which considerable interdependence may occur.

As our description of the autonomous role-sharing marriage in pure form suggests, one set of issues concerns the extent to which each partner should be free to pursue his or her own career interests at the possible expense of marital cohesion. This issue becomes explicit when a couple considers indefinite separations or long-distance commuting associated with career-related moves. The problem was not frequently seen in our sample, but it is becoming of increasing interest (Farris 1978, Gross 1980, Gerstel and Gross 1984). There is need for longitudinal study of this phenomenon. What happens when long-distance commuting (e.g., only weekends or vacations together) becomes a way of life? What is the cumulative effect on marital cohesion of a series of separations resulting from career mobility? Alternatively, what are the consequences of accumulated resentment that one partner may feel over the perceived sacrifice of career autonomy for the sake of the relationship?

Another set of issues concerns the extent to which income and other tangible resources should be "owned" by each partner or pooled. Our data suggest that marital cohesion need not be sacrificed when partners control their own resources, but we had too few cases of more extreme examples to be comfortable about generalizations in this regard. Whether or not cohesion is affected, a number of special issues arise when separate books are kept. How should common expenses be defined? How should inequities in resources be dealt with? Do explicit understandings need to be developed to cover such contingencies as the illness or disability of one partner if both are expected to contribute to common expenses? As these issues become frequent and pointed, they will doubtless raise questions about the meaning of a role-sharing marriage. Consider, for example, a loan to one's spouse to tide him or her over a period of disability.

A third set of issues relates to how domestic and child care labors are divided. As suggested earlier, tasks may be done together or independently. There is need here for more systematic information on different patterns of division—and the extent to which they reflect or influence the partners' autonomy. Does doing "everything together" reinforce a mutually suffocating relationship? For other couples might not greater task interdependency provide some needed cement? To our knowledge, there has been no study of the details of how husbands and wives actually *share* work in the home. (Berk and Berk's [1979] study, using detailed diary reports kept separately by husbands and wives, comes closest to what we have in mind.) What might appear from self-report data to be "doing it together" might, on more detailed analysis, prove to be a rigid separation of subtasks involving little interaction.

Until more couples who are struggling with advanced forms of these three sets of issues are studied, and until more knowledge is obtained about their effects on the marriage as a whole, role-sharing couples can be advised to be alert to implications that have been raised. Further they can be advised to begin to communicate about such contingencies as relocation, income disparities, and financial responsibilities to one another, even if neither partner can foresee them as a source of future issues.

We have discussed at some length the possible relationship between autonomy and emotional attachment and commitment—potentially a major issue for partners in a role-sharing marriage. This issue may have implications for the larger family unit, in addition to the obvious effects that the existence—or lack—of an emotional bond between the parents and commitment to the family unit would have on the children. One implication may involve role modeling and the meaning of a family. It would seem that parents who are autonomous in some ways but actively participate together in other ways would present a meritorious role model for children. This would enable the child to see each parent as an individual who is capable of functioning independently and competently. At the same time, the parents would be seen as a cohesive unit.

It is possible, however, that extremes could lead to dysfunctional family patterns. There is a danger of exclusion of the child or children if the parents are too involved as a couple. This might stem from partners' being very emotionally wrapped up in each other, sharing all their interests in common, or being very involved in their professional work together. We think this type of closeness may be what some of our childless couples did not want disturbed by having a child.

Another kind of dysfunctional pattern might arise if a couple shared the parental role by dividing up children instead of sharing responsibility for child care generally. This arrangement might be emotionally appealing to some parents who would be able simultaneously to concentrate on their favorite children while satisfying requirements of role sharing. It runs the risk, however, of creating symmetrical coalitions within the family: "my" child versus "your" child. This pattern and its problematic consequences, particularly in matters of discipline, has been noted by Rice (1979) in counseling dual-career couples.

Control

Ideally control should not be an issue in the role-sharing marriage. A basic premise of this kind of marriage is equal power between the partners. Unlike most conventional marriages in which spouses have control over their separate role domains and the husband as breadwinner has ultimate control over major family decisions, the sharing of the work-family roles obviates distinctions in family decision-making power. Both spouses should have equal say in all family decisions and the right to make his or her own individual decisions in other matters as long as the welfare of the family is not jeopardized. The line between family decisions and personal decisions may be drawn at different points, depending on how autonomously the partners choose to function.

Disagreements are to be settled through processes of discussion, negotiation, bargaining, and compromise. Giving and taking should be equitably distributed so that no partner can be said to be more in control than the other in the long run.

If reality conformed to the ideal, then control issues might be viewed in terms of the individual personalities of each partner. However, here as elsewhere, traditional patterns in husband-wife relationships exert their influence.

RESOURCES

As Blood and Wolfe (1960) and Bahr (1972) have suggested, power in a marital relationship may depend to a large extent on the relative resources of each partner in the area under consideration. These resources—tangible or intangible, real or imagined—are frequently unequal. The temptation is for the greater control to accrue to the partner perceived as having the edge in relevant resources.

Some examples from our study may make this point clearer. Some spouses who earned more than their partners seemed to have greater say regarding financial expenditures. Although the higher earning spouses were reluctant to admit this, some of their partners did, often explaining the disparity in family power as due to their own perception that they were not entitled to equal say. Our data concerning who made specific decisions also supported this inequity in decision making. Relocation was more likely to occur to advance the career of the spouse with the higher earnings, greater career commitment, or more prestigious job. In our sample, as is true in the general population, the higher earning spouse was usually the husband. A number of couples in our study indicated that they tried to guard against this type of power imbalance, and indeed some appeared to be successful. With our sample, the power imbalance seemed directly related to the size of the income disparity. Mrs. Z, the secretary who earned far less than her criminal lawyer husband, insisted on paying half of her husband's mortgage and of the household expenses to feel the home was hers, too. What she seemed to be saying was not only that she wanted to feel that she belonged there but also that she had a right to control equal to her husband's.

The possession of knowledge and skills in a specific area is an example of an intangible resource. Wives generally have the edge when it comes to maintaining a household and childrearing. Some husbands in our study had a tendency to defer to their wives in these matters, and some wives seemed reluctant to share full control in these areas. Other husbands in our study demonstrated that they could acquire the necessary knowledge and skills to participate fully in the domestic and child care roles. As discussed in chapter 5, tension was likely to occur when the partners had different standards about task performance, particularly when one tried to exercise control over the other's performance.

Role-sharing couples often divide family responsibilities according to who has the greater knowledge, skill, or interest. If followed exclusively, this principle can have a compounding effect since it can lead to even greater discrepancies between the partners. To illustrate, if a couple decides when they have a baby that the wife should be the parent to stay home with the infant since she knows more than her husband about babies, the experience she acquires by doing so will increase her knowledge further. If there is a second child, there is even more reason for her to be the one to stay home to provide child care according to this principle.

DIFFERENCES IN INVESTMENT

Blumstein and Schwartz (1983:283) make the point that the person less committed to a relationship "has the upper hand because the other person will work harder and suffer more rather than let the relationship break up." Support for this contention was found in their large-scale survey of American couples.

The idea, derived from Waller's (1938) "principle of less interest," can apply not only to a relationship as a whole but also to any aspect of it. All that is necessary is for one partner to have a greater investment than the other in a goal but at the same time to be in need of the other's cooperation to achieve the goal. The goal may be as grand as preserving the marriage or as mundane as having a clean sink.

However, it oversimplifies matters to say merely that the person with the greater investment suffers a loss of power. That may be his or her perception as he or she makes concessions to maintain the partner's cooperation, but the partner may feel controlled by the one with the greater investment. It is more accurate to say that this dynamic is the source of a control issue. For example, one wife in our study who had greater domestic skills and higher housekeeping standards than her husband confided to us that she accepts the slipshod performance of his domestic tasks since she is afraid that if she complains or does them over, he will stop doing them altogether. Husbands in this situation sometimes felt that their wives were attempting to exercise control over their performance and would balk at doing more than the minimum they thought was required.

Whether the issue is housework or sex, the combination of a more and less highly invested partner can lead to a control struggle that leaves both less than satisfied. The more highly invested partner feels as if it is necessary to make unreasonable compromises to ensure that the reluctant partner continues to play the game. The reluctant partner, for whom the goal is not that important, may feel put upon to participate at all.

We venture to suggest that this kind of control issue may be more common in the role-sharing than in the traditional marriage. By doing away with customary boundaries in decision making, the role-sharing marriage is likely to require close cooperation from the partners in more areas of family life than the traditional marriage. Hence, for role-sharing couples, there is greater opportunity for differences in investment in particular goals with associated control struggles. Moreover, the ideal of equal say in decisions precludes one partner from having ultimate authority in a particular area. Having one person in charge provides at least a way of bringing an issue to closure.

Is there any reason to suppose that either husbands or wives in role-sharing marriages have any power advantages in such situations? In our study the advantage seemed to be tilted toward the husbands. Evidence of the traditional pattern of greater investment on the wife's part in domestic and childrearing tasks, and in some cases in the marital relationship, appeared to result in concessions to the husband; the wives' lowering their housekeeping standards was the most obvious example. Less frequently, but still sometimes seen, were instances of concessions in the relationship area. Thus, Mrs. U unwillingly went along with her husband's insistence on a sexually open marriage since he made it clear to her that this was a condition of their marriage. This wife indicated that she thought this was the most traditional aspect of her marriage.

SOCIALIZATION

As has been suggested, and as the examples illustrate, characteristics of traditional marriages—greater resources possessed by the husband

and greater investment by the wife in the household, marriage, and family—run counter to egalitarian ideals in decision making. To these outcroppings of traditionalism can be added another—the tendency of wives to defer to husbands in joint decision making. Socialization, if nothing else, prepares women to take a subordinate position, especially concerning important decisions having to do with the family's transactions with its environment—decisions about major purchases, relocations, and so on. The wife's acceptance of the "one-down" position may be part of the implicit contract (Sager 1976) in the marriage. The overt rule of "equal say" may be undercut by the implicit rule of "you decide." As Berman, Sachs, and Lief (1975) suggest, a wife paradoxically may come to see her egalitarian husband as "weak" and her male colleagues at work as "strong" because of covert expectations that a man should be "decisive."

NEW IDEALS AND OLD AGENDAS

In general one can expect tension between the egalitarian ideals of joint decision making and traditional patterns that put wives at a disadvantage in respect to the power they exercise. In our study, this discrepancy tended to be denied at a general level. Almost all couples said they had equal voices in decision making when the question was put to them in general form. When the details and nuances of decision making were examined, however, the tension was often revealed. In some cases there was a simple comment on the disparity on the order of, "My husband has the edge in major decisions but it shouldn't be that way." In other cases contradictory beliefs were expressed. A wife might regard it as proper that her husband, whose income is higher, should have more influence in how money is spent but in another context might say that each should contribute equally to decisions in all matters. In still others, beliefs might be contradicted by behavior. A husband might subscribe to equality in decision making yet act as if his point of view were really the more important.

Power issues are, of course, a part of marriage of all kinds. What is of particular interest in role-sharing marriages is how these issues are played out when power and decision making are presumably equalized. While sharing of control seemed to be the general norm, husbands were likely to have the edge when imbalance occurred.

By understanding the sources of these imbalances in older patterns of sex-role differentiation and prior socialization, role-sharing couples may be in a better position to identify and correct them. Communication about control problems, essential in any case, might be profitably centered on trying to ferret out whatever dynamics might be causing one partner to have an advantage in control. By attempting to understand the problem within the kind of perspective suggested, a couple can perhaps avoid dead ends such as attributing the imbalance to the husband's "dominant personality." Frank discussions of the impact of differences in resources, investments, and socialization may be more illuminating. Thus, a couple may be able to pinpoint the husband's edge in decision making to the unspoken assumption that his greater income should give him the greater say. Once recognized, this dynamic can be dealt with to minimize control issues—perhaps by consciously limiting the husband's edge only to the financial area or by agreeing that his greater income should not matter since it reflects, as several of our couples suggested, the effects of long-term inequities in the work market. Control issues resulting from differences in investment can be usually approached by each partner's attempting to understand the other's position and the rationale for it. As a result the positions of both partners may be modified in more compatible directions. Although the results of socialization are hard to alter, changes can be made if specific attitudes, expectations, and behavior can be identified. As suggested in the previous chapter, both partners can engage in "reverse socialization"—the husband can help his wife be more assertive in certain areas; the wife can provide reassurance that joint agonizing over a difficult decision may be preferable to the conventional norm of male decisiveness. In general, each can help the other to be better collaborative decision makers, putting gender-linked stereotypes about decision making where they belong—in the past.

Tradition and Innovation

Role sharing in marriage departs from those traditions that call for specialized functions for husband and wife. It does not necessarily challenge traditions governing the cohesiveness of the marital union or of the family unit. It offers a pathway to highly independent relationships—what we have termed the autonomous role-sharing marriage.

But couples who take this direction are probably in the minority. The dominant form of this new style of marriage may well be, as our data suggest, one that preserves if not enhances traditional emphasis on marital and family bonds—the cohesive role-sharing marriage.

We have focused on issues in these emerging variations of role-sharing marriages. Essentially the distinctive issues arise from conflicts between the newer ideas and structure, on the one hand, and on the other, the continuing effects of traditional norms of marriage, the past socialization of the partners, and gender biases that are part of the larger social system. Knowledge of the origins of these issues and a range of possible solutions, we assume, will be helpful to role-sharing couples themselves, as well as to those who counsel them.

But greater knowledge will be of little use unless it is combined with freedom of partners to choose the kind of marriage they both want to have. The freedom of choice we have in mind calls for a critical examination of traditional and newer values governing marital and family life and the relationship between men and women. The resulting choice should be made in the light of such scrutiny, even granting that choices will be influenced by the very values being scrutinized. Given the variety of viable options present today, perhaps the worst choices are to do what seems to be customary, what seems to be in vogue, or what others advise.

No form of marriage is inherently unsatisfactory. Each has its own distinctive gratifications, challenges, risks, and problems. For an ambitious career man whose star is rising and a woman who has little desire to achieve in the work place but great interest in being a mother, a traditional marriage may make the most sense. Some couples may find a quasi-traditional arrangement with its opportunities for the wife to combine domestic and career interests the most satisfactory. Many dual-career couples like those in our sample will opt, for reasons already made clear, for some variety of a role-sharing marriage.

In making decisions about the type of marriage, one consideration is paramount in our judgment: the long-range consequences of the choice one makes. The wife who opts for a traditional or quasi-traditional relationship needs to be aware that she is making a career choice, one that favors the domestic world over the world of work. A husband who chooses to share fully child care and domestic responsibilities with his wife should realize that his competitive edge in the work market may be blunted. Directions can always be changed but usually at some cost.

Long-range consequences that may eventually prove to be adverse may be avoided to some extent by long-range planning, including firm understandings with one's partner. For instance, couples who are entering what we have called a transitional stage—couples committed to role sharing but who opt for one spouse to remain at home to care for an infant—need to decide that the stage *is* transitional and plan a way back to full role sharing, if that is what they really want.

Through informed choices and thoughtful planning, and through communicating their choices and plans to one another, couples may increase their odds at finding the right form of marriage for them. With the right form, partners should be able to attain the more important task of developing the right substance.

Appendix A

Study Design and Method

The general purpose of the study was to augment the small but growing body of knowledge on the role-sharing marriage. In particular, we wanted to identify and examine the issues and adaptive solutions that might be found in this kind of marriage.

In terms of a framework we have developed elsewhere (Reid and Smith 1981), the study had primarily an exploratory-formulative function. Although the behaviors and attitudes of the couples may be described in some detail, the main purpose of the description is to provide context for study of issues and solutions. Our approach to the data is essentially qualitative. For example, an issue that we might decide was one of general importance might occur in a small number of cases or even in a single case. Although frequency of occurrence was a consideration, we also relied on our judgment about the issues that might be expected to arise from sources of strain between innovation and tradition in this kind of marriage (see chapters 1 and 2). While some issues posed dilemmas for the couples themselves, other issues could be seen in variations between couples. Such variations may not be issues for the individual couples but could well be for others who need to decide which variation to adopt for themselves.

In order to accomplish our objectives, we interviewed sixty-four couples who identified themselves as role sharing, though as we shall see, some couples were not sharing all major work-family roles at the time of our study. Since our interest was in examining role-sharing behavior and egalitarian attitudes, a purposive or strategic sample seemed appropriate for our study. This kind of sample appeared especially well suited to our research needs because other studies have indicated that role sharing, even among dual-career couples, is still rather uncommon. An additional sample of couples who divide family roles in the traditional manner would have enabled us to make comparisons that our present sample does not permit and therefore to paint sharper descriptions of role-sharing couples. We opted, however, to forgo these comparisons and to concentrate our efforts on role-sharing couples only, in order to gain a more detailed picture of their behavior, attitudes, and particularly of issues that arise in this type of marital relationship. In addition, we expected couples in our sample to vary—and they did—in the extent of their role-sharing behavior, as well as in other variables of interest. Thus, although our sample was purposely selected to consist of self-defined role-sharing couples, we expected enough variation among our respondents to permit comparisons among couples who differed in amounts and kinds of role sharing.

Because of our interest in role sharing with an ideological base, we wanted to restrict the sample to couples who espoused egalitarian attitudes. The indicator we used was whether or not couples, when asked, claimed to be equal in decision-making power in the family. Although this indicator did not prove very discriminating (all thought they met this criterion), it became apparent in the interviews that most of the couples selected did claim to embrace some form of an egalitarian ideology.

We also wanted to limit our sample to couples who had been married for at least a year. We reasoned that couples married for at least that long would have enough experience in managing work-family roles to provide the kind of data we were seeking: how couples develop and maintain role-sharing marriages. Although some of the couples in our study had lived together before getting married, we did not collect systematic data on these periods of cohabitation.

In summary, the main criteria we developed for identification of couples appropriate for our study were that the couples shared the roles of breadwinner, homemaker, and (if they had children) childrearer; had an egalitarian value orientation; and had been married for a year or longer. To find such couples, we solicited from colleagues and students names of couples they knew who seemed to fit our description. After the interviewing began, additional couples were suggested by our respondents. Brief telephone screening interviews were conducted with all couples to determine if they met our criteria. Most of the couples approached stated that they did share work-family roles and family decision making. Of those who did, almost all agreed to participate in our study, but when contacted later for specific appointments, a few couples were dropped because of scheduling difficulties. Toward the end of our data collection, we added another criterion—that the couple have minor children—in order to increase this portion of our sample. We considered it crucial to have enough couples with children because we anticipated that role sharing would be complicated by the added role of parenting or childrearing.

During the telephone screening, we learned that some of the couples were in a transitional category (chapter 1). These couples (n = 21) normally shared work-family roles but were temporarily at a point of imbalance because of a new baby, one spouse's having recently returned to school, or something similar. Consequently, not all of the work-family roles were being fully shared at the moment. We decided to include such couples because we thought they would broaden our understanding of role-sharing behavior and add to the richness of our data. We might learn, for example, under what conditions role sharing works best; when and what kind of adjustments need to be made in the allocation of roles; what problems or dissatisfactions, if any, accompany these changes; how easy it is to be flexible in the handling of family roles; and whether or not role sharing is still feasible under some of these changed conditions. Although these transitional couples did not meet our criteria for role sharing in terms of their situations at the time of the study, their orientation, history, and aspects of their current behavior suggested a basic attachment to a role-sharing pattern. For this reason we generally regard them as part of our role-sharing group, though for certain purposes we consider them separately.

Three interviews were conducted with each couple participating in the study: one joint interview and separate interviews with each partner. The interviews, particularly the initial joint one, were long and probing; altogether from three to five hours were spent interviewing each couple. Semistructured interview schedules were used. Many of the questions were open ended with probes suggested. In addition, the interviewers were instructed to use their own probes to follow up on promising leads in order to obtain more nearly complete information for the study. Although the interviews were exhausting, most of the couples seemed to enjoy them, perhaps because they were able to talk about something in which they were invested and perhaps proud of and because they perceived the interviews as positive recognition of their way of managing the work-family roles.

Second-year graduate students in schools of social work did most of the interviewing. The joint interviews were conducted by two students working as a team, each student interviewing one of the marital partners about a week after the initial interview. All the interviews were taped, but data were also recorded on the schedules during the interviews. Later the tapes were used to record fully information on the interview schedules in order to have the data in a more readily accessible form.

The major focus of the joint interviews was on ascertaining how the work-family roles were shared and how the couple had arrived at this method of handling family responsibilities. Background information was obtained about their parents' marriage, possible role models, and relevant adult experiences before the present marriage. For each of the roles—breadwinner, domestic, and (if applicable) child care—we asked a series of questions about exactly how they handled the tasks and responsibilities involved, how they arrived at this method, and the advantages and disadvantages of their way of sharing the role. We obtained their perceptions of what their families of origin, friends, and colleagues thought of their role-sharing behavior and egalitarian attitudes. In addition, information was obtained about their social life and leisure-time activities, including who took responsibility for what.

The individual interviews were used to round out and clarify information obtained in the joint interviews. Additionally, data were gathered from each spouse about the relationship between their work and family life, focusing particularly on the supports and constraints that their jobs provide for their role sharing. Personal (self-image) and relational (the affective and sexual aspects of the marriage) spheres were also probed. Questions were also asked about possible rigidity in, or discomfort with, their role-sharing behavior and compromises that were made to maintain the sharing of roles.

Appendix B

Scales

Domestic Task Scale

For each of seven domestic tasks (cooking, after-meal cleanup, planning meals, grocery shopping, vacuuming, scrubbing floors, and laundry), the following conversion was made on responses to the question asking who performed the task:

Husband $+2$
Husband Mostly $+1$
Both 0
Wife Mostly -1
Wife -2

The scores for the set of tasks were summed; they could range from $+14$ (husband performing all seven tasks) to -14 (wife performing all seven tasks). The 40- to 60-percent range included scores from $+3$ to -3. The few cases in which the couple had a score slightly above $+3$ (indicating that the husband did more) were counted as shared because of possible bias in this direction due to social desirability. Since the tasks are ones traditionally performed by women, our role-sharing couples, who were generally committed to egalitarian ideals, may have exaggerated the amount of the husbands' participation.

Child Care Scale

The scaling procedure described above was used for responses to questions asking who performed tasks in the following areas: routine care, child's development, emotional support, and child's entertainment. Possible total scores ranged from $+8$ (father performing all four tasks) to -8 (mother performing all four tasks). The 40- to 60-percent range included scores from $+2$ to -2.

REFERENCES

Aldous, Joan, ed. 1982. *Two Paychecks: Life in Dual Earner Families.* Beverly Hills, Calif.: Sage.

Aldous, Joan, A. Osmond, and M. Hicks. 1979. "Men's Work and Men's Families." In Wesley R. Burr, Reuben Hill, F. Ivan Nye, and Ira L. Reiss, eds. *Contemporary Theories About the Family.* New York: Free Press.

Aponte, Harry and John Van Deusen. 1981. "Structural Family Therapy." In Alan Gurman and David Kniskern, eds. (1981).

Araji, Sharon. 1977. "Husbands' and Wives' Attitude-Behavior Congruence on Family Roles." *Journal of Marriage and the Family* 39:302–22.

Bahr, Stephen J. 1972. "Comment on 'The Study of Family Power Structure: A Review 1960–1969.'" *Journal of Marriage and the Family* 34:239–43.

——— 1974. "Effects on Power and Division of Labor in the Family." In L. W. Hoffman and F. I. Nye, eds. (1974).

Bailyn, Lotte. 1970. "Career and Family Orientations of Husbands and Wives in Relation to Marital Happiness." *Human Relations* 23:97–109.

Baruch, Grace and Rosalind Barnett. 1981. "Fathers' Participation in the Care of Their Preschool Children." *Sex Roles* 10:173–93.

Beckett, Joyce O. and Audrey D. Smith. 1981. "Work and Family Roles: Egalitarian Marriage in Black and White Families." *Social Service Review* 55:314–26.

Berk, Richard A. and Sarah F. Berk. 1979. *Labor and Leisure at Home: Content and Organization of the Household Day.* Beverly Hills, Calif.: Sage.

Berman, Ellen, Sylvia Sachs, and Harold Lief. 1975. "The Two-Professional Marriage: A New Conflict Syndrome." *Journal of Sex and Marital Therapy* 1:242–53.

Bernard, Jessie. 1971. *Women and the Public Interest.* Chicago: Aldine.

——— 1972. "Changing Family Life Styles: One Role, Two Roles, Shared Roles." In Louise Kapp Howe, ed. *The Future of the Family.* New York: Simon and Schuster.

——— 1973. *The Future of Marriage.* New York: Bantam.

Bird, Caroline. 1979. *The Two Paycheck Marriage.* New York: Rawson, Wade.

Bird, Gloria, Gerald Bird, and Marguerite Scruggs. 1984. "Determinants of Family Task Sharing: A Study of Husbands and Wives." *Journal of Marriage and the Family* 46:345–55.

Blood, Robert O. and Donald M. Wolfe. 1960. *Husbands and Wives: The Dynamics of Married Living*. Glencoe, Ill.: Free Press.

Blumstein, Philip and Pepper Schwartz. 1983. *American Couples*. New York: William Morrow.

Bohen, Halcyone H. 1984. "Gender Equality in Work and Family: An Elusive Goal." *Journal of Family Issues* 5:254–72.

Boszormenyi-Nagy, Ivan and David N. Ulrich. 1981. "Contextual Family Therapy." In Alan S. Gurman and David P. Kniskern, eds. (1981).

Bowlby, John. 1951. *Maternal Care and Mental Health*. Geneva: World Health Organization.

―― 1958. "The Nature of the Child's Tie to His Mother." *International Journal of Psychoanalysis* 39:350–75.

―― 1969. *Attachment and Loss*. Vol. 1: *Attachment*. New York: Basic Books.

Breckinridge, Sophonisba P. 1928. "Introductory Note." In Edith Abbott, ed. *Women in Industry*. New York: Appleton.

Bryson, Rebecca, Jeff Bryson, and Marilyn Johnson. 1978. "Family Size, Satisfaction, and Productivity in Dual-Career Couples." *Psychology of Women Quarterly* 3:67–77.

Bryson, Jeff B. and Rebecca Bryson. 1980. "Salary and Job Performance Differences in Dual-Career Couples." In Fran Pepitone-Rockwell, ed. (1980).

Carlson, Bonnie. 1981. "Preschoolers' Sex-Role Identity, Father-Role Perceptions, and Paternal Family Participation." *Journal of Family Issues* 2:238–55.

―― 1984. "The Father's Contribution to Child Care: Effects on Children's Perceptions of Parental Roles." *American Journal of Orthopsychiatry* 54:123–36.

Chafe, William H. 1977. *Women and Equality*. New York: Oxford University Press.

Cohen, Leslie J. and Joseph J. Campos. 1974. "Father, Mother, and Stranger as Elicitors of Attachment Behaviors in Infancy." *Developmental Psychology* 10:146–54.

Curtis, Jean. 1976. *Working Mothers*. Garden City, N.J.: Doubleday.

DeFrain, John. 1979. "Androgynous Parents Tell Who They Are and What They Need." *The Family Coordinator* 28:237–43.

Dizard, Jan E. 1968. *Social Change in the Family*. Chicago: Community and Family Study Center, University of Chicago.

―― 1972. "The Price of Success." In Louise Kapp Howe, ed. *The Future of the Family*. New York: Simon and Schuster.

Elshtain, Jean B. 1982. "Feminism, Family, and Community." *Dissent* 29:442–49.

Epstein, Cynthia F. 1971. "Law Partners and Marital Partners: Strains and Solutions in the Dual-Career Family Enterprise." *Human Relations* 24:549–63.

Ericksen, Julia A., William L. Yancey, and Eugene P. Ericksen. 1979. "The Division of Family Roles." *Journal of Marriage and the Family* 41:301–13.

Etaugh, Claire. 1974. "Effects of Maternal Employment on Children: A Review of Recent Research." *Merrill-Palmer Quarterly of Behavior and Development* 20:71–98.

Farkas, George. 1976. "Education, Wage Rates, and the Division of Labor Between Husband and Wife." *Journal of Marriage and the Family* 38:473–83.

Farrell, Warren T. 1974. *The Liberated Man.* New York: Random House.

Farris, Agnes. 1978. "Commuting." In Robert and Rhona Rapoport, eds. (1978).

Fox, Greer Litton, ed. 1982. *The Childbearing Decision: Fertility Attitudes and Behavior.* Beverly Hills, Calif.: Sage.

Gecas, Viktor. 1976. "The Socialization and Child Care Roles." In F. Ivan Nye, ed. *Role Structure and Analysis of the Family.* Beverly Hills, Calif.: Sage.

Geerken, Michael and Walter R. Gove. 1983. *At Home and at Work.* Beverly Hills, Calif.: Sage.

Gerstel, Naomi and Harriet Gross. 1984. *Commuter Marriage: A Study of Work and Family.* New York: Guilford.

Gilbert, Lucia A., Carole Holahan, and Linda Manning. 1981. "Coping with Conflict Between Professional and Marital Roles." *Family Relations* 30:419–26.

Goodenough, Evelyn W. 1957. "Interest in Persons as an Aspect of Sex Differences in the Early Years." *Genetic Psychology Monographs* 55:287–323.

Gottman, John et al. 1976. *A Couple's Guide to Communication.* Champaign, Ill.: Research Press.

Gross, Harriet E. 1980. "Dual-Career Couples Who Live Apart: Two Types." *Journal of Marriage and the Family* 42:567–76.

Grossman, Allyson S. 1982. "Special Labor Force Reports—Summaries: Working Mothers and Their Children." *Monthly Labor Review* 105:59–64.

Gurman, Alan S. and David P. Kniskern, eds. 1981. *Handbook of Family Therapy.* New York: Brunner/Mazel.

Haas, Linda. 1980a. "Parental Sharing of Childcare Tasks in Sweden." Paper presented at the National Council on Family Relations, Portland, Oregon, October 24.

——— 1980b. "Role-Sharing Couples: A Study of Egalitarian Marriages." *Family Relations* 29:289–96.

——— 1981. "Domestic Role Sharing in Sweden." *Journal of Marriage and The Family* 43:957–67.

——— 1982. "Determinants of Role-Sharing Behavior: A Study of Egalitarian Couples." *Sex Roles* 8:747–60.

Haley, Jay. 1963. *Strategies of Psychotherapy.* New York: Grune and Stratton.

Hayghe, Howard. 1982. "Dual-Earner Families: Their Economic and Demographic Characteristics." In Joan Aldous, ed. (1982).

Heckman, Norma A., Rebecca Bryson, and Jeff A. Bryson. 1977. "Problems of Professional Couples: A Content Analysis." *Journal of Marriage and the Family* 39:323–30.

Heilbrun, Alfred B. 1965. "An Empirical Test of the Modeling Theory of Sex-

Role Learning." *Child Development* 36:789–99.

Hesselbart, Susan. 1976. "Does Charity Begin at Home? Attitudes Toward Women, Household Tasks, and Household Decision-Making." Paper presented at the meeting of the American Sociological Association, New York City, August.

Hoffman, Lois Wladis. 1974. "Effects on Child." In L. W. Hoffman and F. I. Nye, eds. (1974).

—— 1977. "Changes in Family Roles, Socialization and Sex Differences." *American Psychologist* 32:644–57.

—— 1983. "Increased Fathering: Effects on the Mother." In Michael Lamb and Abraham Sagi, eds. *Fatherhood and Family Policy.* Hillsdale, N.J.: Lawrence Erlbaum Associates.

Hoffman, Lois Wladis and F. Ivan Nye, eds. 1974. *Working Mothers.* San Francisco: Jossey-Bass.

Holahan, Carole and Lucia Gilbert. 1979. "Conflict Between Major Life Roles: Women and Men in Dual Career Couples." *Human Relations* 32:451–67.

Holmstrom, Lynda. 1972. *The Two-Career Family.* Cambridge, Mass.: Schenkman.

Hunt, Janet G. and Larry L. Hunt. 1982. "Dual-Career Families: Vanguard of the Future or Residue of the Past?" In Joan Aldous, ed. (1982).

Johnson, Frank A. and Colleen L. Johnson. 1976. "Role Strain in High-Commitment Career Women." *Journal of American Academy of Psychoanalysis* 4:13–36.

Johnson, Colleen L. and Frank A. Johnson. 1977. "Attitudes Towards Parenting in Dual-Career Families." *American Journal of Psychiatry* 134:391–95.

Kamerman, Sheila. 1980. *Parenting in an Unresponsive Society.* New York: Free Press.

Kessler-Harris, Alice. 1982. *Out of Work.* New York: Oxford University Press.

Kimball, Gayle. 1983. *The 50-50 Marriage.* Boston: Beacon.

Kotelchuck, Milton. 1972. "The Nature of the Child's Tie to His Father." Doctoral dissertation, Harvard University.

Lamb, Michael E. 1976a. "Interactions Between Two-Year-Olds and Their Mothers and Fathers." *Psychological Reports* 38:447–50.

Lamb, Michael E., ed. 1976b. *The Role of the Father in Child Development.* New York: Wiley.

—— ed. 1982. *Nontraditional Families: Parenting and Child Development.* Hillside, N.J.: Lawrence Erlbaum Associates.

Langlois, Judith and A. Chris Downs. 1980. "Mothers, Fathers, and Peers as Socialization Agents of Sex-typed Play Behaviors in Young Children." *Child Development* 51:1237–47.

Lansky, Leonard M. 1967. "The Family Structure Also Affects the Model: Sex-role Attitudes in Parents of Preschool Children." *Merrill-Palmer Quarterly* 13:139–50.

Lein, Laura et al. 1974. *Final Report: Work and Family Life.* Cambridge, Mass.: Center for the Study of Public Policy.

Lopata, Helena Z. 1971. *Occupation: Housewife*. London: Oxford University Press.

Lopata, Helena, Debra Barnewolt, and Kathleen Norr. 1980. "Spouses' Contribution to Each Other's Roles." In F. Pepitone-Rockwell, ed. (1980).

Maret, Elizabeth and Barbara Finlay. 1984. "The Distribution of Household Labor Among Women in Dual-earner Families." *Journal of Marriage and the Family* 46:357–64.

Masnick, George and Mary Jo Bane. 1980. *The Nation's Families: 1960–1990*. Boston, Mass.: Auburn House.

Matthaei, Julie A. 1982. *An Economic History of Women in America*. New York: Schocken.

Mead, Margaret. 1962. "A Cultural Anthropologist's Approach to Maternal Deprivation." In *Deprivation of Maternal Care: A Reassessment of Its Effects*. Geneva: World Health Organization.

Miller, Joanne and Howard H. Garrison. 1982. "Sex Roles: The Division of Labor at Home and in the Workplace." *Annual Review of Sociology* 8:237–62.

Minuchin, Salvador. 1974. *Families and Family Therapy*. Cambridge, Mass.: Harvard University Press.

Model, Suzanne. 1981. "Housework by Husbands: Determinants and Implications." *Journal of Family Issues* 2:225–37.

Moen, Phyllis, 1982. "The Two-Provider Family: Problems and Potentials." In Michael Lamb, ed. (1982).

Mortimer, Jeylan, Richard Hall, and Reuben Hill. 1978. "Husbands' Occupational Attributes as Constraints on Wives' Employment." *Sociology of Work and Occupations* 5:285–313.

Myrdal, Alva and Viola Klein. 1956. *Women's Two Roles*. London: Routledge and Kegan Paul.

New York Times Poll. 1983. Maureen Dowd, "Many Women in Poll Value Jobs as Much as Family Life." *New York Times*, December 4.

Nickols, Sharon and Edward Metzen. 1982. "Impact of Wife's Employment upon Husband's Housework." *Journal of Family Issues* 3:199–216.

Nye, F. Ivan and Viktor Gecas. 1976. "The Role Concept: Review and Delineation." In F. Ivan Nye, ed. *Role Structure and Analysis of the Family*. Beverly Hills, Calif.: Sage.

Oakley, Ann. 1974. *The Sociology of Housework*. New York: Pantheon.

O'Neill, Nena and George O'Neill. 1972. *Open Marriage*. New York: Avon.

Parsons, Talcott and Robert F. Bales. 1955. *Family, Socialization and Interaction Process*. New York: Free Press.

Pepitone-Rockwell, Fran, ed. 1980. *Dual-Career Couples*. Beverly Hills, Calif.: Sage.

Perrucci, Carolyn, Harry Potter, and Deborah Rhoads. 1978. "Determinants of Male Family-Role Performance." *Psychology of Women Quarterly* 3:53–66.

Pleck, Joseph H. 1977. "The Work-Family Role System." *Social Problems* 24:417–27.

——— 1979. "Men's Family Work: Three Perspectives and Some New Data." *The Family Coordinator* 28:481–88.

——— 1983. "Husbands' Paid Work and Family Roles: Current Research Issues." In Helena Z. Lopata and Joseph H. Pleck, eds. *Research in the Interweave of Social Roles,* vol. 3. Greenwich, Conn.: JAI Press.

Poloma, Margaret M. 1972. "Role Conflict and the Married Professional Woman." In Constantina S. Rothschild, ed. *Toward a Sociology of Women.* Lexington, Mass.: Xerox College Publishing.

Poloma, Margaret and T. Neal Garland. 1971. "The Married Professional Woman: A Study in the Tolerance of Domestication." *Journal of Marriage and the Family* 33:531–40.

Radin, Norma. 1981. "Childrearing Fathers in Intact Families: Some Antecedents and Consequences." *Merrill-Palmer Quarterly* 27:489–514.

——— 1982. "Primary Caregiving and Role-Sharing Fathers." In Michael Lamb, ed. (1982).

Radin, Norma and Graeme Russell. 1983. "Increased Father Participation and Child Development Outcomes." In Michael Lamb and Abraham Sagi, eds. *Fatherhood and Family Policy.* Hillsdale, N.J.: Lawrence Erlbaum Associates.

Rapoport, Rhona and Robert N. Rapoport. 1969. "The Dual-Career Family: A Variant Pattern of Social Change." *Human Relations* 22:3–30.

——— 1971. *Dual Career Families.* Baltimore, Md.: Penguin.

——— 1975. "Men, Women and Equity." *The Family Coordinator* 24:421–32.

——— 1976. *Dual-Career Families ReExamined.* New York: Harper Colophon.

Rapoport, Robert N. and Rhona Rapoport, eds. 1978. *Working Couples.* New York: Harper Colophon.

Reid, William J. 1978. *The Task-Centered System.* New York: Columbia University Press.

Reid, William J. and Audrey D. Smith. 1981. *Research in Social Work.* New York: Columbia University Press.

Reitz, Miriam. 1982. "Model Building for Marital Assessment: A Study of New Marriages on Systemic Dimensions." Doctoral dissertation, School of Social Service Administration, University of Chicago.

Rice, David G. 1979. *Dual-Career Marriage: Conflict and Treatment.* New York: Free Press.

Robinson, John P. 1977. *How Americans Use Time: A Social Psychological Analysis.* New York: Praeger.

Rosen, Raye H. and Twylah Benson. 1982. "The Second-Class Partner: The Male Role in Family-Planning Decisions." In Greer Litton Fox, ed. (1982).

Russell, Graeme. 1982. "Shared-Caregiving Families: An Australian Study." In Michael E. Lamb, ed. (1982).

Ryder, Norman B. 1979. "The Future of American Fertility," *Social Problems* 26:359–70.

Sager, Clifford. 1976. *Marriage Contracts and Couple Therapy: Hidden Forces in Intimate Relationships.* New York: Brunner/Mazel.

Sagi, Abraham. 1982. "Antecedents and Consequences of Various Degrees of Paternal Involvement in Child-Rearing: The Israeli Project." In Michael E. Lamb, ed. (1982).

Sawin, Douglas B. and Ross D. Parke. 1979. "Fathers' Affectionate Stimulation and Caregiving Behaviors with Newborn Infants." *The Family Coordinator* 28:509–13.

Scanzoni, John. 1979. "Strategies for Changing Male Family Roles: Research and Practice Implications." *The Family Coordinator* 28:435–42.

—— 1983. *Shaping Tomorrow's Family.* Beverly Hills, Calif.: Sage.

Scanzoni, John and Greer Litton Fox. 1980. "Sex Roles, Family and Society: The Seventies and Beyond." *Journal of Marriage and the Family* 42:743–56.

Schneider, D. and R. Smith. 1973. *Class Differences and Sex Roles in American Kinship and Family Structure.* Englewood Cliffs, N.J.: Prentice-Hall.

Sexton, Linda G. 1979. *Between Two Worlds: Young Women in Crisis.* New York: Morrow.

Silverman, William and Reuben Hill. 1967. "Task Allocation in Marriage in the United States and Belgium." *Journal of Marriage and the Family* 29:353–59.

Smith, Audrey D. 1980. "Egalitarian Marriage: Implications for Practice and Policy." *Social Casework* 61:288–95.

Smuts, Robert W. 1971. *Women and Work in America.* New York: Schocken.

St. John-Parsons, Donald. 1978. "Continuous Dual-Career Families: A Case Study." *Psychology of Women Quarterly* 3:30–42.

Sweet, James A. 1982. "Work and Fertility." In Greer Litton Fox, ed. (1982).

Szinovacz, Maximiliane. 1979. "Women Employed: Effects on Spouses' Division of Housework." *Journal of Home Economics* 71:42–54.

Tentler, Leslie Woodcock. 1979. *Wage-Earning Women.* New York: Oxford University Press.

Vanek, Joann. 1974. "Time Spent in Housework." *Scientific American* 231:116–20.

—— 1980. "Household Work, Wage Work, and Sexual Equality." In Sarah F. Berk, ed. *Women and Household Labor.* Beverly Hills, Calif.: Sage.

Veevers, Jean E. 1973. "Voluntary Childless Wives: An Exploratory Study." *Sociology and Social Research* 57:356–65.

Walker, Kathryn and Margaret Woods. 1976. "Time Use: A Measure of Household Production of Family Goods and Services." Washington, D.C.: American Home Economics Association.

Waller, Willard. 1938. *The Family: A Dynamic Interpretation.* New York: Dryden.

Weingarten, Kathy. 1978. "The Employment Pattern of Professional Couples and Their Distribution of Involvement in the Family." *Psychology of Women Quarterly* 3:43–52.

Wertheim, Eleanor. 1975. "The Science and Typology of Family Systems II: Further Theoretical and Practice Considerations." *Family Process* 14:103–26.

Wilkie, Jane R. 1981. "The Trend Toward Delayed Parenthood." *Journal of Marriage and the Family* 43:583–91.

Yogev, Sara. 1981. "Do Professional Women Have Egalitarian Marital Relationships?" *Journal of Marriage and the Family* 43:865–72.

Young, Michael and Peter Willmott. 1973. *The Symmetrical Family.* New York: Pantheon.

Zimmerman, Irla Lee and Maurine Bernstein. 1983. "Parental Work Patterns in Alternative Families: Influence on Child Development." *American Journal of Orthopsychiatry* 53:418–25.

AUTHOR INDEX

SUBJECT INDEX

Altruism, vs. equity principle, 14–16; vs. reciprocity, 75–78
Androgynous parents, 32
Attitudes: about outside employment for women, 35, 124; adaptability of, 69; influence on respondents, 123–25; of others toward role-sharing marriage, 123, 137–38, 166–72; vs. behavior, 31, 87, 95, 190–91; *see also* Egalitarian attitudes; Traditional sex-role attitudes
Autonomy, 5, 179–86; and children, 109, 165–66; and commitment to family, 181–82; and emotional attachment, 180, 185; financial, 50, 53–55, 60–62; implications of, 5–6; and interdependence, 5, 179–81; limits of, 5–6, 164–66; loss of, in parenting role, 30, 109; as metarule, 5; in role-sharing marriage, 16–17, 163, 165–66, 179–86; and self-image, 151; and sex equality, 5; as threat to marriage, 7, 181; value placed on, 5

Baby boom, 23
Bank account model of exchange, 78
Biases in data, 45–46; social desirability, 45; "talking dog syndrome," 45
Biological differences, 4
Black women, 20–21, 23
Breadwinner role, 47–50; case examples, 50–60; and family power, 47, 52–53, 177, 186–91; and financial arrangements, 50–51; and income, husbands vs. wives, 49; issues in, 60–69; perception of, 49–50; as

pivotal in role-sharing marriage, 47; responsibility for, 48–50, 140; shared, 37–38

Career(s): competition between spouses, 144–45; conflict with parenting, 101, 111–12, 129; definition of, 28; disruption, 101, 176–77, 179; effects of role-sharing marriage on, 140–43; and marital cohesion, 184; men vs. women, 13, 28–29, 177; relocation, 17, 145–48; sacrifices in, 9, 101, 129, 177–78, 184, 192–93; spouse involvement in, 143–45, 186; *see also* Wife's career
Caretaker role, *see* Child care; Child care arrangements
Case examples, 57–60, 90–94, 97–98, 100–1, 103–7; 119–25; 147–48
Characteristics of sample, 36–37; children, 100; employment, 48–49; extent of role sharing, 37–40; father's participation in housework, 40; income, 49; money management, 50–57; perception of breadwinner role, 49–50
Childbearing, 100–14; ambivalence over, 102–3; as future plan, 105–8; basic considerations, 109; case examples, 100–1, 103–4, 105–7; changing attitudes and behavior, 113–14; child care considerations, 101–2, 107–8, 110–13; costs of, 101, 114; decision-making process, 100, 108–15; decision not to have children, 103–5, 113–14; delayed due to career, 105–8, 113–14;

48,867